SPA... TO NORWAY

ON A BIKE CALLED REGGIE

ANDREW P. SYKES

summersdale

Summersdale Publishers Ltd
46 West Street
Chichester
West Sussex
PO19 1RP
UK

www.summersdale.com

Printed and bound by CPI Group (UK) Ltd, Croydon, CR0 4YY

ISBN: 978-1-84953-990-6

Substantial discounts on bulk quantities of Summersdale books are available to corporations, professional associations and other organisations. For details contact general enquiries: telephone: +44 (0) 1243 771107, fax: +44 (0) 1243 786300 or email: enquiries@summersdale.com.

To Dad, for teaching me how to ride a bike.

Nordkapp

Alta

Tromsø

Bodø

The Arctic Circle

Namsos

Trondheim

Lillehammer

Oslo

Gothenburg

Helsingborg

Copenhagen

Flensburg

Møns Klint

Hamburg

Bremen

Münster

Düsseldorf

Brussels

Cologne

Maastricht

Paris

Orléans

Saumur

Tours

La Rochelle

Arcachon

Bayonne

Benavente

Pamplona

Burgos

Salamanca

Cáceres

Seville

Cádiz

Tarifa

CONTENTS

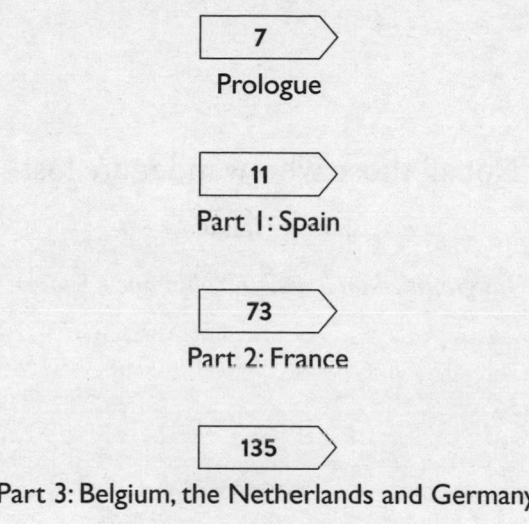

Not all those who wander are lost.

J. R. R. Tolkien

(as graffitied on a wall in Salamanca, Spain)

PROLOGUE

It was Thursday 9 April 2015 and I was standing on the edge of the Isla de las Palomas, less than a kilometre to the south of Tarifa, in southern Spain. For a few moments, my body was host to the southernmost human heart on the continental mainland of Europe. I was Europe's most southerly man. The plan was to cycle from this southernmost point of Europe to the northernmost point at Nordkapp, in Norway, 71 degrees, 10 minutes and 21 seconds (or, to keep things brief, 71°10'21") north of the equator. The plan was to cycle from this southernmost point of Europe to the northernmost point at Nordkapp, in Norway, 71 degrees and ten minutes north of the equator. It would be a journey of just over 35 degrees.

In December 2014 I had said goodbye to my teaching colleagues for the final time. *'Teacher quits to cycle 5,000 miles on a bike called Reggie'* was the announcement blazoned across an inside page of the local newspaper. At least if my cycling endeavour were to end prematurely, I would have moved on to pastures new and the readers of the *Henley Standard* could live the rest of their lives in blissful ignorance of my failings. I packed up my belongings and headed north to the county of my birth, Yorkshire, where, for several weeks, I procrastinated.

A long cycle from A to B in Europe wasn't complicated to plan. I needed to travel through seven countries: Spain, France, Belgium, Germany, Denmark, Sweden and Norway. As I had done on my previous continental cycles, I would be following routes on the EuroVelo network, this time a combination of EuroVelos 1 and 3. Equipment-wise, I had most of what I needed from previous trips, including my bicycle, Reggie: a Ridgeback Panorama World purchased five years earlier for *Crossing Europe on a Bike Called Reggie* (a journey from southern England to southern Italy). The Robens Osprey 2 tent had, despite its slightly sagging back end (it wasn't alone on that score), served me well in *Along the Med on a Bike Called Reggie* (a second journey from southern Greece to southern Portugal) and would hopefully do the same again. I had upgraded my panniers but most of the equipment was tried and tested. I was ready.

On Wednesday 25 February, six weeks before my planned departure from Tarifa, I flew to Malaga, Spain. The final piece in the jigsaw that was 'Career Break 2015' (which deserved to be the name of an Ironman triathlon) was to learn some Spanish. Although a secondary school teacher of languages, I spoke only French. By basing myself in the Andalusian city of Cádiz, where I had enrolled onto a five-week Spanish language course, I would hopefully be able to plug this gap in my CV – and have a nice time doing so.

Alongside the learning, there was plenty of time to explore. One weekend, along with three fellow students, I embarked upon a short road trip of Andalusia: Arcos de la Frontera, Grazalema, Zahara, Vejer de la Frontera and the surfing paradise of Tarifa. Much to my annoyance, I discovered that my intended point of departure – the southernmost point of Isla de las Palomas, or 'dove island', near Tarifa – was inaccessible to all but the *Guardia Civil*, the military police who had a base there. I wondered what the peace-loving doves made of that.

The Isla de las Palomas had clearly been erroneously named: not only did I not spot any doves, but it also was most definitely not an island as I understood it. Perhaps prior to 1808 it had been. That was when a broad causeway had been built, linking it to the continent. In 2015 after more than 200 years of continuous connection to the mainland, I think it is safe to say that it was no longer a proper island. A sign at the point where the causeway met the 'island' informed visitors seeking the southernmost point of the continent that they had found their destination. But they hadn't. There remained half a kilometre of rocky land beyond the closed gates of the military base.

Not being permitted to set off on my quest from the real southernmost point of Europe had perturbed me. The teachers back at the school suggested I ring the tourist office in Tarifa to see if there were any possibilities of being let in.

'¿Hablas inglés?' I enquired.

The woman on the other end of the phone did but there was to be bad news as well as good. Yes, organised visits were permitted but they didn't coincide with my planned departure date of Thursday 9 April. Was I prepared to hang around until the following week? She suggested, somewhat sceptically, that I should contact the *Guardia Civil* directly.

'Estimada Guardia Civil de Tarifa...'

It sounded like grovelling but the teachers assured me it was just the formal way to do these things in writing.

A week later, a response arrived. Much to my relief, it wasn't a *'no'* – more a *'quizás'* or 'perhaps'. I was instructed to seek permission from the Parque Natural del Estrecho.

'Estimado Parque Natural del Estrecho...'

I was learning to grovel quite well.

Four more days passed. Then, an email arrived.

'*According to decree 308/2002 of December 23 2002 approving the Management Plan of Natural Resources...*'

It appeared that I was in.

There were, however, conditions. In order not to infringe decree 308/2002 (etc.), it would be necessary for me to 'realise a project aimed at promoting environmental understanding and education'.

So, here we are at the very start of our journey across the European land mass from the southernmost point – the real one – to the northernmost point. As you read, please bear in mind that in addition to this being a book about travelling, cycling, geography, history, politics and no doubt a few more topics thrown in for good measure, I am under legal obligation – by order of decree 308/2002 – to promote environmental understanding and education. So, once you've finished reading this book, please make sure you recycle it. Thanks.

PART 1

SPAIN

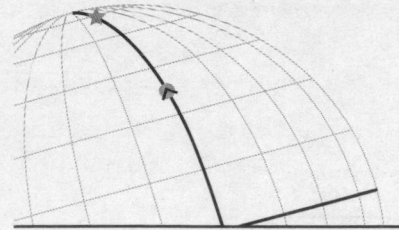

THE FIRST DEGREE
36°–37° NORTH

9–11 April

Reggie had been couriered to Spain and spent six weeks in the underground garage of my Uncle Ron's flat near the coastal town of Estepona, 80 km north-east of Tarifa. The bike – dismantled, transported by van, plane and van again, and then left unloved for a month and a half in a darkened room – needed a good service. Quite what damage such an environment could inflict upon a bicycle, I wasn't sure. Yep Bikes in San Pedro and the shop's German owner, Roman, provided a first-class bike check-up, plus a bright orange T-shirt to alleviate my uncle's concern for my well-being on the streets of the Costa del Sol. The road I needed to cycle along to get to Tarifa – the N-340 – was widely considered to be one of the most treacherous in Spain. At least in my vivid Yep Bikes attire, the speeding, reckless and drunk drivers of the 'road of death' would have no problem in aiming at their target.

On Easter Monday I waved goodbye to Ron and his wife Bea and teetered down the road leading to the N-340, trying to readjust to cycling again on a bike loaded with four heavy panniers. I hadn't done this since the previous summer and it was a skill that took time to reacquire. But reacquire it I did and, via an overnight stop in Gibraltar and after 100 km of cycling, I survived without being maimed or indeed killed on the 'road of death'. Following a long, steady climb south and against a ferocious wind, I found my first campsite – the Río Jara – near Tarifa.

The instructions from the *Guardia Civil* were to present my credentials at 10 a.m. at the entrance to the Isla de las Palomas, wait to be allowed in and then be escorted to the southern tip of the 'island'. After a healthy breakfast of fresh fruit and unbuttered toast, I made my way to the southern end of the causeway. There was, alas, no one there to whom I could present my credentials. A doorbell? Not that I could see. On a wall on the other side of the gate was a camera so I waved in its direction in an exaggerated fashion.

Nothing happened. No one came to investigate why I was standing there. No warning shots were fired.

After I'd been loitering for a few minutes, an unmarked 4 x 4 vehicle approached the gate along the causeway. Inside were four men. The driver wound down his window and said something I interpreted to be a stern warning to clear off.

'¿Hablas inglés?' I enquired, as I proffered him my printed credentials. 'I'm on a mission to promote environmental understanding and education,' I might have added if I hadn't been pretty sure that he was some kind of Spanish secret agent.

After a few moments he smiled broadly and said, in what was approaching Received Pronunciation English: 'Where are you cycling?'

'To Nordkapp in Norway – the northernmost point of Europe.'

'Seriously?'

The man clearly saw in me a kindred secret agent in the waiting.

'Follow me. When you get to the guard's building, show him your paper. And have a good trip.'

With that he was gone to do secret agent things. I was in and the long journey to the southernmost point of Europe was at an end. All that remained was for me to cycle the 7,500 km to Nordkapp.

—

Continental Europe's southernmost beating heart was now thumping a little faster in anticipation of what was to come; a blank canvas of events that had yet to take place lay ahead of me.

Initially, I would be turning my back on the Costa del Sol and cycling northwest along the Costa de la Luz to Cádiz, from where I would head inland to Seville. From there, I intended to follow a pilgrimage path across Spain called the Vía de la Plata, and then turn east and continue along the route of the Camino de Santiago, albeit in reverse, until I arrived in France.

The weather was decidedly average. It had been raining for much of the morning and the temperature necessitated three layers of clothing underneath my waterproof jacket. The wind was blowing but, for the first time since leaving my uncle's flat in Estepona two days previously, it was doing so in the direction I was travelling.

Prior to my arrival in this corner of Spain, I had envisaged the landscape to be bare, flat, colourless and windswept. It was certainly windswept but far from bare, flat and colourless. Most of the hillsides were covered in pine trees that resembled large, upturned sticks of broccoli. More concerning from the perspective of a cyclist were the cactus plants that appeared sporadically and their thousands of sharp needles. I prayed that none would end up in Reggie's new tyres. A pesky cactus needle on day one was most certainly not part of my plans so, as there was little traffic, I positioned the bike in the centre of the road, continued to cycle and hoped for the best.

The wilderness of the Costa de la Luz, compared to the urban sprawl of the Costa del Sol, was a delight. Where development had taken place to cater for the needs of holidaymakers, it had been done without necessitating the building of tower blocks, the concreting over of every available patch of land or the opening of English-style pubs. Even the small industrial town of Barbate where the fishing industry had strewn its onshore infrastructure along the Avenue Generalísimo – Franco liked to spend his holidays in the town – didn't detract from the overall impression of a place where nature thrived.

The main historical highlight of this first day on the bike should have been a visit to the lighthouse at the Cabo de Trafalgar, the Cape of Trafalgar. It was near here that, in October 1805, and after a five-hour battle, the Royal Navy destroyed the Franco-Spanish fleet. It was one of the key battles of the Napoleonic Wars and dealt a severe blow to the French Emperor's ambitions to conquer the whole of Europe. The Battle of Trafalgar was an evenly matched affair: 27 ships on the British side against 33 French and Spanish vessels but by the end of the skirmish, 18 of those 33 had been destroyed and 3,000 of their sailors killed. The British didn't lose a single ship. Admiral Lord Nelson was one of 'only' 500 British casualties and his final words after having been shot on the deck of HMS *Victory* were, 'Thank God I have done my duty.' He was promptly stuffed in a barrel of brandy for the journey back home.

The parting words of the other 499 British sailors don't seem to have been recorded but I'm guessing they were along the lines of 'Ouch!', 'Bugger!' or 'I knew I should have ducked!' My own parting words as I cycled away from the Cabo de Trafalgar were: 'I knew I should have come on a less windy day,' as it proved impossible to push poor Reggie through the sand that had been blown across the road to the lighthouse. Somewhat disappointed at not being able to gaze out to sea to the point where Nelson had got in a metaphoric – as well as literal – pickle, I continued north.

I planned to camp whenever possible. The second-best option would be a hostel and then a hotel. In addition, I was going to seek out WarmShowers hosts. The touring cyclist community's answer to CouchSurfing, WarmShowers had been of good use in the past and prior to setting off from Tarifa, I had attempted to contact half a dozen potential hosts in southern Spain and along the Vía de la Plata. So far there had been no positive responses but it was early days and I remained confident that Spanish hospitality would come to the fore. Apart from being a cheap means of finding somewhere to sleep, it was, above all, an excellent way to interact with the locals. I needn't have been overly concerned about that aspect of the trip, however, as I was about to meet hundreds of 'locals' at Camping Fuente del Gallo, a two-star establishment just north of Conil de la Frontera.

Unsurprisingly for the start of April, campers were thin on the ground and consisted of a few elderly couples sitting snugly in the heat of the sealed awnings of their caravans or mobile homes. It was that time of year when, as soon as the sun set, the temperature fell rapidly so I was eager to get the tent erected and shuffle off to the warm restaurant. My main concern was to pick a patch of empty ground – there was plenty of it – far enough from the handful of other campers so as not to hear them snore but near enough for them to hear me scream should I be attacked during the night. Despite having spent many nights in a tent, I had yet to feel completely at ease when camping alone. But was I? I should have paid more attention to the ground upon which I pitched the tent. The local population that I was about to meet in their hundreds had just arrived: ants. In fairness, I had gatecrashed their party, but I groaned as I grew increasingly aware of the extent of the ant city underneath my tent. I quickly placed everything inside, pulled up the zip and fled the scene.

I woke up surrounded by 'stuff' – indeed, all the 'stuff' that I had methodically laid out on the terrace of my uncle's flat a few days earlier prior to carefully packing it into the panniers. That supreme level of organisation had now been abandoned so as to keep the ants at bay. Normally, I would use the porch area of the tent to store anything that wasn't of great value and that wasn't going to be rendered unusable the following day by a few drops of errant rain. That should have left me luxuriating in the expanse of the tent with just my clothes and valuables. Thanks to the ants, however, everything apart from Reggie was inside with me. It was a tight squeeze.

The coast between Conil de la Frontera and Cádiz left me scratching my head as to why anyone would choose to live or spend their holidays on the nearby Costa del Sol. This beautiful stretch of coastline, only a short drive to the west, was a much more attractive destination in so many ways: modest environmentally friendly development, low levels of traffic, immense blue skies, spectacular sunsets over the Atlantic, flocks of migrating birds, Julio Iglesias and the Madrid Philharmonic providing the campsite entertainment of an evening… OK, that last bit wasn't quite true; Julio never turned up.

The scenery did become a little more urban as I approached Cádiz. A large coastal natural park pushed me inland and through the town of Chicana de la Frontera. I then tentatively joined some suspiciously motorway-like roads through scruffy San Fernando before finally joining the long, straight causeway that joined Cádiz to the mainland. Built upon what was once an island, the old city of Cádiz took up a physically isolated position nearly 10 km from the southern end of the causeway. It was said to be the oldest city in Europe and since its formation over 3,000 years ago, it had seen its fair share of history: from the founding Phoenicians through Roman times to its key role in the relatively recent discovery of the Americas. There you go: three millennia of history in once sentence.

My own five-week stay in the city may not have gone down in the annals of Andalusian history but it had given me a thoroughly enjoyable and vivid glimpse into its people, language, life, culture and, admittedly, local beer, Cruzcampo. The final week of my visit had coincided with the pre-Easter *semana santa* (Holy Week) when great *pasos*, or floats, depicting biblical scenes of a tearful Mary or blood-stained Jesus were hoisted onto the shoulders of penitents and slowly paraded around the city through crowds of people and clouds of eye-streaming incense. On reflection, perhaps that was Mary's problem too. These events, held throughout the day and often in the middle of the night, had been described to me beforehand but nothing could have prepared me for the visual and auditory maelstrom. Spectacular is an overused word but for the Holy Week celebrations of Spain, it was most certainly appropriate.

Upon arrival in the old city, I checked the times of the ferry across the bay to nearby El Puerto de Santa María – it would save me a long journey around the perimeter of the bay of Cádiz – before embarking upon a leisurely circumnavigation of Cádiz to take in a few of my old haunts. I paused for lunch in the pretty square outside the language school where I had studied and I spotted some faces I recognised: the teachers, the barman, the woman who sold bread... but having already said my goodbyes I kept my distance and watched as they interacted with the new students, cajoling them into practising their stuttering Spanish just as they had done so patiently with me. I realised that these were the last familiar faces I would see for many weeks. I smiled and went to catch the boat.

My next stop, 15 km or so away, was Jerez de la Frontera, the sherry capital of Spain, where I had already booked a room at the local youth hostel. The man on reception at the Albergue Inturjoven Jerez didn't seem that pleased to see me. He was on the phone when I arrived and the conversation must have been an important one, as he continued to talk while giving one-word instructions to me, accompanied by loud clicks of his fingers and a fair bit of pointing: '*Pasaporte* (click)... *llave* (click)... *ascensor* (click, point)...' etc.

'*Muchas gracias*,' I replied with *muchas* emphasis on the *muchas*.

Is it possible to click your fingers sarcastically? I wasn't sure. I fought the temptation to do so as I made my way to the lift; it was late in the day and I didn't fancy being thrown out into the street.

The seven-storey building had clearly been designed by an architect who was as disgruntled in his job as the receptionist. Its featureless façade contained not so much as a squiggle of ornamentation. The interior was similarly minimalist and, when I peered through the window of my third-floor room at the rear of the building, I could see an unkempt paved yard surrounded by a concrete fence topped off with a couple of metres of wire mesh. Had I mistaken the youth hostel for the local youth detention centre?

I escaped the building and, after a short stroll around the pedestrian centre of Jerez, my faith in Spanish society was more than restored. Small bands of colourfully dressed men playing lutes and singing in perfect harmony wandered the old, narrow streets, entertaining the locals and a handful of early-season tourists. Families were gathered on the terraces of restaurants, eating, drinking, chatting and laughing. It was a world away from the austere hostel.

By the time I emerged from my room the following morning, *señor* clicky fingers had been replaced by *señorita* happy and smiley. The large breakfast room had been taken over by several youth football teams on a weekend training camp. They were all wearing identical kits and chatting away in that lively manner that only Spaniards and Italians can ever achieve. It was a nice atmosphere in which to munch away at my own breakfast and it put me in a positive frame of mind for the long haul towards Seville across what I suspected to be upwards of 80 km of nondescript countryside.

It was, but – after around 50 of those 80 km – as I cycled along a wide band of spare tarmac by the side of the N-4 road, olive groves to my left and olive groves to my right, I turned a corner that changed my direction of travel from predominantly north-eastern to due north. A few moments later, and unbeknown to me at the time, I crossed the line of latitude that marks 37 degrees north. I had completed the first of my 35 degrees.

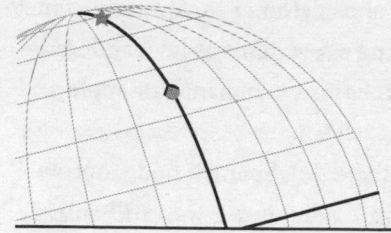

THE SECOND DEGREE
37°–38° NORTH

11–13 April

When you see a touring cyclist on the road, what do you think? *An adventurer? An independent spirit? An explorer?* (Let's not get carried away...) *A vagrant in need of pity and free food?* Hold that thought...

I was determined to adhere to a healthy diet on this journey to Nordkapp. The cycling may be about to provide me with regular exercise, but a regime of stodgy food and red wine had taken its toll on my energy levels in the latter stages of the previous cycles. Perhaps the sizeable town of Los Palacios y Villafranca would be the perfect place to stock up on some of my five-a-day. Lots of banks, estate agents, a few petrol stations, furniture shop and dozens of bars... Greengrocers? Not along the kilometre-long main *avenida* of Los Palacios.

Salvation came in the form of a few Portakabins bolted together in the middle of a large car park a few kilometres north. Oversized pictures of tomatoes on the side of the 'building' confirmed that I had found a greengrocer's, Spanish style. The establishment was staffed by women in green aprons busying themselves stocking the shelves. There appeared to be just one customer in addition to me: a man in his fifties who was selecting a few items as he wandered. I did likewise and presented my purchases – a banana, an apple and an avocado – to the woman at the cash till.

'*Quanto costa?*' I enquired in Italian. My Spanish had improved markedly during my five weeks in Cádiz, but I was still mixing up basic (and alas common) Spanish and Italian expressions. My linguistic faux pas didn't faze the woman serving me.

'*Son gratis.*' They were free. All the women were now chatting and laughing, and I wasn't sure whether it was at my expense or not.

'*¿Por qué?*' I was back on track with the Spanish, enquiring why.

'*Porque…*' started the response, rapidly followed by lots of Spanish that was beyond my linguistic pay grade. Sensing my confusion, the woman pointed at the man who I had thought was another customer.

'*¡El jefe, el jefe!*' He was the boss and, for some reason, had just instructed the woman on the checkout to let me have the fruit for free.

'*Muchas gracias, muchas gracias,*' I responded but unsure as to why.

I sat outside and ate the fruit. *Were these people taking pity on me because I was travelling by bike? Did I have the appearance of a vagrant in need of free food?* I reached for my phone, took a selfie and checked the picture: I was looking well and even clean-shaven after having taken advantage of the facilities back at the hostel in Jerez. The kindness of strangers – how wonderful.

My guidebook informed me that there was a campsite to the south of Seville at Dos Hermanas. Having visited twice before, I wasn't planning to take a day off in Seville, but I did want to carry out a little more research into the Vía de la Plata, the pilgrimage route that I would be following for the next week. I would stay at Camping Villsom overnight before cycling 15 km into the centre of the Andalusian capital on Sunday morning. Finding a hotel in Seville for Sunday night would play havoc with my statistics – I was aiming to average 75 km per day over 100 days – but would afford me the time to plan my onward route.

Pitching the tent in an ant-free environment, I bought a can of meatballs and veg at the rudimentary on-site shop and, for the first time, assembled my new MSR Windboiler stove. I had purchased it for its compactness rather than its ability to remain lit even in storm force winds whilst clinging to the edge of a Himalayan peak. The upside of this was that it could boil a litre of water in well under a minute. The downside was that it wasn't great at simmering meatballs. The flame had two settings: off and fighter jet. Had there been any ants, they would have been cooked alive in the afterburn.

The following morning I fell into conversation with Paul from the Netherlands, the first touring cyclist I had met on the journey so far. In his seventies, he had travelled widely over the years, although he wasn't keen on 'following numbers', which I took to mean cycling routes. I refrained from mentioning the EuroVelos. He was softly spoken and smiled through much of our conversation; if he had grandchildren, I imagine they'd have adored him. Rather than cycle all the way from home, he had taken the train to southern Europe, carrying with him a folding bike. He had no timetable and only a vague plan of action that involved shorter rides out into the countryside near the place where he happened to be staying. He would then take the train a little further before returning to two wheels for more sedate exploration. It struck me as a wonderful way to spend some of the free time afforded by retirement. I could only hope that 30 years down the line, my knees would still cope with the pedalling and my back able to withstand consecutive nights on a thin camping mat. It was sometimes a challenge in my forties so please refrain from placing any bets.

As our conversation drew to a natural end and I turned to go back to my tent to pack away, he called me back.

'Remember that there will always be Mercedes days,' he explained.

'What's a Mercedes day?' I enquired.

'It's a day when it's probably raining, perhaps cold, the scenery is not that inspiring and you tell yourself you'd rather be somewhere else.'

'So, why a Mercedes day?'

'Because it's when you wonder why you didn't just buy an air-conditioned Mercedes instead. I've never bought one because I know that the next day will be so much better.'

I smiled, shook his hand and wished him well. I wondered how many Mercedes days I would experience over the coming months. I had certainly had to endure them in the past but, just as Paul had said, the next day was always so much better.

—

Seville was the same, rather beautiful, Seville that I had discovered on my previous visits. I found a central hotel, the Convento la Gloria which, as the name suggested, was a former convent. The decoration suggested that the nuns had left quite recently and in a hurry, as biblical scenes and statues of the Virgin Mary were still dotted around the place, looking down upon my every move. Away from her prying eyes, my preoccupation for the afternoon was to seek out as much information as I possibly could about the Vía de la Plata.

Plata is the Spanish word for silver and the name is often translated as the 'Silver Way', but its origin is in the Arab word *balat*, which refers to a paved or cobbled path. It was built by the Romans and is now considered one of the main pilgrimage routes to Santiago, which is why I had been able to access quite a bit of information about cycling along it from the dedicated Vía de la Plata website. A suggested itinerary split the route from Seville to the northern coast at Gijón into 12 days, ranging between 46 km and 105 km. I envisaged only using the first nine of these sections as far as Benavente, at which point I would head east. The first suggested leg was to the town of Monesterio and it would be 105 km. That was no bad thing, as my average since leaving Tarifa had slumped to only 67 km per day. A longer day in the saddle was needed and, after my rest day, I was up for the challenge.

A charming woman at the *oficina de turismo* had provided me with a map indicating interesting diversions en route and a business card for the Amigos del Camino de Santiago de Sevilla Vía de la Plata (Friends of the Vía de la Plata). Their office was in the western part of central Seville. Adopting a flagrant disregard towards one-way signs, I located it within a few minutes in a covered alleyway off the Calle Castilla. How wonderful it would be to start my journey along the pilgrimage route by having an in-depth chat with a group of real experts! I'd tweeted to say I'd be visiting and they'd rapidly retweeted, perhaps thrilled at having a prestigious cycling writer come to pay them a visit. They might even want to take a photograph. (Had I shaken off the vagrant look?) It was all potentially very exciting.

The office was shut.

Horario:
Mañanas: Miércoles de 10,00 h. a 12,00 h.
Tardes: de Lunes a Jueves de 19,00 h. a 21,00 h.

I could hang around to see them at 7 p.m. or come back on Wednesday at 10 a.m. The office itself wasn't the tourist-friendly welcoming point that I had envisaged. They'd gone more for the inner-city youth club design, with a painted metal door and bars across the window.

I stood for a few moments, and looked up and down the street. I wasn't even sure which way I should be going.

'*¡Buen camino!*'

The comment – the traditional good luck salutation to pilgrims – was directed at me by a man who was clearly out for a long walk; wherever he was heading, I needed to be heading too.

'*¡Perdón!*' I called as I tried to catch him up. '*¿Dónde es el camino?*'

His name was Antonio and he patiently answered my questions as to where exactly I should be heading, using the kind of map that I wish I had invested in. It even included dotted-line variants for when the cycling path deviated from that of the walkers. He pointed to one of the seashell signs that I should be looking out for, wished me well and off we went at our different speeds.

As the seashell signs were primarily intended for walkers rather than cyclists, they were easy to miss. With a few twists and turns, I eventually made it to the Río Guadalquivir, having travelled the epic distance of about... 2 km from the centre of Seville. I had already lost count of the number of times I had stopped cycling to search for a directional seashell.

'*¡Buen camino!*'

It was another walker. He read bemusement on my face and explained I should follow the yellow arrows. Whereas the seashells were official, the yellow arrows were very much unofficial. Most had been daubed or sprayed on the ground, a building or anything else that happened to be handy (a confused cyclist?). They were much more useful than the seashells in that they indicated the direction when it wasn't all that clear.

Alas, on the other side of the bridge over the Río Guadalquivir, the arrows directed me down a steep bank and towards a rough track running alongside the river. I looked ahead of me; there was no alternative access route to the track so, reluctantly and very hesitantly, I pushed Reggie down the bank, fighting to counter the effects of gravity on his fully laden frame. We eventually made it to the bottom, where I remounted and started to cycle along the track. Within a couple of hundred metres, it had degenerated into freshly churned mud. Not wishing to return to the main road and climb the steep bank that I had earlier descended, I persevered. For much of the time I pushed; where I dared, I rode. Was this a taste of things to come?

After another 5 km and with my enthusiasm for the Vía de la Plata waning considerably, the track passed under the motorway – the Autovía Ruta de la Plata – and across the N-630, subtitled on the signs as the Ruta de la Plata. I paused under the awning of a BP petrol station to ponder the situation. My high hopes of being able to cycle along quality off-road paths had been dashed. It was developing into a Mercedes morning.

I looked at the map of the Vía de la Plata given to me by the tourist office. Three long lines linked Seville with my destination, Monesterio: on the left was the pink walking/cycling route, in the middle was the white motorway and on the right was the red N-630. All three had a legitimate claim to call themselves the Ruta de la Plata. For a cyclist, the *autovía* was not even an option, but the N-630 most certainly was. In fact… surely the N-630 had more of a claim to call itself the Ruta/Vía de la Plata than the other two? The *autovía* was a modern-day construction. The walking/cycling route was surely a *relatively* modern path born out of the pragmatic desire to keep walkers (and a few cyclists) away from the main road, right? The N-630 was, I conjectured, the modern name given to a road that had existed in various states for hundreds of years. Perhaps even a couple of thousand years, dating all the way back to the Romans. The original Ruta/Vía de la Plata was the N-630!

However plausible or implausible my reasoning, in terms of cycling the decision was an excellent one. The N-630 was a wide, good quality road almost devoid of traffic. All but a handful of cars, lorries and buses had decided to make use of the toll-free A66 motorway, leaving those who hadn't to trundle past Reggie and me in an amiable fashion. They were presumably on short journeys to and from the smaller towns and villages not served by the *autovía*. Even the ascent from sea level in Seville to around 500 metres at the northern border of Andalusia was sufficiently stretched out over 80 km that it could hardly be called taxing. The air was increasingly cool but the sky was blue and I was making real progress north. This had been no Mercedes day.

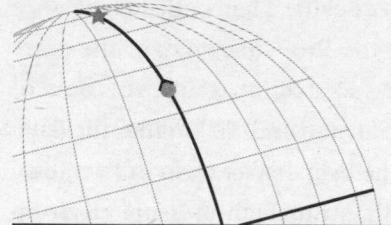

THE THIRD DEGREE
38°–39° NORTH

13–16 April

I was excited about moving into the next Spanish region, Extremadura, for no better reason than the fact that it wasn't Andalusia, where I had now spent over six weeks. But I had little idea as to what to expect.

My guidebook referred to 'the harsh landscape of Extremadura cradling ornate conquistador towns built with riches from the New World' but as I dug a little deeper, one inhabitant of the region was given more than his fair share of column inches: the pig. This was no ordinary pig; this was the acorn-fed Iberian pig. In Monesterio there was even a museum dedicated to him. The town announced itself as the *Ciudad del Jamón* – the city of ham – but that's where the excitement finished. I didn't spot the museum but I did find a basic €25 room for the night and a small basic bar which served basic food. It was a basic kind of place.

The most pig-like thing that I could find in Monesterio the following morning was Reggie. I pushed him out of the garage of the *hostal* and leaned him against an adjacent wall. He was still covered in mud from the previous day's foray along the rough tracks of the Vía de la Plata, north of Seville. I had noticed that since our encounter with the banks of the Río Guadalquivir, the gears were slipping and the brakes were scratching against the rims of the wheels. I put all this down to the mud and, 20 km into the day's ride, I eradicated most of it with the help of a jet wash in Fuente de Cantos. But even more exciting than this high-pressure clean-up was the sighting of my first group of Iberian pigs.

From a couple of hundred metres, the pig farm created an idyllic rural scene: to the left, the farm buildings on a gentle slope. Beyond them a large expanse of undulating green hillside and to the right, some fenced-off brown fields containing lines of tent-like shelters. Huddling together in a group to one side of the 'tents' were around ten well-built muddy black pigs. I stood and watched them. The size of the animals suggested that they were nearer the butcher's hook than perhaps they realised. There was, however, something amiss. No acorns – or rather, no oak trees from which the acorns could fall. Since reading about their diet, I had envisaged these premier league pigs spending their days wandering around dense forests of oak trees, snuffling out acorns at their leisure. Perhaps they did elsewhere but not here in this oak-less, indeed treeless, landscape.

—

Much of the next two days of cycling was downhill. It was the reward following the long climb to Monesterio and my average speed on the bike climbed to over 20 km/h. With minimal traffic, the N-630 felt more like a wide cycle lane than the major highway it must once have been prior to the arrival of the *autovía*.

The short 45 km ride to Zafra dented the daily average once again – it now stood at only 66 km – but at least the town looked more promising from the perspective of a tourist. The Hotel las Palmeras was a world away from the previous day's *hostal*. For one additional euro, I had a cracking second-floor room with a balcony overlooking the attractive, cobbled and traffic-free Plaza Grande.

Sunglasses were on my mind though not, alas, on my nose. Pair number one had been left inadvertently at the campsite in Tarifa. In Seville I had bought a cheap replacement pair from the El Corte Inglés department store. Perhaps a little *too* cheap as, within 48 hours, one of the lenses had fallen out and I was back in the market for pair number *three*.

Should I go for the cheap option again or should I 'invest'? As any cyclist worthy of the name will know, the best place to 'invest' is a dedicated bicycle shop. I went online and discovered that my LBS – local bike shop – in Zafra was Bicicletas Rodríguez. Rod's Bikes was on the southern edge of Zafra, a kilometre away from the centre. I was soon standing outside a rather impressive emporium dedicated to everything two-wheeled that didn't have an engine.

Once inside, I didn't have to search for long to find what I was looking for. To the right of the door was a cabinet. Behind lock and key were four glass shelves upon which a small number of brightly coloured sunglasses had been placed. It's probably a closely guarded secret in retail management circles that anything placed inside a locked glass cabinet can have its mark-up doubled instantaneously, but I wasn't thinking of such marketing ploys as I visually inspected each pair of sunglasses in turn.

'*¿Gafas?*' asked the sales assistant. He was referring to the glasses.

'*Si… Quiero gafas de sol.*'

'*¿Inglés?*'

'*Si.*' My response didn't have the desired effect of him abandoning Spanish.

'*¿Para el ciclismo?*'

'*Si.*' But I was managing. I tried to keep things simple.

'*Quanto costa?*' Err… And in Spanish: '*¿Cuánto cuesta?*'

'*Ciento veinte euros.*' Mmm… €120. I was tempted to point out that only 24 hours earlier I was being offered free food. Not remembering how to say 'Have you anything cheaper?', I went for the more direct approach.

'*¡Es caro!*' It's expensive!

I was sensibly escorted away from the glass cabinet towards some more reasonably priced glasses.

'*Cuarenta euros y el quince por ciento de descuento hoy.*' I'd arrived on a special day; everything in the shop was being discounted by 15 per cent. So… About £25. Yes, that was in my price range. The deal was done.

I took another selfie to check out my new look. I was happy. The bright red sunglasses gave me the appearance of someone who was taking the whole enterprise of cycling across Europe seriously which, of course, I was. Most of the time.

But, aside from red sunglasses, how does a traveller prove that they have elevated themselves to the ranks of a serious adventurer? By getting hold of a GoPro camera, of course. I had only used it a few times since purchasing it earlier in the year but had so far created cinematic masterpieces such as *My Cycling Commute Meets The GoPro Hero 4* and the all-time classic *Sunset At The Beach In Cádiz*. The technology of the GoPro was outstanding but the camera could be a little fiddly to control.

Hence, my departure from Zafra the following morning was delayed by considerable fiddling.

I had to be very careful not to overwhelm the ability of my iPad mini to store any resultant film and edit it, so making anything in 4K Super HD quality was out of the question. I settled instead for standard 4:3 HD. If I were to set the camera to take one picture every 10 seconds, that would mean that, when played at a frame rate of 30 images per second, every hour of real time would be squeezed down to 12 seconds on screen. A four-hour journey – the time I estimated it would take to cycle to Mérida – would play out in 48 seconds. Once uploaded to YouTube, in our digital world of limited attention spans, that might have a few people watching it to the end before giving in to the temptation of finding a cute cat video.

I attached the camera to Reggie's handlebars, switched it on and set off.

Just outside the pedestrianised part of Zafra, I had a short conversation with another cyclist. He was about the same age as me, from Germany and, I assumed, on a pilgrimage. Unlike me, he was – perhaps religiously – sticking to the cycling route that I had abandoned. He said it had been tough going but he had persevered and managed so far. He was cycling a standard, well-worn bike, using old panniers, wearing a crumpled linen shirt, staying in pilgrim hostels every night and certainly not filming things with a GoPro.

It was an interesting contrast and one that played on my mind as I cycled towards Mérida. I saw more faults in my approach than his. For no better reasons than his understated cycling 'look' and his unwillingness to choose the easier option of following the N-630, I suspected that he might be a priest and I wondered if I would bump into him again further north. I had more questions to ask about his motivation for cycling the Vía de la Plata. Although a non-believer myself, I had always found the concept of and belief in a god to be fascinating. He wouldn't be able to convert me but here was a guy who could, perhaps, enlighten me.

It was the seventh cycling day of the journey to Nordkapp and it was downhill all the way. Save for a few small, fluffy white clouds, the sky was blue and there was little wind as I trundled under the force of gravity from 600 metres at Zafra to under 300 metres at Mérida, the ancient capital of the Roman province of Lusitania. It promised me more Roman ruins than you could shake a GoPro selfie stick at and, as I cycled over the very modern Puente Lusitania, I was able to see an extraordinarily well-preserved Roman bridge spanning the wide Río Guadiana a few hundred metres upstream.

The deserted campsite 3 km on the other side of Mérida was not enticing. Would I be happy leaving all my worldly goods there while I returned to the centre to explore? Probably not. As there were numerous *hostals* and cheap hotels listed online for around €25, I was beginning to wonder why I was even bothering to look for campsites in the first place, given that they were invariably only a few euros cheaper. The Hostal Residencia Senero charged me €26 and, after checking in, I wandered off to the Plaza de España to watch it rain.

The map that I picked up from the tourist office told me there were 31 points of interest in and around the centre of Mérida. They were ordered in what would have created a continuous yet tortuous extended tour of the city; the almost complete aqueduct at number 31 looked impressive in the photo although I wondered how many people ever made it that far. With limited time available,

I decided to concentrate my attention on numbers 1, 2 and 3: the amphitheatre, the theatre and the Roman garden.

One payment gave access to all three attractions and, according to the ticket, I was visitor number 569,124. I wondered how many of the previous 569,123 people had been just as impressed as me with what they had stumbled upon. There was, of course, much to stumble upon – watch your feet on those 'granite blocks which functioned as speed bumps' for example – but the extent to which the buildings were, or appeared to be, intact was remarkable.

The theatre was, perhaps, the standout attraction. When in use by the Romans, it could seat 6,000 but, due to its simple yet brilliant design, none of those 6,000 would be further than a few tens of metres from the stage. I climbed to the top of the semicircular seating area and tried to imagine I was a citizen of the Roman Empire enjoying an afternoon of tragedy or comedy. I then remembered that I had only studied Latin for one year at school and the storyline became a bit hazy to say the least. My focus slowly drifted away from the imaginary scene being played out on the stage below me. From my elevated position I had a view across the ruins, the suburbs of Mérida and the large expanse of predominantly bare countryside beyond the city walls. Out in the fields, fat Iberian pigs were undoubtedly continuing to chomp through their piles of acorns. Here in the city, however, I was discovering that there was much more to life on the road in Extremadura than just snouts, trotters and future legs of *jamón*.

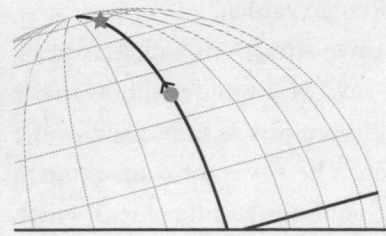

THE FOURTH DEGREE
39°–40° NORTH

16–17 April

I had, through my cycles around Europe, become somewhat of an expert in the quality of road signage. Briefly... Italian signs: dreadful – place names with seemingly random numbers placed next to them. Greek signs: not quite as bad as the Italian ones. Swiss signs: disappointing. French signs: the benchmark for excellence – clear, accurate and everywhere. But there was a new kid on the block: Spanish signs.

I defy anyone travelling along the N-630 in western Spain to ever feel that they had no idea where they were. Not only were the standard town/city/distance signs clear – and, as far as I had noticed, accurate – but every transition from *comunidad* (region) to *comunidad* and *provincia* to *provincia* was proclaimed via a large green sign. I was never in any doubt as to who was ruling over me.

On a more practical level, I was always aware of just how far I had travelled thanks to the neat arrangement of distance posts that had been set up along the side of the road. Every 50 metres was marked with a simple white post. After every 100 metres there was an identical white post with a number counting up from 1 (100 metres) to 9 (900 metres). The passing of every kilometre was noted with a red-and-white sign reminding me that I was travelling along the N-630 and that I had reached, say, the 599 km point. Finally, every 10 km mark was celebrated with not just the road number and the distance travelled, but also the royal crest of the Spanish state. Now, that's the kind of clarity that doesn't just rival the French – it beats it hands down.

Signage might have been amusing my mind but it wasn't warming my body. Thursday 16 April was turning out to be much colder than its recent predecessors so, following the short climb away from Mérida, I paused to layer up. On went my merino wool arm warmers, jumper, bright blue wool hat, neck-warming Buff and a pair of thick waterproof socks. It wasn't raining, but combined with a pair of summer cycling sandals, they ensured that my feet were warm and snug. My thoughts turned toward Scandinavia and especially Norway. If everything went to plan, I would be there in July but that was no guarantee of good weather. Wrapped up as I was, I wondered whether this level of thermal insulation would become the norm once I had passed through the Arctic Circle. Getting comfortable with cycling while dressed as the Michelin Man was, perhaps, no bad thing.

The road continued to be comically quiet. Occasionally, the twisting route of the walkers' Vía de la Plata would cross the N-630 and a warning sign next to the road would alert me to human traffic ahead; the pilgrims were perhaps the most treacherous obstacle out there. However, near the town of Alcuéscar I did spot something travelling towards me on the other side of the road at relatively high speed. I say 'relatively', as the only things I had to compare it with were myself, the ramblers and the occasional sheep or fat pig. A brisk jogger would have had me moving aside so as not to get caught up in the turbulence.

The approaching object turned out to be John from Birmingham, and he was riding a recumbent bicycle. He was the first fellow Brit that I had met so it was nice to chat freely without the barrier of language to impede us. I say 'chat' but it was more of an interview, as I seemed to be asking all the questions. Having spent a considerable length of time being a full-time carer for his now-deceased father, John had decided to sell his house, give up his job and go off cycling for a year. He'd caught the ferry from Portsmouth to Santander in northern Spain and was heading initially to Gibraltar but with the hope of getting as far as Greece over the next few months. He had cycled through the night, as he hadn't spotted a suitable place to string up his hammock; this guy had taken wild camping to the next level and was wild hammocking.

My questions kept coming. Surely, I thought, at some point he would express an interest in what I was doing, where I had come from, where I was going... Eventually, I gave up.

'Well, good luck with the rest of your trip,' I said, as I began to move back onto my side of the road.

'I have a question,' called out John. *At last*, I thought; he wants to know something about me and my own little adventure.

'What do you think are the advantages of using a recumbent?' he enquired.

I couldn't think of anything that would outweigh the disadvantage of being squashed by a truck driven by someone who hadn't seen me, but I took a guess at 'comfort'.

'Yeah, spot on. See ya!'

I didn't mind if fellow cyclists were a bit grumpy at times. On occasions, I certainly was. However, John wasn't grumpy in the least. He was a cheerful, affable chap but one who appeared to have little interest in anyone outside his recumbent bubble. He probably made it as far as Gibraltar and then Greece, but I wonder how much he learnt along the way. For me, there was delight to be had in travelling from A to B, seeing new places and experiencing new things. But there was also the joy of meeting new people, hearing their stories and exchanging experiences. It's what I'd had the opportunity of doing with Paul (of the 'Mercedes days') back in Seville and what I was hoping to do with the cycling German pilgrim if I bumped into him further north.

—

Casting my eyes skywards, there was much ornithological action to attract my gaze. Birds of prey circled above, hovered for a few moments and then swooped to seize their victims. Swallows darted in front of the bike almost as if they were clearing a path for me through an invisible crowd of people. Storks peered down from their lofty positions on top of electricity pylons where they had made their nests. The landscape reminded me of the Yorkshire Dales in the early months of summer: vibrant green grass, colourful flowers, drystone walls, cattle and sheep... The final third of the cycle from Mérida to Cáceres was the prettiest since leaving Seville.

As I approached Cáceres, I was joined by a lean, Lycra-clad cyclist. He was Spanish and his name was Santiago. Over the next few kilometres we chatted, in Spanish, about cycling, Spain and each other in a way that I had failed to do with John. Cáceres was much bigger and busier than I had expected, with wide boulevards lined by seven-storey apartment blocks and offices. Santiago continued to cycle with me until the junction where he could point me in the direction of Camping Cáceres, which was down a hill a few kilometres to the north of the town.

The further down the hill I cycled, the less enthusiastic I felt about camping. I had been staying in town centre *hostals* and hotels for several days by now and was very much appreciating the proximity of bars, restaurants and nightclubs. Admittedly, I had yet to visit any downtown Spanish discos but it was good to know that they were there should I feel the urge to dance the night away.

As a consequence, it was always going to be a hard sell for Camping Cáceres. The young woman on reception was keen to tell me about each pitch having its own individual toilet shed but it would cost me €21 (there was no option of ignoring it and making use of a nearby bush). So I was soon pedalling back into the centre to the Hotel Iberia where, for only a few extra euros, there was no mention of having to crap in a wooden box.

I found a laundrette and an hour or so later took great joy in pulling on my freshly laundered clothes while they were still warm. It is an underrated pleasure of being a touring cyclist and as I wandered into the old town of Cáceres, I glowed, ever so slightly. What I had seen of the place so far was nice and modern but as I approached the Plaza Mayor in the old town, I was taken aback to notice before me a long, open square of white buildings to my left and the pale, red stone of something decidedly medieval to my right. The sky had now darkened to a beautiful deep blue and at the base of the white buildings were the awnings of restaurants, illuminated from above. It made for a perfectly harmonious southern European scene and I suspected that I might have stumbled upon a highlight of the trip.

After finding something to eat, I didn't have much time or inclination to explore but the following morning I was back in the square, this time with Reggie in tow.

A long flight of steps connected the Plaza Mayor with the elevated cluster of buildings where the main attractions of the *Ciudad Monumental* were to be found. I paused at the bottom of the steps to read my guidebook, while at the same time wonder how I was going to drag a fully laden touring bike to the top. Fortunately, a long cobbled ramp hidden behind a row of bars and restaurants came to our rescue. Once inside the *Ciudad*, we wandered and I admired the almost-too-pristine buildings that made up the sides of each of four interlocking small squares. Apart from the odd delivery van, they were free from traffic and the buildings unblemished by modern-day shop fronts. They were a mixture of churches and government offices; the former clearly identifiable by their grand entrances and towers, the latter by a set of three flags – region, state and European – fluttering above the doorways. It came as no surprise to discover that the *Ciudad Monumental* had been designated as a World Heritage Site.

Back on the N-630, a sign told me that Salamanca was 197 km away. The 'official' cycling route of the Vía de la Plata split the journey into three stages, with stopovers in Carcaboso and Béjar, but the N-630 took a more direct route away from Carcaboso and through Plasencia. It was Friday and I reckoned that I could get to Salamanca by Saturday evening. The incentive for doing so was my first proper rest day on Sunday.

A new high-speed railway – the Línea de Alta Velocidad Madrid-Extremadura-Frontera Portuguesa – was taking shape north of Cáceres. Long and straight, it cut through the undulating landscape without mercy, and gracefully spanned rivers and reservoirs across half-completed high bridges. How strange that these unnatural, man-made constructions of steel and concrete could fit so harmoniously into an otherwise untouched piece of countryside.

More feats of great engineering were on the cards for later in the day but this time on a more personal level. As I approached the small town of Grimaldo, I noticed a wobble. *Was it last night's pizza lying heavily in my stomach?* The road surface wasn't great so I initially dismissed any fears that something could be amiss with Reggie (or indeed me). I pulled into a service station to buy peanuts but had to make do with an 'energy' bar which required more calories to be expended in opening the watertight wrapping than those gained in consuming the contents. A little dejected by my failure to top up the fuel tanks, I cycled across the forecourt of the garage. The front of the bike was very springy. Too springy? Yes. I stopped and squeezed the front tyre. It was not good news: I had a puncture.

I leaned Reggie against the wall of the service station in an area that was clear of refuse. My technical skills were limited. Even the challenge of changing an inner tube made my heart sink, but I knew that one of the keys to success in the procedure that I was about to perform would be in remembering how I dismantled everything, so I could put the bike back together again. I found the box of tools, laid them out on the bare patch of ground and carefully started to remove the wheel. This was not mechanics; this was surgery. I released the brakes, deflated the tyre and manoeuvred the hub of the wheel away from the forks and through the narrow pannier rack. Stage 1 was complete. I proceeded to insert the levers between the tyre and the rim, and ease it away from the metal…

Ten minutes later I stood back and admired my handiwork.

'Nurse, I think he will live.'

Patients can stay in bed for a week and recuperate. No such luck for Reggie. I was anxious that, although I had checked very carefully for anything inside the tyre that could have caused the deflation, I had found nothing. I inspected the operating theatre floor to ensure that we had everything; it was just as empty as when I had started. Very tentatively, I started to cycle down the road.

After 15 km, with a tyre that was still as hard as when I had pumped it up at the service station, I approached the outskirts of Plasencia. I had, it appeared, successfully managed to repair my bike without any outside intervention. Perhaps there was a God after all.

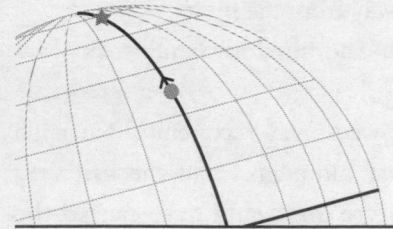

THE FIFTH DEGREE
40°–41° NORTH

17–20 April

With the existence (or not) of God on my mind, I cycled through the southern suburbs of Plasencia, past the optimistically named Funexpress funeral parlour and into the centre of the old town where, somewhat to my surprise, I met Jesus. Kind of.

I had reserved a room at the Albergue Santa Ana, a short walk from the main square. I was looking forward to meeting a few other travellers – religiously motivated or not – in the relaxed environment that the photograph I had seen online suggested would be a world away from the large youth hostel back in Jerez. Upon arrival, the two-storey *albergue* looked promising, except for one thing: it was closed. The door was locked but, behind heavy metal bars, one window was open. Although it was dark inside and there was no activity, the open window suggested that the *albergue* was only shut until someone returned rather than until the summer. I waited, stretching out on a convenient and unexpectedly comfortable concrete bench outside the door.

After ten minutes of dozing, I noticed that a young man had appeared. He was on a bike, albeit one that had seen better days, probably in the mid-to-late 1980s. He had a large, rolled-up sleeping bag on the back of the bike and a couple of well-worn panniers. I sat up from my horizontal position and he turned to face me. His clothes were tatty, his skin was a shade of reddening mahogany and his scruffy beard was only outdone by his unkempt hair.

Jesus, I thought, unsure as to whether to add an exclamation or question mark. The man in front of me could have easily passed for a young Robert Powell in his Nazareth days.

When he spoke, his voice was soft. His name was Marcos and he was from South America but his functional English and my functional Spanish kept conversation to a minimum. Unlike me, Marcos wasn't willing to wait to see if anyone turned up to open the *albergue*, so after a few minutes he was off. He mentioned meeting up with a friend further north and seemed confident of finding alternative accommodation before darkness fell. I returned to my horizontal resting position, unsure as to whether I had just experienced the Second Coming or not.

I was reluctant to make alternative arrangements for the night, as I had already paid my €17 to the hostel online. My patience eventually paid off. A rather apologetic man arrived in a car, unlocked the door and gave me instructions. Despite my high hopes of sharing bread and fish soup with some other travellers along the Vía de la Plata, I would have the place to myself. Even the guy with the key wouldn't be spending the night at the *albergue*. He left me to choose my own bed in the 12-bunk dormitory and fend for myself.

The ride to Salamanca would be a long one so I was up early. I crept around the hostel in a manner that implied the light-sleeping society of Spain had arrived for their annual conference. They hadn't. I estimated that the cycling day would be one of around

130 km, eclipsing the 102 km between Seville and Monesterio by quite some margin. What's more, the route profile suggested that there was some serious climbing to be done and, only a kilometre out of Plasencia, that became more than apparent. I paused for a few moments to look across the valley that had opened up beneath me. Sandwiched between a cloudless blue sky and the green of the trees that blanketed the wide plain was the thin slither of a distant range of mountains.

What I could see was the southern flank of the Sistema Central, the rather prosaically named swathe of mountains that mark a 500 km line across the Iberian Peninsula where the south-east stops and the north-west begins. To get to Salamanca, I would have to climb them.

Again, it was turning out to be a cold day. Having consulted the forecast before leaving Plasencia, I was wrapped up, as were the many other cyclists who had hit the N-630 that Saturday morning. Most exchanged a cheery '*hola*' or even '*buen camino*' as they passed me at speed. Unlike me, they were not carrying any weight on their bicycles and not much on their bodies either. Near a small town called Hervás, just as I was beginning to feel the vertical effects of the Sistema Central, I paused for a drink and was joined by one of the SMAMILs (Spanish middle-aged man in Lycra). The topic of conversation was topography, and we 'chatted' easily by supplementing our altitude-themed exchange with hand gestures and a fair amount of incredulous intonation.

As our voices repeatedly raised and lowered in tone, and our hands etched out the contours of the land, it was clear that the period of significant climbing was about to start. My fellow cyclist, glancing down at the four panniers, was full of admiration for what I was about to attempt. When I mentioned that I intended to continue as far as Salamanca, the level of adulation went up a notch. Was I about to bite off more than I could chew?

My newly acquired fan wished me luck and sped off up the road. I set off at a more sedate pace, edging onwards both vertically and horizontally. My slow progress gave me the opportunity to admire the view, which was gradually changing back into one of winter. The trees were now predominantly bare of leaves and snow still capped some of the higher peaks. Altitude was clearly the major factor but latitude also played a role. I was moving away from Andalusia and its gentle maritime spring climate. Indeed, it struck me that although I may not have been as speedy as most of the other cyclists on the road, I was still progressing north more quickly than the season. That, at least, put a smile on my face.

Towards the end of the long climb, the wind picked up considerably but crucially it was heading in the same general direction as Reggie and me. The summit – the Puerto de Vallejera – was announced by a sign telling me that I had climbed to 1,202 metres. Although this was good news, I was still only halfway to Salamanca and from what I could see in the distance, I doubted it would be downhill all the way. It wasn't.

I was now in the region of Castilla y León and, for a period, the local authorities had adopted a much more casual approach to the upkeep of the N-630. On several occasions it morphed from the deserted major highway I had become accustomed to, into an inconsequential minor and much neglected back road. Gone were those wonderfully clear distance markers and, at times, I felt decidedly lost. I had been following the road since leaving Seville a week earlier and the realisation that it was no longer there was disconcerting to say the least. Gone were the elongated and carefree periods of gazing at the countryside; I was again required to think about where I was going.

The appearance of the pig-dominated town of Guijuelo prompted the region of Castilla y León to start using the N-630 signs again. And when I say 'pig-dominated', I mean just that. Almost without exception, the businesses along the N-630 had some role in the rearing, slaughtering or selling of pigs. Even those that didn't were keen to associate themselves with their four-trottered friends by incorporating into their name or logo something linking them to the not-so-humble pig. They all had their snouts in the trough. On the northern side of the town, distressed squeals emanated from a large concrete building and I sensed that a few more Iberian pork joints were about to start the ageing process.

My eventful day of cycling was not yet at an end. Following a final climb back up to nearly 1,000 metres, the remaining 25 km of the ride to Salamanca were predominantly downhill. The deep blue and cloudless sky of the morning and early afternoon had been replaced by a foreboding bank of black cloud to the north. I noticed a few forks of lightning linking the land to the sky but was not overly concerned, as the wind was still pushing me, and presumably the clouds, further north. Then, abruptly, the direction of the wind changed and within minutes the storm was no longer a distant thing to admire; it was overhead and I was in trouble.

Cycling in the rain could be tolerated, dare I say even enjoyed. Cycling through a storm of forked lightning was not going to be so enjoyable but with Salamanca so relatively close I was reluctant to stop cycling and seek shelter. I paused to put on my waterproof (alas not lightning-proof) jacket and headed into the storm. The open countryside offered little protection should I have chosen to stop; surely it was safer on the open road rather than under one of the few trees. My childhood had taught me that, as well as accepting sweets from strange men, standing under a tree in a storm was to be avoided at all costs. Better off on a bike with rubber tyres, hopefully.

The rain was now approaching a horizontal angle and so was most of my body, as I ploughed through the wall of water. It was also cold. Not the crisp, breathe-in-and-fill-your-lungs-with-gallons-of-freshness cold but painful, numbing, soaking wet cold. A combination of it being late afternoon and the black clouds above my head made it sufficiently dark for me to reach for my bike lights for the first time since leaving Tarifa. For the next 20 km I pedalled, without stopping, until I reached the safety of the centre of Salamanca.

The magnificent Plaza Mayor, the hub of Salamancan life, didn't look so magnificent through the prism of a dark, rainy evening – and even less so from the perspective of a cold, wet cyclist whose only desire was to thaw under a hot shower. Finding a hotel wasn't a problem, and within 15 minutes of arriving in the city I had (brace yourself) stripped naked and was standing in a bath waiting to be drenched in a good way.

Another five minutes later and I was standing (fully clothed) back at the reception desk.

'I'm sorry sir but we don't have any other rooms. The shower will be repaired in the morning.'

My second choice of hotel, the Estrella Albatros, not only had vacant rooms but also showers that functioned, and warmth could return to my numbed body.

The magnificent Plaza Mayor (remember, that hub of Salamancan life) did look much more magnificent through the prism of a bright Sunday morning. Even more so from the perspective of a cyclist who had now thawed, dried out and benefitted from a good night's sleep. I found a bar in one corner of the *plaza* and filled in my diary, noting down the statistics of the previous day's cycling. The ride from Plasencia to Salamanca had been 133 km, bringing the total for the ten days of cycling from Tarifa to 754 km, or an average of 75.4 km per day. My late afternoon of toil and suffering had been worth it and the goal of completing the 7,500 km to Nordkapp in 100 days seemed a little more attainable. I deserved a day off and I was about to benefit from one.

Salamanca was full of frogs. Handbags, T-shirts, postcards, mugs, paperweights… Anything that your average tourist could possibly purchase was embellished with one. The street vendors were selling plastic ones with remarkably authentic croaks for only €2. But why? Walk down the Calle Libreros along one edge of the main building of the Universidad de Salamanca until you arrive at two red doors and you might find out the answer. Top tip: bring your binoculars.

The entrance, with the intricate façade above it, is known as La Puerta de Salamanca, or the door of Salamanca. If you stand in front of *la puerta* and can find the tiny frog amongst the mass of stone swirls, seashells, bearded men, crests, flowers and birds, it will, allegedly, bring you good luck. Even if you have remembered your binoculars, you'd be hard-pressed to find the little blighter. He sits on top of a skull on the right-hand side of the 400-year-old façade, more than a little worn down by four centuries of weather. Second top tip: if you can't find it (very likely), google it. That's what everyone, including me, appeared to be doing.

The origins of the frog are a little ambiguous and the three possible theories resemble a round of *Call My Bluff*. Was it... put there for students to find and give them good luck in their exams? A symbol of sexual temptation to warn the then all-male cohort of students away from disease-ridden prostitutes? Or a certain Doctor Parra who failed to save the life of Prince Juan – represented by the skull – who died in 1497 at the tender age of just 19? Discuss.

Leaving the Salamancan set of a 1970s panel game, I chose to get my dose of culture at the other university, the Universidad Pontificia, and was duly escorted around the building with a group of Spaniards, in Spanish. I was required to persist with the tour of all things Baroque in order to access the tower. It appeared from the street that it would offer good views over the city and surrounding countryside, and I wasn't disappointed. Looking south, beyond the fat layer of red tiles of the old city of Salamanca and a thinner band of modern suburbia, I could clearly see the mountains that I had climbed on the previous day. Turning to the north, I saw no mountains, just a distant patchwork of hazy green, yellow and brown fields. My onward journey promised to be a little less strenuous, for one day at least.

Returning to street level and the constant croaking of plastic frogs, I did what should be done in all old towns and cities: I went for a wander in the hope of getting lost. I wasn't totally successful, in that a few minutes later my attention was drawn by a banner hanging from a first-floor window of the Centro Documental de la Memoria Histórica. Below an old black-and-white photograph of a soldier wearing a thick overcoat and a tin hat, with a rifle slung over his right shoulder and a wicker basket of food in his left hand, it read:

Documentos de una guerra: España 1936–1939

When I was in my mid-teens, the first travelogue that I ever read was Laurie Lee's *As I Walked Out One Midsummer Morning*. It recounts Lee's journey from his home in the Cotswolds to London and then, in the summer of 1935, to Spain. He started his own journey across Spain in the Galician port of Vigo, before heading east via Zamora – my next stop – and Valladolid to Madrid. Playing his violin to earn a little money, he continued south to Seville and then towards the sea at Cádiz. He wasn't a great fan, referring to the city's 'dismayed and half-mad citizens'. He then travelled to Tarifa to drink whiskey with fishermen and a 'mysterious dandy' from Cuba – no mention of healthy breakfasts – before being rescued, reluctantly, by a British destroyer in Gibraltar.

It's difficult not to read *As I Walked Out One Midsummer Morning* and Lee's subsequent books about his experiences during the Spanish Civil War in a romanticised haze, especially from the distance of over 80 years, and there's a part of me which would have loved to rediscover that seedy Cádiz of 1935 and meet its 'dismayed and half-mad' population.

If a counterbalance were needed, however, it was provided in abundance in the Centro Documental de la Memoria Histórica, where there was little romanticism on display in the exhibition of Civil War documents. The posters, photographs and paintings organised into sections labelled 'political ideas', 'republican propaganda', 'repression' and 'exile' emphasised just how divisive and brutal the fight between Franco's Nationalists and the Republicans had been. I wondered what was going through the minds of the other visitors, especially those who had lived a significant part of their lives under the rule of the dictator Franco.

In reality, I know that the harsh life of Spain in the 1930s would have me scuttling back to twenty-first-century Spain faster than an EasyJet flight to Malaga. Since Franco's death in 1975, the Kingdom of Spain has rebuilt itself as a strong and enduring democracy, whose citizens now enjoy all the freedoms that most other countries in Western Europe have had since the end of World War Two. Far better to be travelling in 2015 rather than 1935. Perhaps.

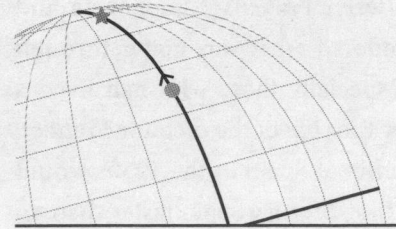

THE SIXTH DEGREE
41°–42° NORTH

20–21 April

Not only had the hills disappeared as I cycled north from Salamanca in the direction of Zamora, but so had most of the sheep, cows, bulls and pigs. Central Castilla y León was much more arable. Cycling through a flat landscape of crops didn't make for the most exciting of days on the bike but the sun was shining and I was happy to keep my mind active, as I contemplated the journey ahead through Spain and beyond.

My thoughts may have been on future adventures but, only a few metres from the road, there was a reminder of those from the past: an abandoned railway line. There was a substantial network of 'Vías Verdes' – literally 'green ways' – in Spain: disused train tracks that had been converted for use by people travelling on foot or by bicycle. Before leaving Salamanca, I investigated the Vías Verdes network but didn't find any routes heading in my direction of travel. Perhaps the disused line from Salamanca to Zamora was on the 'to do' list.

At one point a side road cut across the railway track and I was able to investigate it in more detail. The rusting rails had yet to be removed and a thick carpet of greenery had grown to cover the sleepers. A sign beside the defunct level crossing warned of non-existent *trens*. It would have been impossible to cycle along the line but I suspected that the Vía de la Plata's walking pilgrims would make good use of it. Then again, who needed an abandoned railway to cycle along when there was a perfectly good and all-but-abandoned major highway available? Perhaps this was why it remained on the Vías Verdes 'to do' list. The sleepers in this corner of Spain had been left to doze.

—

I had little expectation of Zamora being anything other than a quiet, overnight stop. It was only mid-afternoon on a sunny spring day so I cycled into the centre without making any effort to pause and read up on accommodation options. I found the Plaza Mayor; it wasn't of Salamancan standards but, then again, few were. A large Romanesque church dominated the scene, and I stretched out under its shadow and did nothing but relax.

'The joy of Zamora lies in its quiet old-town quarter… and its 22 pale-stone Romanesque churches…,' according to my guidebook. I looked up and glanced around. It was certainly quiet. Opposite the church, the terraces of several bars were open for business but remained almost empty. To my right, a huddle of taxis and police cars had been parked, waiting for their respective drivers to either pick up a fare or chase a criminal. For a few moments, I was happy watching life pass slowly by…

I then noticed a cyclist in the far corner of the Plaza Mayor. He had panniers on his bike, and I wondered where he was coming from and going to. The shadow of the church tower had moved and my feet were beginning to feel the benefit; I shuffled the rest of my body into the sun to make the most of the warming rays, closed my eyes and resumed my state of relaxation.

'¡Hola!'

It was the cyclist. I held up my hand to shield the sun from my eyes and responded.

'¡Hola!... Ah! Hola!'

It was the German guy I had met a few days previously in Zafra, the one I suspected of being a priest on a pilgrimage, the one I wanted to talk to about being a *proper* pilgrim. Here was the opportunity I had been hoping for.

His name was Dirk: he was in his forties and from Hanover. Since meeting in Zafra, he had continued to use the 'official' route, although he did admit to resorting to the N-630 at times when things became a little tough. He was staying – usually for free – in the pilgrim hostels. I felt embarrassed to admit that I hadn't veered from the N-630 in days and that the greatest hardship I had encountered as far as accommodation was concerned was the broken shower in my first hotel in Salamanca. I suggested we continue our chat later in the evening and he proposed that we meet up at 8 p.m. for a beer. I decided it would be at that point that I would delve deeper into his religious soul.

After checking into yet another cheap hotel, I returned to the centre of Zamora. As the bell in the clock tower of the Iglesia de San Juan struck eight, I entered the Plaza Mayor from one side just as Dirk approached from the other. That's British and German timing for you. We chose one of the bars in the square and sat outside to indulge.

'I'm not a priest,' laughed Dirk.

'Sorry, I just imagined that… Well, you being a pilgrim and…' I was stumbling over my words, as I couldn't think of another reason why I had thought he was a priest apart from him looking like one.

'I'm a journalist. I used to work for the popular German newspaper *Bild*.'

Whatever alternative occupations for Dirk might have passed through my mind, tabloid journalist hadn't been one of them.

'I'm not even very religious. I liked the idea of taking a bit of time out to think.'

He explained that, since leaving the newspaper, he had worked as a political advisor for the German politician David McAllister, the former Prime Minister of Lower Saxony. Finding himself again 'between jobs', but having previously embarked upon some serious cycle touring in South America in his younger days, he had left his wife and young daughter to fend for themselves for a few weeks in Hannover while he rekindled his two-wheeled passion. Religious enlightenment would have to wait for another day.

Dirk talked about the problems of not using the roads for his journey. The surface quality of the paths wasn't great and he was spending much longer than me in the saddle. Since our initial meeting in Zafra, we had covered the same straight-line distance but – by following a route that deviated tortuously across, below and occasionally over the N-630 and the *autovía* – he had cycled much further. However, as he talked, I thought about my uneventful day. I could see the attraction in his way of doing things. I asked if he would mind me cycling with him the following morning and we agreed to do just that.

The pilgrim hostels that Dirk was using may have been cheap – often free – but they did have their downsides. If you weren't back in the building by 10 p.m., the doors would be locked and you would need to make alternative arrangements. This was going to severely curtail our evening of beer and tapas. What's more, although he had met many interesting people, some did have their idiosyncrasies.

'Are there a lot of other cyclists in the hostels?' I enquired.

'Not many but there was one guy last night in Salamanca who was with his girlfriend. In the middle of the night we started hearing loud panting in the dormitory. They were having sex.'

It was a pity that Dirk no longer worked for the tabloid newspaper back in Germany; this had all the potential of a good story.

'He was from South America: dark skin, beard…'

'Marcos?'

'Yes, that's him.'

I could now see why Marcos – the Jesus lookalike from Plasencia – had been so keen to make progress north; he clearly had things on his mind. Dirk really had witnessed the second coming, perhaps even the first.

—

It was with renewed enthusiasm for travel that I met up with Dirk the following morning. I was looking forward to doing things 'properly' along the Vía de la Plata, for one day at least. That said, it wasn't until after about 15 km that the pilgrims' route deviated away from the N-630. Perhaps I hadn't been doing things so wrong after all, but Dirk was in charge and I would follow.

Compared to the mud lane I had attempted to cycle along near Seville, the off-road sections north of Zamora were OK. Our pace was slow but as it wound its way through the countryside, the path got us up close and personal with nature in a way that I had been missing. The boring fields of crops became flying carpets of vegetation above which birds swooped. Distant ramshackle buildings revealed themselves to be abandoned and crumbling ghost-filled castles when viewed at close quarters. And the disused railway was about to become altogether more interesting.

We noted from the map that there was a river ahead but no apparent bridge. The path was disappearing fast into undergrowth and the adjacent railway line was no longer anywhere to be seen. Was this the reason why following the road was a much better idea? Dirk was more confident. Presumably, this was the kind of dead-end problem he had been encountering all week. He consulted his guidebook.

'According to the directions, the path is up here,' he explained, pointing up a steep bank that was almost entirely covered in thick vegetation. A small, graffitied building gave some glimmer of hope that we weren't the first humans ever to pass this way. 'I think there's a bridge of some description.'

A minute or so later I was at the top of the bank – the embankment of the disused railway line, which would have been impossible to cycle along since the rusting rails and sleepers were still in place beneath the weeds. To my left, however, there was indeed a bridge, and what a bridge it was. Over the river, the rails shot off seemingly to a point of infinity. They had been laid over iron supports, and Mother Nature had yet to encroach on the lattice of Meccano-like ironwork. Between the rails, metal sheets had been laid, allowing anyone who discovered the bridge to walk or cycle easily to the other side of the river. I shouted down the embankment to give Dirk the good news but when he appeared from the jungle of vegetation, he seemed somewhat less surprised than I had been.

'It's just what it said in the guidebook directions,' he commented, Germanically.

Our destination – Benavente – was now not far. It turned out to be not as well-kept as Zamora but just as quiet. We found a bar near the centre of town and sank a couple of beers to toast the successful, mainly off-road, day of travel. I wondered what I had been missing by following the N-630 so religiously but reasoned that with such a long journey ahead of me, I had made the correct decision to play it safe and not risk damage to myself or Reggie along the rough country paths.

For the time being, however, I remained in learning mode and Dirk remained in charge of my pilgrimage education. He explained that he needed to find the tourist office as, according to his guidebook, it held the key to the pilgrims' hostel. He also needed a stamp for his pilgrimage passport. He had already collected a few stamps earlier in the day in bars. I wasn't quite convinced and wondered whether he really needed them or if it was just an excuse to have another beer. His attitude to alcohol during the day was very liberal compared to my own no-beer-until-the-cycling-stops rule.

I felt a little uneasy about exploiting the Vía de la Plata pilgrim thing. I wasn't a pilgrim and I had only been following the pilgrimage path for one day with Dirk.

'But it's free,' stated Dirk.

'Good point,' I replied, rapidly casting my morals aside.

We decided to spend our money elsewhere and, after leaving our bikes and kit at the deserted hostel, we headed for the nearby Parador. The Paradores chain of hotels is to Spanish tourism what Château Lafite Rothschild is to French wine: usually expensive but always classy. The verb *parar* means to stop or stay. It doesn't translate as to sit on a terrace, drink beer and eat good food but that's what Dirk and I did at the Parador in Benavente. There are 94 Paradores across Spain and they tend to be located in castles or former monasteries. The first opened in 1928 on a site chosen by none other than King Alfonso XIII and, on and off, they have been thriving ever since. The Parador de Turismo in Benavente was a converted castle with origins in the twelfth century but its unblemished, somewhat plain, walls and turrets gave little indication of it having seen much military action since then. Inside, brick beams and arched ceilings overlooked large rooms of heavy oak furniture, but Dirk and I chose to eat al fresco in a small garden. Guests of the hotel were far outnumbered by staff, making me wonder whether we weren't the only tourists to have opted for the cheaper option of a pilgrim hostel. Although it had appeared deserted earlier on, our hostel might, perhaps, be somewhat less so when we returned later in the evening.

More drinking ensued back in the centre of Benavente – Dirk was certainly leading me astray – but whereas I stuck to beer, he opted for doubles of gin and tonic. We eventually swayed our way back to the hostel late in the evening for a night of free slumber. When it came to rest, it didn't matter where I laid my head: Parador or pilgrim hostel, sleep was sleep. That said, your chances of being woken by a Brazilian having sex with his girlfriend in the bottom bunk were somewhat less in the former. I would have to take my chances.

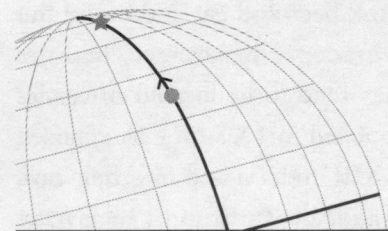

THE SEVENTH DEGREE
42°–43° NORTH

22–28 April

My quest to traverse the 35 degrees of latitude between Tarifa and Nordkapp was about to slow significantly. Over the course of the next week, as I made my way towards the forty-third degree of latitude – somewhere near the French border – I would need to cycle through four degrees of longitude. As far as longitude went, I had hardly budged an inch since leaving Tarifa on 9 April. It would be a long lurch to the east.

Most of the day spent cycling from Benavente to Palencia was monumentally uneventful. I sensed that Dirk wasn't a morning person when I poked my head into his dormitory to say goodbye. Or was it the gin? I surmised that it was most likely a combination of the two, shook his hand, wished him luck for the remainder of his journey to Santiago de Compostela and was off.

Not only did I have to cope with no longer seeing Dirk – he'd been good company but I soon got over it – but my long-term relationship with the N-630 was about to hit the rocks. It was a parting of ways that was entirely predictable, as the Ruta de la

Plata highway continued north towards the coast and I turned east towards France along the N-610. The N-630 had been quiet and the landscape surrounding it impressive. The N-610 was very different: kilometre after kilometre of the same view of tarmac and fields. No big hills to climb or descents to enjoy – just one long, cold, drizzle-infused trudge into a headwind, alongside speeding cars and articulated trucks. Those wonderful Spanish signs celebrated each diabolical kilometre: 80, 70, 60, 50… minor excitement when I discovered the Museo del Queso (that's cheese) in Villalón de Campos, but it was closed… 40, 30… a canal… 20, 10… Palencia. A Mercedes day of cycling if ever there was one.

My destination did, however, promise excitement. WarmShowers, the accommodation social network for cyclists, had finally given me the chance of staying with a local. Of the ten requests so far sent, three had replied negatively and six hadn't responded, but finally I had received positive news. Juan, an English teacher in a local primary school, had offered me a bed for the night.

Talking of school, the drizzle had now graduated from college and become a full-blown heavy downpour with rumbles of thunder in the distance. I took cover in a bar opposite the cathedral in the centre of Palencia to wait, a little nervously, for Juan to come and pick me up.

The next two days were to provide me with the perfect antidote to the Mercedes day of cycling I had just experienced: welcoming people, fabulous countryside, interesting towns and a couple of nights of quality accommodation. When he arrived to meet me, I could see that Juan fitted the cycling stereotype much better than I did: tall and thin with a Bradley Wiggins beard. He lived alone in a centrally located flat, where he put together a simple but delicious meal of cured ham and bread. As we ate, we discussed our respective adventures on two wheels. A fellow teacher, he too had the opportunity of using the long summer holidays to venture a little further afield and for a longer period of time than many, and he harboured ambitions of one day travelling around the world. Alas, his most recent long-distance trip – cycling home from the north of France – had ended somewhat abruptly in Brittany following an accident with a car that resulted in a broken wrist. It was a reminder of just how easily great plans could be turned on their heads, and I prayed that between now and the end of my own trip I wouldn't succumb to a similar fate. It was one of those thoughts that was worth the effort of trying to forget.

Later in the evening we headed out to meet up with his friends. Juan was the only member of our small group who spoke both fluent Spanish and English but, oiled with a few beers, the conversation flowed surprisingly well. The five Spanish thirty-somethings around the table – three women and two men – expressed admiration at me having cycled from Tarifa to the north of Spain. I played down my 'achievement' but smiled with just a hint of pride. Eventually, the mental exhaustion of concentrating on every word uttered finally got the better of all except Juan and we headed home.

The following day was a bank holiday in Castilla y León so, as an employee of the state, Juan had a day off. He proposed that he escort me for the first part of the journey towards Burgos – an offer I gladly accepted – and we set off towards the hills.

The only direct road from Palencia to Burgos was the A62 *autovía*. Had I not been cycling with Juan, I may have followed the *vía de servicio*, a side road for unauthorised traffic that most Spanish motorways seemed to have. But local knowledge was about to pay dividends in abundance, as Juan guided me into open countryside far from any traffic. The views were similar to those of the previous day but without the rain, wind, cars and lorries, and with a bright sun illuminating the immense carpet of crops, I could have been cycling on a different continent.

After about 25 km of steady climbing, we arrived in the pretty village of Astudillo for mid-morning coffee. We chatted as we sipped our espressos in the peaceful main square; a few young children were running around the pruned trees, three white-haired old men and a dog were sitting on one of the benches, chewing over life (or a bone in the case of the dog), and the sun was popping in and out from behind the clouds... Perfect. Had I reached such a level of contentment with cycling since leaving Tarifa? I doubted it.

North of Astudillo, I continued my cycle alone but near the small rural town of Castrojeriz I began to encounter pilgrims walking to Santiago de Compostela along the route of the Camino de Santiago.

'¡Buen camino!'

'¡Buen camino!'

It was a Thursday afternoon in late April. Not, I would have thought, the busiest time of the year for pilgrims, but over the course of the next 30 minutes I encountered perhaps 50 walkers. That meant a lot of 'buen caminos'. After so many days spent ruling the road as a lone cyclist, it was all a bit bewildering. I imagined that by embarking upon a pilgrimage you might be hoping for peace and solitude. Little chance of that happening on the Camino de Santiago. You'd have found more solitude on a stroll around Piccadilly Circus.

In fairness, it was a novelty to have the company, albeit fleeting, as our paths crossed. Most did respond to 'buen camino' but some didn't. I wondered about the pilgrims' motivations for taking on such a physically demanding challenge. Why were they there? What were they thinking about? Was it living up to their expectations? What I was sure about, however, was that every single one of them was wondering: 'Does that bloke know that he's cycling in the wrong direction?'

———

Plan A involved campsite A, about 20 km to the west of Burgos, but it was too close to the motorway on one side and a large construction site for the new Burgos to Valladolid high speed train line on the other. I opted for plan B instead, without knowing if campsite B existed. Fortunately, it did, and it was called Camping Fuentes Blancas, located a short cycle from the centre of Burgos. It was my kind of site: municipal (i.e. cheap), friendly, no hedges preventing casual fraternisation with potentially interesting neighbours and no riff-raff.

Indeed, my near neighbour was about as far from riff-raff as you could get without feeling obliged to bow your head. His name was Peter and he was travelling with his wife Linda in a modern VW camper. It was a palace on wheels that had transported Peter – a former 'Controller of European Services' at the BBC World Service – and Linda to most parts of Europe. He was a linguist, and his knowledge of the world and its languages made him not only good company, but also a useful source of practical information about my onward journey across the continent. He also had words of advice about my next few days in Spain.

'Whatever you do, don't stay at Camping Bañares. It's terrible,' he explained the following morning. 'The campsite in Logroño is great, but avoid Camping Bañares at all cost – screaming kids everywhere...'

By the time I left Burgos – the impressive historic buildings of the city centre were too good to simply ignore – it was already approaching midday and the possibility of cycling as far as Logroño, over 100 km away, was remote. It was, however, good cycling country: a gentle climb to the Puerto de la Pedraja at 1,150 metres before a long, almost continuous descent towards the small region of La Rioja.

The first town in La Rioja was Santo Domingo de la Calzada. Its narrow streets were full of the pilgrims that I had been continuing to encounter all day, as the walkers' path ran parallel to the road. There were numerous hostels in the centre and even a Parador hotel; I was tempted, but the previous night in the tent had been my first for over 11 days and it had rekindled my enthusiasm for camping. I decided to push on a further 5 km to Camping Bañares. It couldn't be that bad, could it?

It resembled a mini city, with roads, junctions and not just hedges marking out each pitch, but high fences. These had, by all appearances, been constructed by the absent residents of the mobile homes that dominated the site. I was left with a small patch of rough ground next to the wash block. The staff were friendly enough but I was soon regretting not taking the plunge, digging into my pocket and luxuriating for one night at least back at the Parador in Santo Domingo de la Calzada.

The countryside of La Rioja was gorgeous. With mountains forming an ever-present but distant backdrop, the valleys through which I was cycling were home to some of the most picturesque views I had yet to encounter in Spain. The cultivation of grapes dominated the landscape in a way that the rearing of pigs hadn't dominated back in Extremadura. Lines of vines crossed the gentle inclines of most of the fields of red earth. For a country that was the third largest producer of wine in the world, I found it curious that it was only here, in the north-eastern corner of Spain, after more than 1,000 km of travel that I had seen my first vine.

It was now the weekend – Saturday to be precise – and I was seeing many more cycling pilgrims along the Camino. They were just as diverse as their walking counterparts. I chatted to a couple of retired Belgian cyclists. Like me, they were sticking to the roads but a few kilometres further along, two young Germans explained that they were happy to remain loyal to the official route despite its uneven surface. Perhaps it was an age thing. Or, indeed, a German one.

Just as Peter had promised, Camping La Playa in Logroño was a much better site. I spent the evening contemplating my three remaining days in Spain which would form a cycling-Pamplona-cycling sandwich. East of Logroño there was no mistaking that the Pyrenees were fast approaching. During the day, I sweated through three significant ascents and numerous minor ones, climbing in total over 1,000 metres into the sky. The rewards were ever-more-inspiring views of green valleys, distant outcrops of rock, and small towns and villages clinging to the edges of the riverbanks. The climbs and the views were intrinsically linked: without one there wouldn't have been the other, and I had no complaints whatsoever.

The final ascent of the day was a crawl of over 300 metres to the top of one of the hills surrounding Pamplona, the Alto de Perdón. I was congratulated on hauling myself to the top by two Spanish cyclists who were out for a Sunday afternoon spin. Our conversation, translated, went roughly as follows:

Spanish cyclist 1: 'Where have you come from?'

Me: 'Tarifa.'

SC1: 'Goodness. That's impressive. I must shake your hand.'

Spanish cyclist 2: [Who had just arrived at the top of the hill and been given the low-down on my efforts in high-speed Spanish by his mate] 'I must shake your hand too.' [Which he did.]

[Assorted chit-chat followed about our respective cycling endeavours.]

SC1: 'Don't forget to wear your helmet.'

SC2: 'If the *Guardia Civil* catch you not wearing it, they will fine you €200.'

Me: 'Well, I've been passed by lots of *Guardia Civil* cars and they haven't yet stopped to fine me.'

SC1: [Now bent double, laughing and pointing in the direction of SC2] 'Ha! He's a *Guardia Civil* officer!'

SC2: 'Well, err…'

Me: 'Err…'

I was reminded of a conversation that I had had with Roman, the German guy who ran the bike shop in San Pedro, near my uncle's apartment. He had explained that the wearing of helmets was compulsory in the countryside, but not in urban areas. However, there were three exemptions to this rule. Firstly, you didn't need to wear your helmet 'during periods of excessive heat'. No one could describe Sunday 26 April 2015 in north-eastern Spain as being in the middle of one of those. Exemption two: if you are a professional cyclist. My speed alone would have made that a hard one to plead in mitigation. Exemption three: on steep hills. The climb to the Alto de Perdón was certainly that – I was off the hook.

—

Despite the rain, the dark charm of Pamplona, capital city of Navarra, was evident. Or should I say Nafarroa? Or even Navarre? But isn't this the Basque Country? Or Euskal Herria? Hang on, you said Pamplona? Shouldn't that be Iruña? And what about the bit over the border in France? Isn't that the Basque Country – *le Pays Basque* – as well?

The Basque Country, or Euskal Herria, extends over 21,000 km², half of which is the Chartered Community of Navarre. Ninety per cent of the population live in the part of the Basque Country situated in the Spanish state and the rest in France. The Basque Country is divided into the 'historical territories' of Araba, Biscay, Gipuzkoa, Lapurdi, Navarre, Lower Navarre and Zuberoa. Today the territories in the Spanish state are divided into two self-governing administrative regions: Navarre and the Basque Country (Euskadi). The territories north of the Pyrenees are within the French *département* of the Pyrénées-Atlantiques. Let's not mention the Treviño enclave…

There was much evidence of the region's semi-autonomous status. Many buildings sported pro-Basque graffiti, Basque flags were draped from countless windows and the Basque language was ubiquitous, used in parallel with (and often instead of) Spanish. The Basque Country may not have achieved full independence from the Spanish and French states but, from the evidence to be seen in its capital, here was a region wallowing in almost full autonomy.

After a night in a dry and warm hotel, I was back in the main square, preparing for a day of exploration – my second day of rest of the trip.

Salamanca had had its croaking frogs; Pamplona had its raging bulls. They were decidedly quieter than their reptilian counterparts further south, however, only to be seen on posters, in souvenir shops and, strikingly, in one spectacular statue situated along a rather anonymous shopping street near the bull ring. The Monumento al Encierro depicted in frozen and bloodless detail the infamous running of the bulls that takes place every July. At 8 a.m. each morning from the 7 to the 14 of July, six bulls charge along the fenced-off 800 m course through the city centre towards the bull ring. Locals and tourists who are brave (or stupid) enough to run with the animals have only a rolled-up newspaper with which to defend themselves. My suggestion would be to go for a Sunday broadsheet rather than a tabloid.

The running of the bulls is not unique to Pamplona, of course, and it will come as little surprise to discover that every year many men (for it is men who seem to participate most frequently) are killed taking part in it. In Pamplona, 15 lives have been lost in the last 100 years. Across Spain, 2015 was one of the deadliest years on record, with ten people being killed, including four people over the course of just one weekend in August. One of the ten people to lose their lives was too busy filming the event on his mobile phone to notice that a bull was about to gore him in the neck from behind.

It seemed unlikely that something so close to the Spanish heart – occasionally all too literally – would ever be banished from the kingdom but austerity may be giving a helping hand to those who want to see it outlawed. Cash-strapped local authorities are beginning to prioritise funding schools over bloody bull festivals. You can see their point.

I wasn't sorry to have arrived in Pamplona nearly three months too early to witness any running; the evocative statue would suffice for me. I was happier getting up close and personal with the pilgrims who were walking along the Camino and for whom Pamplona was their first major stop. Usually in small groups of three or four, they were easy to identify with their sticks, rucksacks and brightly coloured waterproof jackets. At this point of their own adventures they were still visibly enthusiastic about what was to come along the road to Santiago. The following morning – my final morning in Spain – I continued to pass them as I approached the forty-third degree of latitude. It was only 10 km from the border with France and 1 km south of the first Spanish stop on the Camino, Roncesvalles.

It was a steady climb from Pamplona at 450 metres towards Roncesvalles at 900 metres, but there were many small cafés along the route through the foothills of the mountains. I made the most of their facilities when hunger got the better of me and chatted with a few of the pilgrims. They had a long way to travel to their destination but so did I. As I cycled those final few Spanish kilometres, I spent most of my time reflecting upon my months in Spain: Cádiz, my uncle's place in Estepona, the cycle through Andalusia, Seville, the Vía de la Plata, Salamanca, German Dirk, Spanish Juan, English Peter, frogs, bulls, pilgrims… It had all gone pretty well. And then I thought about what was to come, not in the medium to long term, but in the very short term; I still had to cross the Pyrenees.

PART 2

FRANCE

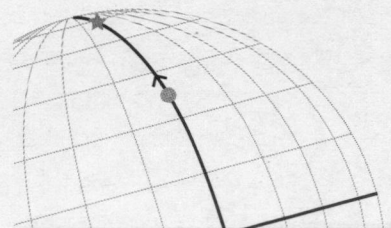

THE EIGHTH DEGREE
43°–44° NORTH

28–30 April

I paused for lunch at Roncesvalles, my final destination in Spain. Imagining it to be a sizeable town, I was surprised to find it small, quiet and isolated. One building dominated the village: the Real Colegiata de Santa María de Roncesvalles, a former hospital for pilgrims, around which a cluster of other pilgrim-serving enterprises had been established, including a couple of hotels and a *hostal*, Casa Sabina, which also served food. I sat outside the building, ordered a sandwich and contemplated the climb to come.

Fifteen minutes later I remounted and started the long crawl over the Pyrenees in the direction of the French border and the town of Saint-Jean-Pied-de-Port. In front of me was the Michelin map booklet of the Camino de Santiago, which broke down the walking route into 34 stages, each of approximately 25 km. Above each map was a height profile of the stage. I noted that between Roncesvalles and the highest point of the first day of the walk, I needed to ascend a further 500 metres.

After 10 km, the climbing had still to begin in any serious way. This was a little concerning, as I reasoned that the longer it didn't happen, the steeper the incline when it did. I continued for a few more kilometres and arrived at the Puerto de Ibañeta, the mountain pass, where the sign told me that I was now at 1,057 metres. A modern church to one side of the road also marked the spot. I paused for thought. Strange... Where were the remaining 400 metres?

My error was in assuming that the walking path and the road upon which I was cycling were one and the same. A couple of kilometres to my right, the pilgrims were reaching the heights noted on the altitude profile. My contemplation of great physical efforts to come whilst munching on a sandwich back in Roncesvalles had been misplaced. Disappointed? A little. But disappointment severely muted by a fabulous 20 km freewheel ride along the narrow valley to the unmarked border with France.

—

My plan was to follow the west coast of France as far as... Bordeaux? Royan? La Rochelle? I hadn't yet decided, but I did plan to cycle along the Loire Valley before heading to Paris.

My first night in *La Belle France* would be in Saint-Jean-Pied-de-Port, the traditional starting point for pilgrims setting off along the Camino de Santiago. My guidebook spoke well of the small-yet-perfectly-hyphenated town and it delivered on most levels. I was almost overcome with emotion to find the kind of campsite upon whose grass I could happily have spent the rest of my life. Cheap, basic and in a prime location near the centre of town; it could only be the famous French municipal campsite. The reception was closed but I pitched the tent, D-locked Reggie to a lamppost and wandered off for something to eat.

'How was the journey from the coast?' was my first question the following morning to a fellow touring cyclist and neighbour at the campsite who was heading in the direction of Spain.

'*Valloné*,' he replied. Up and down. The poor bloke hadn't slept well.

'Did you hear all those people talking last night?' he enquired in French.

I hadn't. I had spent much of the late evening in my tent – just a few metres away from his – catching up on episodes of *The Archers*. Having lost my earphones, I had been playing the everyday story of country folk through the speakers of my iPad... Ahh...

'I didn't hear a thing, sorry...'

The route to the coast wasn't at all *valloné*. It was a continuation of the gradual descent that had started on the previous day at the mountain pass. The French drivers did, however, seem a little faster and closer than their Spanish counterparts, so after a short recuperative pause at Cambo-les-Bains, a spa town seemingly dedicated to offering therapeutic procedures mastered in the nineteenth century, I extracted myself from the main road and sought out more tranquil back routes. The plan worked a treat and before you could say 'soothe me with a moist white flannel and a sulphur-infused glass of spring water', I was standing outside a Portakabin bearing the words *Office de Tourisme de Bayonne*. The geometrically intriguing building shrouded in scaffolding next door was, I assumed, the angular tourist office of the future.

Having decided to hug the French Atlantic coast, it seemed a good idea to follow the Vélodyssée. This was the portion of the EuroVelo 1 cycle route that started at the coastal border with Spain and finished at Roscoff, in Brittany. I enquired at the temporary tourist office if they had a Vélodyssée map.

'*Err... Joséphine? Joséphine? La Vélo— Pardon monsieur, pouvez-vous répéter?*'

'*La Vélodyssée,*' I repeated.

'*Non. Je suis désolée monsieur. Nous n'avons pas de brochure pour La Vélo...*'

It struck me as strange that a major tourist office – even one in a Portakabin – had never heard of the route. I trundled north out of Bayonne in the hope that I would bump into a sign for the cycle route and, shortly after crossing the Adour River, I did. The good news, however, stopped there. The sign indicated I had reached the point after which the cycle path had yet to be built, at least here in Bayonne. The route did continue but along the road rather than as a segregated track.

In my ideal world, we wouldn't require any special facilities to be built for bicycles, because cyclists would feel safe and confident in using the extensive network of cycle paths that already exists. This intricate lattice of routes has been developed over many centuries for people who wish to travel from street to street, village to village, town to town and occasionally city to city, and is commonly referred to as 'the road network'. Not 'the motor road network' or indeed 'the cycle road network' but 'the road network'.

Alas, we don't live in my ideal world and what's more, as a cyclist, I want to have my cake and eat it. I like the idea of having cycle paths from which vehicles have been excluded, mainly down to reasons of noise and pollution. It's never going to be a reasonable goal that cycle paths link everything in our societies together in the same way the current road network does. Well, not unless you live in the Netherlands. It is, however, a very reasonable goal that the road network be transformed into a desirable resource for all travellers, not just those who move quickest and all too often shout the loudest.

In the meantime, in the absence of dedicated cycle paths or at those points where there was a '*Fin provisoire d'aménagement*' as in Bayonne, cycle route designers have often adopted an altogether different approach: sending the cyclist on a tortuous obstacle course that incorporates more twists and turns than your average tango. The northern suburbs of Bayonne were not unpleasant but why I needed to visit so many of their streets I wasn't quite sure.

As I neared the town of Cap Breton, only 50 km north of the peaks of the Pyrenees, the landscape began to adopt a softer feel, as the pine forests of western France started to become the dominant feature of the landscape. Away from the sphere of interest of the women at the tourist office earlier in the day, the Vélodyssée had now become the fully-fledged, segregated and wonderfully smooth cycle path I had been dreaming about prior to my arrival in Bayonne. It cut a narrow path through the tall pine trees of the forest; a kilometre to my right were the unseen towns of Tarnos, Ondres and Labenne, and to my left were their equally hidden coastal offspring: Tarnos Plage, Ondres Plage and Labenne Océan. Here, I ventured west towards the sea to pause, sit and stare out over the water. It was the first time I had had the opportunity of doing so since leaving Cádiz and I revelled in the momentary sense of achievement of having travelled under my own steam from ocean to ocean, albeit the same one.

I assumed that it wouldn't be difficult to find a campsite along this stretch of the coast, but many places hadn't yet opened at this early stage of the season. I eventually stopped at a municipal establishment to the south of Cap Breton where, over a leisurely mug of wine, I spent the evening chatting with a young British lawyer called Pete who had taken time out to cycle to Spain. Pete, young and lean, made me wonder if I had taken my own career break 20 years too late. My concerns eased with the overnight arrival of French cyclists Pascal and Laurent, who pushed our average age (and waist size) to beyond that of my own. I didn't feel so over-the-hill after all.

They were also cycling south and concurred with Pete that the journey through the pine forests had been much hillier than they had expected. We all went our separate ways, with me scratching my head. My maps and limited knowledge of the area had me believe that the ride from here north would be as flat as an *étang de canards* (duck pond). What hills could possibly be hiding out there in the forests of pine? It was one of those questions that would normally require me to spend a good 30 minutes sipping strong black coffee and eating a croissant or two for breakfast in a pristine French square in the spring sunshine, so I proceeded to do just that.

'*Vous avez des croissants aux amandes?*' I asked the smiley lady in the *boulangerie*.

'But of course,' she replied, in perfect English. 'Is that everything?' she asked, giggling with delight. Cap Breton was a delightful little place. Almost *too* delightful.

I crossed the road to sit on a low wall in the square. I put on my sunglasses, as the sun was bouncing off most of the surfaces surrounding me: the whitewashed buildings, the scrubbed floor, the teeth of the locals... The only surfaces absorbing light were their mahogany skins. They all appeared very happy. *Too* happy? Time for a coffee:

'*Un petit café, s'il vous plaît.*'

'*Absolument monsieur. Avec plaisir.*'

Had I wandered into a French version of *The Truman Show*? I glanced around to see if there were any off-message extras lurking behind the *hôtel de ville* having a crafty fag and looking glum. Not that I could see. Conclusive proof that there was, at the very least, something in the water came when I went to *la poste* to send some documents back home. No withering glances. No complaints that I hadn't filled in the form properly or wrapped everything securely. Very strange.

Pine trees were omnipresent in Les Landes – the French *département* through which I was now cycling – especially along the coast. Unlike many corners of the world where deforestation is rampant and the decline in the number of trees seemingly unstoppable, the story of the pine forests of Les Landes was one of careful management and growth. Today it is a forest of about one million hectares, four times its size compared to the end of the eighteenth century. Up until that time the trees were limited to naturally drained areas and were systematically cleared to use the land for the grazing of sheep. The nineteenth century, however, saw the introduction of effective drainage and the development of a flourishing timber industry that continues to this day. So said the information boards erected to educate the masses about such things. There was more...

The management cycle of your average maritime pine from planting to chopping down is 50 years. Periodically, I cycled through parts of the forest where a few hectares had been cleared of all their trees. It made for an ugly duckling of an area but it was just evidence of the cycle starting again after 50 years. That meant that the efforts of workers back in 1965 was only now reaching fruition and, in turn, those workers had been living off the back of the tree huggers of 1915. What a wonderful thought. It was actually a little more subtle than that, as four periods of *éclaircie*, or thinning out, took place during the 50 years, but essentially the sweat and toil of the swinging 1960s were providing us with soft four-ply toilet tissue today. Now there's a thought.

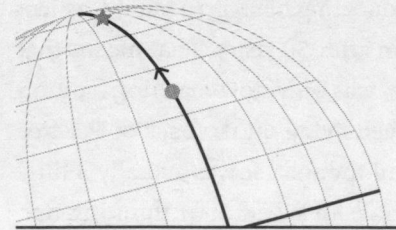

THE NINTH DEGREE
44°–45° NORTH

30 April–3 May

Cycling through the forests on a well-maintained tarmac track was very easy. The Vélodyssée/EuroVelo 1 was clearly signposted and every ten or so kilometres, where the path intersected with one of the east–west roads leading to the beach, easily negotiable wooden barriers prevented any nasty collisions. That said, the area was almost deserted of people, cyclists or cars into which I might crash. On several occasions I cycled for more than an hour without seeing any other signs of human life. What's more, there was barely any wind so when I paused, the only things to be heard were the waves crashing onto the unseen beach a few hundred metres to my left.

The roads I was crossing created umbilical cords to small towns and villages a few kilometres from the coast. After 70 km of travelling due north from Cap Breton, I took my chances with Saint-Julien-en-Born, where I found another municipal campsite, albeit one that had closed for the evening. When I returned to the reception the following morning to pay, it remained shut. I made a point of hanging around for a few minutes and toyed with the idea of pushing €10 through the letterbox in an envelope, but didn't. Had the owner of one of the static caravans not spent most of the previous evening strimming every blade of grass in his vicinity, I may have felt more charitable. I would call him and his annoying strimmer as witnesses should the matter of my non-payment ever make it to court.

The morning was wet and grey, and a quick 360-degree glance around the sky gave every impression that the rest of the day would turn out to be equally miserable. I attempted to shake the tent dry in a small undercover area assigned to the washing of dishes. As I did so, I pondered life under canvas.

Tents must rank as one of the oldest forms of human habitation, just a few rungs up the ladder of longevity from the cave. They were not invented with forty-something men on recreational career breaks in mind; they were, of course, created out of necessity. At the bottom of Maslow's hierarchy of needs are the physiological requirements without which any human couldn't survive: water, food and oxygen. But let's face it, it's also nice to wear clothes and have some form of shelter before we start to worry about such trivialities as safety, love and belonging. And this was just as true for the first humans as it is for their modern-day descendants. It seems a reasonable assumption that if you didn't have a handy cave to sleep in but you did have a few animals that you were in the habit of killing for their meat, one day you would pull one of their skins over a branch to keep out the rain at night. The tent had been invented.

Scroll forward in time to the summer of 1980 and a large field near Benllech on the island of Anglesey, just off the north coast of Wales. A long line of canvas tents had been erected and in each of them were four 11-year-old children trying desperately to stay warm at night. In the morning they would spend several minutes flicking earwigs from their sleeping bags and several more minutes wondering why it had ever seemed like a good idea to sign up for first-year school camp. I was one of those children and I was experiencing my first-ever week in a tent.

In the several tens of thousands of years between its invention and my trip to Wales, the tent hadn't fundamentally changed. It was still a large expanse of thick material lifted above the ground by a wooden pole. I dare say my tent in Anglesey was just as draughty, just as insect-ridden, just as heavy and just as difficult to dry as the tents of early man.

But look what has happened in the last 30 years. Should I be so inclined, I can drive to my local outdoor shop and, within half an hour, have purchased the kind of tent about which Edmund Hillary (and I in 1980) could have only dreamt. For a couple of hundred pounds I can buy a hydrostatic (waterproof to you and me), lightweight (under 3 kg) and fire retardant tunnel tent (with a porch no less) designed with a double skin and manufactured from a mixture of breathable polyester and siliconised nylon, all supported by alloy DAC (not quite sure what that stands for) anodised poles – and it will come complete with an earwig-resistant groundsheet (i.e. no gaping holes through which they can crawl). Should I have a friend (or get lucky on my travels), it will comfortably sleep two and the whole thing can be packed into a bag that's only 41 cm long.

A couple of years ago, I did feel so inclined, and the description above is that of the tent I bought and have been using ever since. As with everything 'outdoor', many of its specifications were wasted on a casual adventurer such as me, but it was good to know that the innovations were there, should I ever decide to go commando. The fact that it would stay erect in winds of up to 150 km/h – that's off the Beaufort scale by some way – was reassuring the next time it got a bit breezy.

Following on from my experiences as an 11-year-old boy, I've notched up a significant number of nights in a tent. Although many of these have been during cycling trips, they are outnumbered by the several hundred nights spent under canvas – and it *was* canvas, not polyester – when working for Eurocamp, the British tour operator specialising in camping holidays around Europe. The pay was pitiful, the work menial and the days long, but the camaraderie amongst the employees was good. As part of a small group of other twenty-somethings who fancied a little adventure but didn't have the inclination to climb the Himalayas or the money to finance a year of doing sod all on a beach in Thailand, we travelled across Europe putting up tents. We were the 'erection team' or, as the company preferred to call us in French, the '*montage*' team. Can't imagine why. But was it proper camping? Tents equipped with (brace yourself…) double beds, thick mattresses, mains electricity, fridges, freezers, gas cookers, full sets of kitchen equipment, barbeques, wardrobes, tables, chairs, sun loungers, parasols… It was glamping before glamping had even been invented.

My tent-shaking technique back under the watery sky of Saint-Julien-en-Born was reaping few results. Despite its many other technological features, the designers of my tent had drawn the line at making it shake dry. All I could do was set off in the drizzle and hope for a break in the weather later in the day.

Although in no way could my journey along this stretch of the coast be described as strenuous, I was beginning to understand why Pete and the Frenchmen had called the terrain 'hilly'. Ahead of me there was always a small, short incline to contemplate as I ascended and then descended a seemingly endless string of sand dunes. Occasionally, the wind would pick up slightly and I needed to protect my eyes from the airborne grains of sand. What I couldn't prevent, however, was the extent to which the sand was getting into the workings of the bike. On numerous occasions I paused, found a stick and cleared the chain of gunk, but within a couple of hours a new layer had built up. Perhaps I could find a bike shop that could clean the bike thoroughly? They might also be able to explain why Reggie had developed a rather annoying click. Was it the gears? Or the bottom bracket? (Or even me?) Whatever its origins, it didn't sound at all good.

Had the sky been blue, had the rain never fallen, had I been warm, had I been carrying a dry tent, had the bike been purring like a contented cat, had I been in a better mood... I might have stopped at the famous Dune du Pilat to explore. I could see the outsized mound of sand – the tallest dune in Europe – rising 100 metres or so above the road and it was impressive. But on a cold, wet day was climbing a sand dune anything other than a poor choice of leisure activity? I cycled on.

My hopes for a break in the weather weren't materialising. I had cycled well over 100 km and as there was little prospect of me spending a dry night in the tent, I reached for my phone, went online and booked into a dry hotel in Arcachon. The three-star Grand Hôtel Richelieu was outside of my price comfort zone but I reasoned that having paid nothing for the previous night, I could stretch my pocket just a little.

Arcachon could be renamed Bordeaux-sur-Mer, as it was here that the residents of France's great city of wine flocked whenever they fancied a bit of fresh air, or perhaps a detox. Even on a wet bank holiday in May – it was *la Fête du travail* – Arcachon had a nice seaside charm. It was clean, pretty and maintained to a level that many coastal towns back in Britain seem even unable to aspire to, let alone achieve. Many of the architecturally interesting buildings dated back to the heyday of turn-of-the-century Victorian meets Edwardian mass tourism. I don't know whether Victoria or Edward ever ventured this far themselves but if they did, the Arcachon they would have found couldn't have looked so different to how it looked when I rocked up in town in 2015.

That said, however pleasant Arcachon might have been, however clean its streets and however well maintained its promenade, it wasn't going to dry my tent. Although my last day off had only been four days ago in Pamplona, I was feeling washed out and, after carefully consulting my ride statistics, I decided upon a plan of action. I had made good progress during the week and my average daily distance would still be over 75 km per day if, after my night at the hotel, I simply trundled a few kilometres down the road to the *camping municipal* near Gujan-Mestras and prayed for sunshine.

I cycled off, pitched the wet tent and started praying. By the middle of the afternoon my tent was indeed dry. Primarily because of the weather, my mood had sunk in recent days and giving myself the opportunity to do some mundane tasks – wash my clothes, sleep, think, plan and clean the bike – turned out to be good therapy.

Come Sunday morning, the wet weather had abated somewhat. It had rained overnight but I tried to avoid the error of wrapping up the tent when it was excessively wet. This resulted in a slightly delayed departure, but by mid-morning I was ready for the off and I started the longish trek around the perimeter of the Bay of Arcachon. I had been told that I could catch a ferry across the narrow mouth of the bay to Le Cap Ferret but this would mean retracing my route back to Arcachon and, for complex psychological reasons, that was something I was reluctant to do.

By cycling around the bay I was also continuing to follow the official route of the Vélodyssée. It in turn was following the route of a disused railway line from Biganos to Arès, the two towns at each corner of the bay. Thereafter, it was a return to the pine forests and the dunes, but not the high-quality, well-maintained track that I had been cycling upon south of Arcachon. It wasn't so much Vélodyssée as *Vélo-tout-terrain-odyssée* – or, in English, mountain bike odyssey. All too frequently tree roots had deformed the surface of the track. Where concrete slabs had been used instead of tarmac, they were in desperate need of TLC, as was Reggie after many kilometres of being shaken about.

I found solace in venturing to the beach along a long wooden walkway and watching the Atlantic crash into the land. I studied the map and reasoned that there was only one more day of pine forests ahead of me. Although I didn't doubt my decision to stick to the coast, I was beginning to yearn for something a little different and that change of scenery was now only a day or so away, on the other side of the Gironde estuary in Poitou-Charentes.

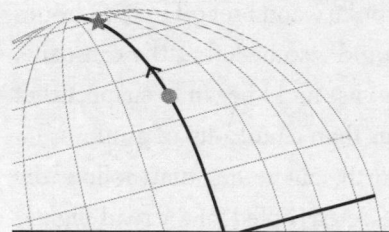

THE TENTH DEGREE
45°–46° NORTH

3–6 May

The cubicles in the wash block at the four-star Camping Airotel l'Océan didn't provide luxuries such as toilet paper so, surprised it could ever be considered optional, I trotted down to the small campsite supermarket to buy a roll.

'C'est combien?' I asked politely.

In a manner reminiscent of the receptionist at the youth hostel in Jerez, the man serving me clicked his fingers and pointed at the electronic display above the till. In turn, I clicked my own fingers and pointed at my pocket containing cash.

Alas, that's not true. The French call it *l'esprit d'escalier*: the annoying realisation that you have come up with the perfect *bon mot* when you are wandering off to bed and it's just too late to say or in this case do it, hence the 'spirit of the staircase'.

The following morning I set about trying to remove all the gunk from Reggie's chainset with the help of several buckets of hot water and a rag donated by a cleaner who was busy smoking a cigarette outside the wash block. I successfully transferred much of the oil-infused sand from the bike onto the grass next to the toilets – the cleaner glared at me through her smoke – and I set off in high hopes that Reggie's annoying clicking would also be left at the campsite. Unfortunately, this wasn't to be the case and I began to suspect that it might be something more serious than a build-up of gunk.

I continued to click my way north, but rather than follow the Vélodyssée through the sandy pine forests, I opted for the road slightly further inland. This brought me into contact with *boulangeries, cafés, supermarchés…* and, in smart Maubuisson, a bike shop owned and run by two of France's friendliest bike mechanics.

'You're going where?' asked Christophe, one of the owners, half in admiration, half in horror.

With that, Christophe and his colleague François seemed to elevate me to cycling royalty. They were, on reflection, the kind of guys who elevated all their customers to cycling royalty but I was happy to bask in my delusion of grandeur.

I explained my predicament – Reggie's clicking – and François set about trying to sort out the problem. He cleaned the chainset, not with a toilet cleaner's rag, but with a high-pressure jet of air. Having been on the road for nearly a month I was tempted to ask him if he wouldn't mind pointing it in my direction too.

Then came the Berner Super 6+ Universal Spray.

'It's what the professionals use,' explained François. I was already sold on the stuff. 'And it's from Germany.' That had me reaching for my cash quicker than a campsite supermarket manager could click his fingers. It was clearly, as I'm pretty sure the French don't say, *les couilles du chien.*[*]

---

[*] Pardon my French but… 'the dog's bollocks'.

Alas, after only a few kilometres, the clicking returned. In the same way that a vibrating dashboard doesn't affect the quality of the drive, the clicking was in no discernible way affecting the quality of the ride. It was just bloody annoying. In a car I would have been thumping the dashboard; on a bike, thumping anything whilst cycling wasn't the best of ideas so on it went: click, click, click...

The pine forest was beginning to appear rather middle-aged in that it was most certainly thinning out. I was reacquainted with the sea at Soulac-sur-Mer, where I was stopped in my tracks by a miniature version of the Statue of Liberty on a plinth in the middle of a traffic island. The diminutive Liberty was looking out to sea and a plaque explained why she was there.

It was all to do with aristocrat and Franco-American hero Gilbert du Motier, marquis de La Fayette. With a name like that, he was perhaps destined for great things when he was born in 1757. He didn't like the British, but in fairness he had good reason not to do so, as his father had been killed by one of their cannonballs a month before little Marie-Joseph Paul Yves Roch Gilbert could celebrate his second birthday.

His elevation to a marquis had been inadvertently fast-tracked and so, it seemed, was much of his life. An officer in the army at 13, married at 17 and a major-general (and a father) at 19. It's enough to make the average man feel inadequate. During the late eighteenth and early nineteenth centuries, if it involved France or the nascent United States of America, La Fayette was on the scene. His first voyage to the Americas was in 1777 on board the schooner *La Victoire*:

We can only imagine that the Médoc coast, and in particular the beach at Soulac were probably the last views of France that La Fayette took with him before his journey to the American continent.

So read the text below Liberty's toga. He did return to France and we'll pick up his story again in Rochefort.

It was nice to travel under the steam (well, diesel fumes) of a boat again. It had taken La Fayette two months to reach South Carolina on *La Victoire*; it took me 20 minutes to reach Royan on *La Gironde*. Perhaps that didn't qualify me for a statue of my own, especially as my gaze was to the north, where I could see a long sandy beach and a distinctly twentieth-century town sitting upon it.

Royan stood in stark contrast to the dozens of villages, towns and cities through which I had so far travelled. I cycled off the ferry and along the esplanade where I stopped to take in its right angles and white concrete. A couple of hundred metres inland, poking up above the other buildings, was an edifice that resembled a space shuttle on its launch pad. A church? I didn't require the assistance of a historian to realise that Royan had been flattened during World War Two and subsequently rebuilt in line with the tastes of the 1950s and 1960s.

I had reserved a room at the Hôtel Arc en Ciel, the rainbow hotel. Appropriately, it appeared to be the only building in central Royan painted anything other than white. The hotel's cheerful owners were just as warm and welcoming as the yellow façade of their building, and they set about making sure that I was fully informed about the city and its attractions.

However, no mention was made of the space shuttle church so the following morning I went to investigate. A large black-and-white photograph had been erected next to what was described as the '*cathédrale de béton*' – the concrete cathedral – showing the devastation of the town as a result of the events of 5 January 1945. 'Have a thought for the 442 victims of the useless and tragic bombardments,' it said, in French. Tragic, certainly. Useless? It seemed a strange choice of word, laden with subjectivity.

From the viewpoint of the twenty-first century, it is easy to consider such deaths as the price worth paying for freedom but, digging a little deeper, that probably wasn't the case in Royan. By early 1945, the Third Reich had been pushed out of most of south-western France. They remained in just two places, on either side of the mouth of the Gironde, to hinder the Allies in refuelling their ships. According to the French historian Guy Binot, the citizens of the city were living in 'medieval conditions', cut off by the remaining German troops and lacking any communication with the outside world.

A decision was taken to bomb Royan and orders were given to evacuate the city. It was assumed that the remaining civilian population was small and that those who did choose to stay were collaborators. But with 'no radio, no mail, no newspapers', Binot argues that it's difficult to see how any order to evacuate could have been received. Messages from the Free French Forces on the ground that the city *hadn't* been evacuated didn't get through to high command and in the early morning of 5 January, two waves of Lancaster bombers dropped their payload on the city, destroyed 85 per cent of the buildings and killed the 442 civilians. 'Only' 47 German soldiers perished. American bombers came to finish the job in April 1945 with napalm. The surrender came later that month.

Ironically, most of the German concrete fortifications remained intact. It may have been a suitable material for military buildings, but concrete didn't make for a great religious one. The rebuilt cathedral in Royan was simply ugly and, alas, getting uglier by the day. It opened in 1958 but within four years it was leaking and the concrete decaying. In the 1980s it was listed as a *monument historique* but, one can only imagine, as a symbol of what it represented – the rebirth of a city – rather than its intrinsic aesthetic appeal.

—

Twenty kilometres into my coastal cycle towards Rochefort I was, for the first time in France, cycling alongside the beach. Pine trees were growing on the low dunes surrounding me and, beyond the narrow strip of beach, brown mud flats reached out across the Baie de Bonne Anse towards a distant horizon. A couple with their two young children were playing in the sand below a sky of blue and wispy clouds of white. There was a light breeze and the only sounds were those of the birds. The small towns along the coast were delightful, consisting mainly of belle époque residences, many of which had been carefully renovated and painted in pastel shades of yellow, blue and green. The contrast with Royan and its Église Notre-Dame was welcome.

It is often better to stumble upon things rather than to contemplate them in advance and before arriving in Rochefort, I was about to do that not once but twice. First was the isolated fortified town of Brouage. It had once been on the coast but land reclamation had repositioned it a few kilometres inland. It had been built to a small grid pattern and encased within thick fractalesque outer walls, now all but redundant apart from giving tourists something upon which to stroll. There was a story about a pining discarded girlfriend of Louis XIV, a few small shops selling art… and a bicycle museum.

I tried the door but it was locked. '*Fermé le mardi*' the sign stated. The Musée du Vélo promised 'a collection of 80 bicycles alongside models dressed from the time retracing history from 1817 to the present'. I peered through the window and could see the bikes and models on their day off. It resembled a neat jumble sale. Perhaps my arrival on a Tuesday had saved me €5.

The second unanticipated attraction was to be found over a wide curve of the meandering Charente River, which I needed to cross. There was a high modern bridge that I had seen from some distance away, but what was the other structure spanning the river a few hundred metres further upstream? Its shape was that of an excessively wide and overly tall set of rugby posts, with no obvious way of accessing the metal cross beam. I had found the Pont Transbordeur de Martrou or, as they call them in Middlesbrough and Newport, a transporter bridge. How exciting.

Only 26 such transporter bridges have ever been built and, of those, half have now been demolished. They tended to be constructed in places where tall ships needed to navigate the river but lack of space or money prevented access roads to a high bridge being built on either bank. A gondola (think large section of road in a cage rather than anything from Venice) was suspended from the high span of metal and moved from one side of the river to the other. In the modern era of mass transit they're useless. But if you're a tourist on a bike they're perfect and, along with a dozen or so other holidaymakers I paid my €4 fare and was off. Great fun, albeit at a very sedate pace.

I was discovering an unexpectedly rich vein of history in this part of France: La Fayette, World War Two, seventeenth-century military towns, belle époque houses and old bridges… and, once settled at the campsite in Rochefort that evening, I took time to catch up via my guidebook. My research, however, only served the purpose of creating more gaps to fill. Pierre Loti? The Royal Ropeworks? The *Hermione*?

The following morning I went off to explore. Pierre Loti – naval officer, adventurer and writer of exotic novels – had lived in Rochefort but his house was, disappointingly, closed, as it was undergoing substantial refurbishment. So, moving on, I located the curiously (but not unsurprisingly) long Royal Ropeworks by the river. This being a naval city, it was useful to have a handy 374-metre-long shed in which to twist the hemp. But being built in seventeenth-century France, it was a very beautiful shed indeed, more in the style of an elongated *château*.

Next door to the former rigging factory was the *Hermione*. Or rather, she would have been there had I turned up two months earlier. We were back to our friend and all-round French hero Marie-Joseph Paul Yves Roch Gilbert du Motier, marquis de La Fayette. We left Marie-Joseph on a ship, gazing at the beach at Soulac-sur-Mer. His trip to North America was successful and, to cut a long story very short, he went on to become a hero of the American War of Independence from Britain.

True to his desire to get on with things – don't forget that he was an officer at 13 – he arrived back in France in February 1779 and spent the year trying to organise an invasion of Britain, while at the same time ensuring that his wife was kept busy by getting her pregnant. She gave birth to George Washington in December. Yes, it's true. Not *the* George Washington you are thinking of but one George Washington La Fayette, named after the first US President.

In 1780, leaving childcare duties in the hands of his wife (and, no doubt, a legion of servants), La Fayette set off again for America, this time on board the good ship *Hermione*. In 1782 he returned to France, got his wife pregnant again, survived the French Revolution, spent five years in jail courtesy of the Austrians, became a politician and then, as all great men and women have been doing ever since, went on a speaking tour of America.

The *Hermione* had been constructed in Rochefort but after many years serving the cause of American independence, she ran aground and was wrecked just north of Saint-Nazaire. However, in 1997 construction started in Rochefort on a replica. It took nearly two decades to build and test the new *Hermione* but in April 2015 she set off on a tour of the east coast of the USA. All I was able to see was the empty dry dock. Some you win, some you lose and some are either closed on a Tuesday, shut for restoration or have buggered off on a jolly to America. It was time, perhaps, for me to move on too.

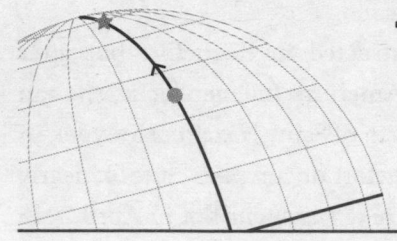

THE ELEVENTH DEGREE
46°–47° NORTH

6–9 May

I was back on the Vélodyssée for the last time, picking up the route by accident a few kilometres north of Rochefort. It hugged the coastline like never before, often vying for position with the regional train line to La Rochelle. I was cycling almost as much to the west as I was to the north and, due to a strong breeze blowing onshore, the effort required to make progress was a step up from anything that I had become accustomed to since arriving in France.

Helpful signposts loitered on most street corners as the route of the Vélodyssée turned left and right at every opportunity, navigating the higgledy-piggledy layout of small houses crammed close to the sea wall. It was a fun, if at times confusing, cycle but after only a few hours I began to see La Rochelle in the distance. On land were the town's distinctive medieval harbour towers. On the sea was what must surely be one of Europe's largest marinas, with dozens of horizontal floating piers and hundreds – probably thousands – of vertical yacht masts twitching from side to side as the boats bobbed in the water.

It was only 3 o'clock in the afternoon; I had arranged accommodation via WarmShowers and agreed to meet my host, Chris, at 9 p.m. I hadn't envisaged arriving in La Rochelle so early in the day and now had six hours to fill with meaningful activity. I had plenty of experience keeping myself busy for much longer periods of time when taking a day off for example. But on those occasions I could wander aimlessly – *flâner* in French – without a bicycle, four pannier bags and a tent. My ability to *flâne* in La Rochelle would be severely curtailed by my two-wheeled friend and all my luggage.

I needed to find activities that would involve leaning Reggie against a wall and sitting in one place for a long period of time. First up was a small outdoor jazz concert taking place next to one of the old towers. I was happy tapping my feet to the music until lack of movement in the rest of my body began to get the better of me and I started to feel the cold. Later, perhaps inevitably, I found a quiet backstreet bar, ordered a glass of wine and started to read the local paper from cover to cover.

Three stories dominated the front page: 330 jobs being lost at a car component factory, the progress of the good ship *Hermione* on her tour of the eastern United States and a large picture of a rather gaunt-looking David Cameron under the headline '*Vote crucial pour l'Europe*'.

The British general election of May 2015 was about to take place, and the question of the United Kingdom remaining in the European Union was being mulled over by the columnists in the newspaper and by me in the bar. Here I was, benefiting from a united and peaceful Europe. The European Union was by no means perfect – few people had ever argued that it was – but whatever faults could be found in the European institutions of the twenty-first century, they were surely incomparable to the fault lines that had fractured Europe in the first half of the twentieth century, as I'd recently been reminded when learning of the senseless killing of hundreds of civilians in Royan. That wasn't ancient history. Was it worth the risk if, taking a lead from a British exit, the Continent again became fragmented and factionalised? Over the next few days, I would have one eye on the road and one eye on the political comings and goings back home.

As 9 p.m. and my rendezvous with Chris were approaching, I retraced my steps back to the marina, having agreed to meet him at the end of pier 41. I felt a little uneasy hanging around a port – even one as civilised as this – at dusk, waiting to meet a complete stranger. Chris arrived, on an engineless scooter, just after 9 o'clock. He shared a flat in one of the nearby modern housing blocks with his girlfriend, Audrey. Both were scientists. His specialism was digital animation and he was a researcher at the university, while she worked in a water quality laboratory. With computer gadgetry taking up much of the living room, a large fish tank on the dining table, and science-themed books and magazines filling most of the gaps, there was something of *The Big Bang Theory* in their flat that night, and Chris' resemblance to the main character of the hit American comedy series only added to the slightly surreal atmosphere.

By the time I woke, Audrey had already left for work but I shared coffee and croissants with Chris at a café a short scoot from the flat.

'Have you ever seen *The Big Bang Theory*?' I asked.

'No, I don't think so…' replied Chris.

I left it at that, to avoid digging myself a grave out of which I might find it difficult to climb in French.

Before leaving La Rochelle, I popped into the tourist office. Rumour had it (well, someone had told me on Facebook) that a new cycle path was about to open, linking La Rochelle with the northern coast of France on a route that crossed the Loire at Saumur. This was my next medium-term destination, as it was where I could hook up with the EuroVelo 6. It was this kind of cycling serendipity which made me feel proud that I hadn't wasted too much time at the pre-trip planning stage.

Initially, the young woman in the *office de tourisme* looked perplexed. She glanced over her shoulder to an older woman who was hovering behind her. The older woman whispered something in her ear.

'He's English. You'll get used to it,' she probably said but, whatever it was, it prompted the younger woman to stand up and announce: '*Un instant.*'

A few *instants* later she returned and I was presented with a hot-off-the-press brochure for La Vélo Francette. She went on to explain that the route hadn't yet officially opened – that was due to happen in early June – but that everything, including the brochure and the signage, was in place.

I was reminded of the moment many years ago when, during a period living in France, I went to my bank to sign up for the fledgling internet banking service. It was explained that I was the first person to express an interest.

'*Ah! Je suis un cochon d'Inde!*' I exclaimed – I'm a guinea pig!

The woman dealing with me looked up with a confused expression on her face.

'*Ah oui? C'est intéressant…*'

The appropriate expression should have been '*Je suis un cobaye*', *un cobaye* also translating as guinea pig. Perhaps the woman in the bank worked all this out as I was standing in front of her. Or perhaps she was experiencing the same level of bewilderment as a cashier in NatWest who had just been informed by a customer that he was a hamster ('Security!').

'*Merci. C'est très utile*,' I responded to the women at the tourist office, avoiding any mention of rodents.

I went outside to examine the brochure. La Vélo Francette was a godsend: 600 km of signed cycling of which I would be following the first 250 km from La Rochelle to Saumur via Niort, Parthenay and Thouars.

Although not yet hot, the sun was shining brightly in a sky of only sporadic high clouds. I reached for my sunglasses and… one of the lenses had a large crack in a corner. They had been the third pair since setting off from Tarifa. In hope of more sunny days to come, I detoured to the La Rochelle branch of Decathlon, where I managed to ignore the mass of advice and multitude of options available and plumped for a pair that looked good.

My new sunglasses gave everything an Instagram tint that made the greens even greener and the blues ever bluer. This being spring in an already very green and pretty corner of France, under a bright blue sky, it was almost too much to take in, but I wasn't complaining as I headed east in the direction of Niort. Much of the cycling was along the towpaths of canals and rough tracks, as directed by the signs of La Vélo Francette. It made for a bumpy but traffic-free ride and the advantages of the latter more than compensated for the inconveniences of the former.

On a macro level, the terrain was as flat as a boy band singing live, but I refrained from bursting into song myself as I trundled from one picturesque village to the next. This was a part of France that I had never previously considered, let alone visited, and it was rather nice. I was cycling through the Marais Poitevin, an area where the marshes had been drained in the seventeenth century by forward-thinking Dutch engineers. Forward-thinking because, whatever their motives at the time, it had provided me and all the other Thursday afternoon tourists with somewhere very nice to do what we were doing.

It was turning into an almost perfect day. Yes, Reggie was still making that annoying noise but after 85 km of cycling I arrived in Niort and booked into the Hôtel Particulier La Chamoiserie. We would call it *boutique*. The owners called it *cosy-chic*. With its modest prices, I couldn't understand why I was the only customer. Of the 16 rooms, just one was occupied, by me. I was a prince in his palace. There was no waiting to be endured and no issue finding somewhere to store the bike – indeed, no problem that couldn't be addressed immediately and to my full satisfaction.

After a meal on the edges of a vast square in the centre of Niort, I returned to my palace to follow events back in Britain via the satellite TV in my room. David Dimbleby was sitting in his usual place, looking no different to how he has looked for most of my adult life. His thick mane of white hair gave him a level of dignified gravitas of which the likes of me could only dream.

At 11 p.m. French time, the exit poll was announced and it appeared at the bottom of the screen below the unflappable Dimbleby:

CONSERVATIVES LARGEST PARTY
CON +9 LAB -19 SNP +52 LD -47

I had been hoping for a rather boring status quo. Consensus politics; agreement and compromise seemed the way forward. It might not have been as exciting as a landslide but at the risk of sounding like a wishy-washy liberal, the coalition appeared to be working well and had prevented the real political nutters from imposing their agendas. Perhaps that's why I was also such a fan of the European Union: countries trying to get along with each other in a complicated, difficult world and, on the whole, succeeding.

As Mr Dimbleby, his colleagues and their guests spent the next few hours discussing a result that was already clear-cut, I fell asleep on my comfortable *cosy-chic* bed.

I descended for breakfast at around 8.30 a.m., the only person to whom breakfast needed to be served. I felt embarrassed to the point of apologising for the fact that the chap attending to my every need had had to drag himself out of bed and get dressed. He had certainly kept himself busy, however, as before me was a large feast: toast (brown and white), butter, jam, marmalade, cheese (three varieties), ham, pickle, muesli, corn flakes, milk, tea (several options), coffee… Everything was laid out on a small table beside the one at which I was sitting. This wasn't a buffet; it was all for me. At least the amounts were modest – except, that is, for hard-boiled eggs, of which there were five. Five. I feel obliged to write the number twice to avoid ambiguity. *Cinq*. I peeled one of them and ate it. The other four (four) were left for lunchtime egg mayonnaise… But for whom?

Much of cycling days 28 and 29 was run-of-the-mill stuff, certainly when compared to number 27. My aim was to arrive in Saumur on Saturday sufficiently early in the afternoon to be in with a chance of having Reggie's noise investigated properly. According to its website, if I were to follow the exact route of La Vélo Francette, I would need to cycle 166 km. Having only had a few hours' sleep, however, I wanted a short Friday cycle followed by a long Saturday one. I located a campsite at a place called Parthenay – 40 km from Niort – and decided to aim for that. I reckoned that by cutting out a few of the meanders of La Vélo Francette and opting for the roads instead, I might be able to shave off a good 10 or 20 km. It seemed like a good plan.

What wasn't part of the plan was the weather. In depressing contrast with that of the previous day, it was cold, blustery and wet. I had no desire to cycle along muddy tracks so I opted for the D743 – one of those long and uncompromisingly straight secondary roads that criss-cross France – all the way from Niort to Parthenay. The rain never stopped but fortunately it was another bank holiday in France so there were no HGVs on the roads, just lots of cars. I pulled the hood of my raincoat over my helmet and cycled until, after about three hours, I arrived at my destination.

Perhaps on a sunny summer's day, Parthenay shone. But it wasn't shining on Friday 8 May. A quick cycle around the town centre had me fleeing to the campsite – Camping du Bois Vert – where, by the time I arrived, the rain had finally stopped falling. I erected the tent, gave it half an hour to dry out, inflated my camping mat and snoozed for most of what remained of the afternoon.

The short day of cycling had, for the first time since my stay with Juan in western Spain, pushed my daily average to below 75 km. It now stood at 74.4 km. This was only a difference of some 0.6 of a kilometre but the more days I cycled, the more difficult it would be to close the gap. If I wanted to be in with a chance of cycling the estimated 7,500 km in 100 days or fewer, I couldn't afford to have too many more lazy sleep-in-a-tent-all-afternoon days. From now on I needed to be hitting not just 75 km per day, but well in excess of 75 km per day.

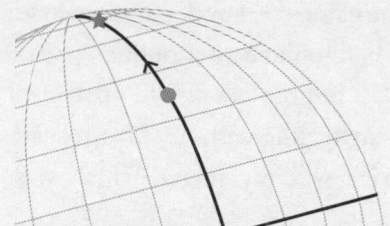

THE TWELFTH
DEGREE
47°–48° NORTH

9–15 May

Upon arrival in Saumur in 1993 as an employee of Eurocamp, I discovered a delightful, quintessentially Loire Valley town complete with fairy tale castle, medieval squares and lots of sparkling wine. I also discovered a great municipal campsite on an island in the middle of the Loire where I worked during that long, hot summer season. Twenty years later, the town had barely changed, or so it seemed. Camping l'Île d'Offard, on the other hand, had changed significantly. It had been privatised and therefore was no longer run by the local council. Gone were the open-air swimming pool (*'condamnée'* according to the receptionist), the shop run by friendly Jean-Claude and the incomparable views of the *château*. That's not quite true. The view was still there, but you had to be staying for more than one night to be allowed to camp on the hallowed part of the site from where you could appreciate it. I was allocated a pitch on the other side of the island with a less-than-majestic view of a green metal fence and some bushes.

But enough reminiscing; I had a bike to mend. With most of what I was carrying deposited at the campsite, I cycled into town to locate VéloSpot, a bike shop that I had found earlier online.

'*J'ai quelques problèmes avec... le...* bottom bracket?' I explained to Patrice, the owner of the shop, struggling with my bike-related vocabulary. Of more use to Patrice was my finger, which was pointing at *le bottom bracket.*

'*Le jeu de pédalier?*' he suggested.

'*Oui, c'est ça!*'

'*Oui, je peux le changer,*' he replied.

'*Et le...* stand? *Je ne sais pas comment dire* "stand" *en français,*' I admitted.

As for '*le bit of plastic that holds the CatEye computer to the frame*', I didn't even attempt its French translation and just let my finger do the talking.

Up close, Saumur wasn't looking quite as good as it had done from the other side of the river. The rose-tinted sunglasses of time could play cruel tricks on the mind and the years of growing up from being a twenty-something casual campsite worker to being a forty-something middle-aged grump had me noticing every crumbling pavement, every piece of discarded litter and every abandoned shop. The Trianon restaurant – my favourite – had closed and the bar where we used to challenge the locals at pool on the Place Saint-Pierre was now a busy upmarket bistro. The rest of the square was filled with trendy bright young things creating memories that they would one day look back upon and cherish unjustifiably.

I picked up Reggie late in the afternoon and cycled him back to the campsite, praying that the clicking had disappeared. The journey was short and he was unladen. Everything *seemed* to be OK. I dined, alone, on a baguette, some cheese and a bottle of wine, next to the fence and the bushes. I had been looking forward so much to this portion of the trip but so far it had turned me into a melancholic reminiscer of days that were probably nowhere near as good as I remembered them. Was this the shape of things to come over the next week or so, as I made my way along the familiar Loire Valley towards Paris?

In the morning, my mood remained low. Upon being served a croissant in a local *boulangerie* by a woman who gave every impression of having just lost her entire family in a plane crash, I didn't hold back: '*S'il vous plaît, madame; soyez polie avec vos clients!*'

I was impressed with my use of the subjunctive as I admonished her for her attitude; the customer behind me was impressed with my courage in saying what I did (he smiled, discreetly) but the recipient of my words was not impressed. She glared at me and remained silent but I could read her mind, which was shouting, '*Get out!*'

I needed to relax, chat to someone and smile. Fortunately, I had arranged to meet Lynne from the cycling website FreewheelingFrance.com. Lynne, an Australian by birth, was now based near Bordeaux and we had only ever communicated online, so it was good to put a face to a name. She happened to be in Saumur because she was also cycling La Vélo Francette with a friend in anticipation of its official inauguration the following month. Over coffee and a croissant we chewed the fat of being on the road: the highs, the lows, the miserable bastards who ran local *boulangeries*... Her positive Aussie spin on life shamed me.

What did I have to complain about? I was on a cycling odyssey across a continent, travelling through gorgeous landscapes, visiting beautiful villages, towns and cities, and meeting people who were almost always charming, helpful and polite. I didn't have much to complain about at all.

It being a Sunday morning, there was a relaxed atmosphere on the roads. I would be following the route of the EuroVelo 6 as far as Orléans. Much of the cycling was either away from the main road or on a segregated cycle path. For all but a short period north of Chinon, where a nuclear power station was positioned next to the water, the wide expanse of the Loire was either a few metres to my left or to my right. I cycled through places that had become familiar during my previous life in the valley: Montsoreau, Langeais, Cinq-Mars-la-Pile, Saint-Cyr-sur-Loire… each name conjured up a different memory. I then crossed the river for the final time over the long Pont Wilson into the centre of Tours.

Following the summer of 1993 in Saumur, I returned to France in 1994 but when my work on campsites finished in the autumn, I needed a reason to continue living in the country. I eventually found a job teaching English at a private language school in Tours and stayed in the city until 1999. I had revisited on a couple of occasions after that but on this trip I was struck by how much Tours had moved into the twenty-first century. It had always been a very pleasant place to live – its people, its culture, its location, its climate – but I had the distinct impression that the city was embracing a new kind of living. This was most evident in the Rue Nationale. For nearly one kilometre the wide boulevard had been all but pedestrianised and four long, straight rails had been sunk into the shiny stone to guide sleek and almost silent trams from north to south and back again. If Saumur had let itself go a little in recent years, Tours had most certainly done the opposite.

Cycling was permitted in the newly environmentally friendly Rue Nationale and I gloried in weaving along a street where, if I had done such a thing 20 years earlier, I would have been mown down by a truck travelling at high speed. Now there was just the small risk of being shunted by a very quiet tram.

Many corners of the city had, however, changed little and I spent time cycling here and there, reminiscing and smiling. I used to live in a small first-floor studio flat in the Rue Colbert; it was still there, as was the children's bookshop on the ground floor. The pretty Place Foire le Roi where I occasionally visited the chain-smoking doctor, the 8 à Huit supermarket that was never – and still wasn't – open from 8 a.m. until 8 p.m., the laundrette, the Lapin Qui Fume restaurant (it wasn't just the doctor's bad habit)... and even one or two vaguely familiar faces. I glanced in their direction but went unrecognised; I was, after all, just another passing tourist. It was nice, however, to be back.

I had never sat down and worked out the exact distances, but when looking at the map of Europe, it seemed that Tours was about a third of the way to my ultimate destination of Nordkapp. To mark the end of this first third I planned to take a couple of days off. Rest days three and four would be consecutive and spent with a friend and former colleague from the language school. Her name was Liz, she was still teaching English and lived with her British farmer-turned-lorry driver husband Roger near a small village called Couture-sur-Loir, about 40 km north of Tours.

So on Monday morning I caught the train to the town of Château-du-Loir, from where I cycled the 30 km to Liz's house near Couture.

Although approaching retirement, she was as bright and breezy as I remembered her being from our time at the language school. Roger was away on a driving job so the two of us spent a relaxing couple of days ambling around the local countryside, taking in the crumbling tower of the Château de Fréteval where Thomas Becket had met Henry II in the twelfth century and then a curious railway tunnel in which Hitler had spent the night before meeting the puppet leader of the Vichy regime, Philippe Pétain, in nearby Montoire in 1940. My meeting with Liz may have been of less historic proportions but, on a personal level, equally memorable. It was good to catch up with an old friend.

I used the opportunity of having a hot tap nearby to give the bike a good wash. No corner of Reggie's metallic body went untouched, including the spokes, one of which fell out in my hand. I was confident that a touring wheel containing 35 more spokes would not be an issue when cycling back to the train station at Château-du-Loir. It was, however, a problem that I would need to sort out once back in Tours.

The trains from Château-du-Loir to Tours were few and far between so it was a choice between either 9 a.m. or 1.15 p.m. I chose the former, which meant a very early departure from Liz's house, but she was up to see me off with a good breakfast.

'You won't be able to take that on the bus mate,' a railway employee informed me in French, pointing at the bike, as I waited on the platform.

'It's OK, I'm taking the train.'

'At 1.15 p.m.?'

'No, at 9 a.m.'

'It's a bus.'

To be informed that your comfortable train journey has been replaced by a rail replacement bus is never welcome news. To then remember that you are travelling with a touring bike, four panniers and a tent only makes the heart sink further.

A few moments before 9 o'clock the bus arrived and, after a short discussion, the driver reluctantly informed me that I had one minute to place Reggie in the storage area. Quite how he would have explained to his boss the presence of half of my stuff in his hold if he *had* driven off after just one minute, I wasn't quite sure.

Back in Tours, I pushed Reggie down the road to a bike shop. It was a busy place but one of the employees hoisted Reggie onto a stand immediately and started work. He could clearly see that I was a man on a mission. The young guy was a mechanic of few words but, using the small number that he had been allocated to use on Wednesday 13 May, he explained that the spokes that I had brought with me on the trip were all too thin. Once the replacement spoke had been fitted, the others checked, the wheel rebalanced and my old spare spokes exchanged for ones of the correct size, I was presented with a bill for just €15. Perhaps I had been charged per word.

For the next two days I continued to follow the Loire in the direction of Orléans. Wednesday's ride was a short one. With my departure from Tours being delayed due to the spoke issue and having already cycled 30 km from Liz's house to the train station, my legs were flagging. The spacious municipal campsite in Amboise was too good an option to cycle past in the hope of finding an alternative some 10 or 20 km further to the east. This again dented my daily average – now less than 73 km per day – but it was the correct pragmatic decision to make. And there were worse places to spend a few hours than Amboise, a smaller, smarter version of Saumur.

—

Paris was now looming. Through an unlikely coincidence, it seemed that I would be passing through the French capital at the same time as a group of pupils and former colleagues from the secondary school in Henley-on-Thames where, until the previous December, I had worked. If I could split my journey into three or four parts – to Orléans, followed by Fontainebleau and then to Paris, with an intermediate stop along the way – I would arrive just in time for a reunion.

The wind was heading east and so was I. For much of what remained of the cycle to Orléans, the route adopted a raised position on top of the levees keeping the Loire at bay at times of flooding. The high wind and my elevated position combined to allow me to pick up considerable speed – touching 30 km/h at times – and in only five hours I cycled the 107 km to my destination. Along the way I passed many other cyclists heading in the opposite direction, battling against the forces of nature. A few laughed, some smiled, many grimaced. A handful ignored my cheery '*bonjour*'. Had I been cycling with them, I would probably have done the same.

As an educated Englishman, I was very aware of the part my 'Great' country had played in world history. During my travels around Europe I had had many opportunities to see the results of the actions of my forefathers. It was fair to say that, over the centuries, we had been an interfering lot. Sometimes with good reason: the gradual liberation of France in 1944 and 1945 brought with it some horrendous destruction but the aim was honourable and just. Sometimes with bad reason: was it necessary for Lord Elgin to prise those marbles from the Parthenon? A little further back in time, we English saw fit to burn at the stake those who didn't quite see things our way. Setting fire to a French teenager in 1431 wasn't one of our greatest achievements.

The teenager in question was of course Jeanne d'Arc – Joan of Arc, La Pucelle, the Maid of Orléans. Cycling into the centre of Orléans, she was difficult to avoid, whether it be in the form of hotels, schools, cafés, roads or statues. Some people in France consider the bank holiday on 8 May not so much a celebration of the end of World War Two but of the life of Saint Joan, and the date is commonly referred to as simply *Jeanne d'Arc*, especially by supporters of the right-wing Front National. It was on 8 May 1429 that an army, led by Joan, liberated Orléans from an English siege.

The woman herself, invariably described as a martyr, saint, warrior and military leader was (so the official story goes) born into a humble family in eastern France. As a young child, she started to have mystical visions encouraging her to seek permission from the future Charles VII to lead an army to defeat the English. I imagine that in the days before Snapchat, WhatsApp and Justin Bieber, he was inundated with such requests from teenage girls. He took some persuading but, eventually, persuaded he was and off she went to fight the English.

Her downfall came when she was captured not by the English but by the pesky Burgundians. For 10,000 francs they sold her to the English, who in turn handed her to the Church who charged her with witchcraft, heresy and dressing like a man. She was burned at the stake in Rouen on 30 May 1431. I'll leave it to others to decide whether the English really were to blame.

I was in two minds. Not about the guilt of the fifteenth century English army but as to whether to cycle the 7 km to a campsite recommended by my guidebook or stay in a city centre hostel. I took a chance and cycled off to the southern suburbs towards Camping Municipal d'Olivet. My decision turned out to be a very good one indeed as, for a modest €7.60, it was a fabulous idyll, with friendly and welcoming staff, free camping area for cyclists, heated wash block, eco-friendly credentials and achingly picturesque. It was a campsite in desperate need of some kind of award.

Three single-person tents had been erected in the area set aside for people travelling without cars – the free camping area – and their bikes were leaning against a tree. But the cyclists were nowhere to be seen. By the following morning, the view hadn't changed: three tents, three bikes. They must have been out late and were now sleeping it off.

My tent was damp from the morning dew so I dragged it away from the grass to the reception area to give it a good shake and allow it a few minutes of direct sunlight. There was no shortage of that. An already very picturesque campsite had become a beautiful one. I looked through the branches of a large tree above my head which was full of pink blossom. The sky was cloudless blue. Life was good. One of the cyclists had now emerged from his tent. I nodded in his direction and he nodded back but I sensed that he might not be in the same state of mind as me to appreciate the bright blue sky.

Then a text message from home arrived to darken my mood. It was from my sister-in-law, informing me that an old school friend had just died. I hadn't seen him for 15 years but the shock was nevertheless real. Somewhat numbed by the unexpected news, I packed away the tent and set off back into the centre of Orléans.

I took my morning coffee in the Place Sainte-Croix, in front of the distinctive cathedral. Despite being a person devoid of religious belief, it seemed an appropriate place to reflect upon the life of someone who had died far too young. Not quite as young as Jeanne d'Arc but, in the small community that was my secondary school, someone who was just as popular. I could only imagine that he had remained so after we had all headed off on our respective paths in life. Mine had brought me to Orléans, France, on a beautiful if chilly morning in May with the prospect of an interesting few months of travel ahead of me. As I headed east beside the canals and along roads of the pleasant but unspectacular Loiret *département*, I had much for which to be grateful, and I was.

THE THIRTEENTH DEGREE
48°–49° NORTH

15–19 May

I had an ambition of venturing regularly into the adventurous world of wild camping during the cycle to Nordkapp. Once a week? After a few days of cycling through Spain this had been amended to once a fortnight and then once a month. You can see it wasn't going well. By the time I had crossed the forty-eighth degree of latitude in the centre of Montargis I had spent 38 nights on the road: 16 in campsites, 15 in hotels, three in hostels, two with WarmShowers hosts, two with a friend… and zero wild camping.

I used to trot out the excuse that Europe wasn't such a wild place. Then, in 2013, I met a Ukrainian cyclist in the south of France who told me he had wild camped every night since leaving Kiev. The encounter had made me feel pitifully inadequate. On the great scale of adventure, I was somewhere down at the end with all those holidaymakers I had once looked after during my Eurocamp days.

Thus, I had so far failed abysmally in embracing the simple life of wild camping. But perhaps that was about to change.

Camping de la Forêt in Montargis was on the edge of an immense forest – a short cycle uphill from the train station but, once inside, the trees were densely packed and the ground uneven, with large patches of moss blanketing the extensive network of roots. At its centre was a cluster of buildings: the reception, a communal TV room and a large wash block but, looking east into the forest, you were in the wild.

In high season, with kids everywhere, vertical lines of barbeque smoke and the gentle chit-chat of people, it was probably a nice place to be. On a damp evening in mid-May, with little evidence of other campers – just a distant pop-up tent and a few rusting caravans – it verged on threatening: the kind of place where good-looking teenagers in American movies get murdered. Undeterred, I paid my €6.55 at reception and pitched the tent, choosing a spot that would give me a fighting chance of making it back to the gate should anything untoward happen.

Two women in their late twenties were using the communal wash block. Next to one of the sinks was a bottle of vodka from which they were swigging. Their skirts were short, their tans a shade too dark for spring and their lipstick distinctive. They ignored me and I made no effort to engage them in idle campsite banter. I suspected these businesswomen were preparing to sweat their assets elsewhere.

Darkness fell. Rarely had I felt so uneasy in a tent and my mind wandered to places that I had no wish to explore. Around midnight I started hearing voices but this was no Joan-of-Arc-asking-François-Hollande-for-permission-to-raise-an-army moment. They were real. I peered out of the tent and could see three men sitting around the pop-up tent. They had lit a fire and were drinking beer from cans. There was no car. Why would they be there? It made no sense. Were they homeless? 'Business partners' of the two women I'd seen earlier? Whoever they were, I didn't want to meet them in a dark, deserted forest in the early hours of a Saturday morning. My good-citizen urge to point out the 'no fires' sign was easily quelled.

It was a long night of little sleep and I had time to reflect upon the whole wild camping thing. It may have felt like wild camping, but it wasn't. This was just creepy camping on a dodgy campsite. My ambition to wild camp at some point before Nordkapp was not diminished but it would take a little more thought.

Buoyed somewhat by the realisation that I had survived the night, I set off in the direction of Paris, almost exactly 100 km to the north. If I arrived in the capital on Sunday afternoon, it would be perfect timing for my Monday rendezvous with former colleagues and pupils, so I decided to make it a two-day cycle via the Palace of Fontainebleau.

From Montargis to Nemours the River Loing competed for space with the canal, the railway line, the main road and a side road. As to whether I was following the 'official' route of the EuroVelo 3, it was anyone's guess. Sometimes I probably was, but for most of the time, I probably wasn't. When I sensed I was within a few kilometres of the palace, I stuck to the road.

I had expected the Palace of Fontainebleau to sit in glorious isolation, surrounded by grand symmetrical gardens, but in reality it was a little more connected to the outside world, appearing rather suddenly behind ornate metal railings. Those lucky enough to find a parking space in the square opposite its façade had, without doubt, a cracking view of its Renaissance beauty. France was usually so good at maximising the visual impact of her heritage – think of the Louvre in Paris – but I couldn't help but think that here in Fontainebleau, she had let herself down a little.

The campsite in nearby Samoreau – the busiest I'd yet visited and in complete contrast to the one in Montargis – was in a great position next to the Seine. It shouted, '*Set up that expensive camping chair that you brought with you, sit in it for the rest of the day and relax!*' But I had come to Fontainebleau specifically to see the *château* so although my heart (and, after an almost sleepless night, most of my body) was saying, '*Sod that!*' my head was saying, '*You really should go and absorb some French culture despite it being back up that steep hill.*'

I had forgotten that to appreciate a monumental chunk of culture, you needed an equally significant chunk of the day and a body that was up for the challenge. I had neither but went through the motions of cycling up the hill, purchasing a ticket and joining the hundreds of other tourists to be directed on a strict route around the former apartments of kings, queens, emperors, empresses and one Pope.* In retrospect, I should have taken my camping chair, erected it in the gardens and admired the view. As it was, much of the undeniable beauty and majesty of the palace escaped me.

Upon arriving back at Camping Grange aux Dîmes, I noticed much commotion taking place in the car park. A large maypole was being erected by a group of Germans, so not a maypole but a traditional *Maibaum*. A helpful local explained that every two years, residents of the Bavarian town of Bernried visited Samoreau to complete the task. The job of lifting the impressive length of

---

* Pius VII, who first visited in 1804 and was subsequently held there under arrest between 1812 and 1814. His 'cell' was very comfortable.

wood to a vertical position was being done without any mechanical intervention. Burly Bavarians huffed and puffed until 90 degrees was achieved. Physical effort aside, it was a wonderful sign of international friendship.

Indeed, the entire campsite had a very international atmosphere. When I went to the reception the following morning to pay my bill, a sizeable number of young Dutch people were in negotiation with the campsite manager. From what I could understand, a window had been smashed as a result of alcohol-fuelled high jinks and the French woman behind the counter was reluctant to return the group's deposit. After much discussion, everything was resolved amicably. Well-built Germans, drunk Dutch students, an exasperated Frenchwoman and an Englishman on his bike; rarely had I felt so thoroughly European.

—

Having attempted to cycle several times along the Thames Valley into central London following the National Cycle Network route 4 and, on every occasion, having lost my way (usually around Chertsey), I didn't rate my chances of cycling uninterrupted along the valley of the Seine into central Paris. It was time to call California and see what Google Maps had to say.

The suggested route worked out just fine and, until I was close to the orbital *périphérique* motorway – only about 5 km from the centre – I followed Google's every twist and turn. I crossed the Seine for the first time at Bois-le-Roi, cycled through the centre of Melun, stumbled over a block of stone in Lieusaint used to define the metre in pre-revolutionary France, dodged joggers in the Sénart forest and then hit Paris itself… Well, not so much Paris as a Japanese tourist who was far too eager to cross the road, but let's not dwell upon that inglorious moment of this adventure.

Once over the *périphérique*, the landscape was increasingly familiar: along the banks of the Seine, past the cathedral of Notre-Dame, over the multi-padlocked Pont des Arts, beside the Louvre, through the Jardin des Tuileries, over the cobbles of the Place de la Concorde and finally along the length of the Avenue des Champs Élysées to the Arc de Triomphe. Who needed an open-top bus when you could do the whole thing for free on a bicycle?

I parked Reggie near the middle of what must surely be the world's most prestigious traffic island and sat for a few minutes to admire the view down the busy thoroughfare along which I had cycled. You couldn't have wished for a more pleasant spring day, with the sun high in the blue sky and a light breeze – sufficient to breathe life into the oversized French tricolour dangling from the triumphal arch behind me but insufficient to take the edge off the warm afternoon. Having just achieved the feat of cycling from the southern tip of Europe to one of the continent's pre-eminent capitals, I was triumphant, and where better to be than an arch dedicated to that very emotion?

I'm in Paris! Look forward to seeing
you at the Eiffel Tower at 10.30-ish.

> *Great news. Thierry is up*
> *for looking after Reggie.*

So went the text conversation with my former French teaching colleague Kerrie. The school group had arrived in Normandy a few days earlier and would be travelling up to Paris early the following morning. Thierry was their coach driver and he had accepted the challenge of minding the bike for the day. The plan was coming together well.

All that remained to do was for me to find somewhere to stay. In most cities I would have shuffled off to the nearest modestly priced hotel, but this was Paris. Did such things exist? My guidebook told me that the nearest campsite to the centre was Camping Indigo, on the other side of the Bois de Boulogne. If Hyde Park is one of the lungs of London, the Bois de Boulogne is the artificial respirator of Paris, slung over the shoulder of the *périphérique* and a stone's throw from the Arc de Triomphe. Within 15 minutes, I was outside the gates of the campsite, a small cluster of rather stylish reception buildings before me and beyond them a pitch beneath a tree that would be my home for the next 36 hours.

I cycled a rather slimline, pannier-less Reggie back through the Bois de Boulogne the following morning. The weather was OK, neither good nor bad. Despite this, many vehicles were parked along the roads criss-crossing the park and their female drivers had removed many of their clothes – far too many clothes for them to be comfortable in the freshness of a May morning in Paris. In some cases they had stripped down to their bra and pants. Could it have been an issue with the air conditioning? Were they waiting for a mechanic to turn up? Some of the ladies had abandoned waiting in their vehicles and were perched on nearby benches, their legs wide open in the hope of the cool air penetrating even the most inaccessible areas of their bodies. Lacking the necessary mechanical skills to offer assistance, I smiled and cycled on.

My former colleague Kerrie hadn't told the pupils that they were about to be reacquainted with one of their former teachers.

Whether this was because she didn't want to deal with insurrection in the student body ('What? You're dragging us to Paris to see Mr Sykes?!') or whether this was to add an element of happy surprise into their day akin to that which would be provoked by them bumping into their favourite pop star or professional footballer, I shall leave for others to judge. But the children certainly gave the impression of being pleased to see me and it was a genuine delight to see their familiar faces.

As a teacher, it was strange to be surrounded by familiar children but not have anything other than a passing moral responsibility to keep them safe and well. Aside from Kerrie and two other French teachers, the group of four adults accompanying the pupils from Henley-on-Thames was completed by my good friend David. Away from the classroom, his interests were very much of the two-wheel variety. A fellow northerner – in his case from Lancashire – he had spent many years living and working in the Thames Valley and had even worked in the bike shop in Caversham from where I had purchased Reggie. He had coached cyclists at the Reading cycle track, and was able to talk with enthusiasm and passion about cycling in a way that wasn't just mindless waffle.

David had helped me to keep my nerve prior to embarking upon the trip from Tarifa to Nordkapp with his regular injections of supportive words and advice. At times I questioned my decision to leave my job and venture off along the cycle paths of Europe but David never did. It was good to see him again and, as the kids went off to explore the Eiffel Tower and have their portraits painted in Montmartre, we chatted about the cycling and the travelling in a way that I hadn't been able to do with anyone in months. Who needed performance-enhancing drugs when I had a performance-enhancing friend? By the end of the day, my motivation to complete the task of cycling to Nordkapp was high and I was in good mental shape for the challenges ahead of me.

As the coach trundled off along the Avenue de New York and I stood waving on the pavement, I felt a sudden pang of loneliness. I had spent seven hours amongst the people of my old life and now they were gone. Once again I was alone, surrounded by strangers. I carried Reggie up the steps of the Palais de Chaillot, pushed him around the Trocadéro roundabout and cycled back towards the Bois de Boulogne. The women were still there, waiting for someone to come along and repair their air conditioning. Just as I had done earlier in the day, I smiled sympathetically and cycled on.

THE FOURTEENTH DEGREE

49°–50° NORTH

19–21 May

So, Picardy, excite me! I might have shouted if I hadn't been spending so much of my time and energy battling the wind. North of Charles de Gaulle Airport, I paused to examine my large paper map but after several comical minutes of struggle, I gave up. Mother Nature had beaten me. She refolded the map in a manner she saw fit and I chose a road that was heading roughly in the direction that I needed to be travelling. Between the centre of Paris and the airport, traffic had been fairly heavy so it was with a sigh of relief that I was now able to turn off the main road and head for... somewhere.

Southern Picardy was a flat landscape of cultivated fields. A few modest settlements and the occasional copse added a small drop of diversity to proceedings. I was beginning to suspect that this northernmost section of France wasn't going to be the most interesting portion of my trek to Nordkapp. I tweeted as much and when I checked my phone a little later, one follower had replied: 'Look out for the castle at Pierrefonds. It's worth a visit.'

It was in the direction I happened to be heading. Something to look forward to. In the meantime, the lingering inner glory of having cycled as far as Paris was keeping a smile on my face and, however mundane the ride through Picardy was turning out to be, it felt comfortable.

Nearing Pierrefonds, I had been on the bike for over four hours and had knocked off in excess of 80 km, helping to nudge my daily average distance in the correct direction again. I wanted it to be pushed significantly above 75 in the flatlands of northern France, Belgium, Germany and Denmark, before heading into the more mountainous areas of Scandinavia. A few days of 80, 90 and 100 km or more would be useful at this stage. With few things to stop me in my tracks, I saw no reason why this shouldn't be possible.

I was then stopped in my tracks.

My view had been restricted by trees on either side of the road but suddenly, ahead of me, poking up above the greenery was a cluster of pointed turrets. Passing coaches parked to my left and a pretty yet crumbling white church to my right, I cycled a little further and looked up. I wasn't expecting that.

I had found the *château* of Pierrefonds, an edifice of considerable size. Cylindrical towers supported ramparts with conical roofs. Between the towers were high walls resembling those of a mighty dam, their smooth surfaces interrupted only by a few small windows. Embedded into the wall of each tower was a statue. The building had been constructed on a mound to one side of the town centre. The fact that I hadn't seen it coming was perhaps one of its greatest attributes and all credit to its medieval builders.

Yet something was not quite right. The medieval castle had somehow failed to age. The walls were blemish-free, the tiled roofs too pristine. Where were the cannonball scars? There were hints of a Disney castle and it looked faintly familiar. I reached for my guidebook.

... built in the twelfth century, dismantled in the seventeenth and restored by order of Napoleon III in the nineteenth to create a fantastic fairy-tale affair of turrets, towers and moat.

In the main square below the castle I noticed a couple of painters busy at their easels. A third person – a man – flitted from one to the other, offering advice. A black Range Rover with a British personalised number plate was being used to keep them supplied with paint, brushes, rags and whatever else one requires to paint a 'medieval' castle. I pushed Reggie to a position where I could see their paintings and fell into conversation with one of the artists.

'Do you know *Merlin*?' she asked.

'Not personally...'

'No, the TV series *Merlin*. The one with Victor Meldrew. Well, the actor who played him.'

'Richard Wilson?'

'Yes, that's him. It was filmed here.'

'I don't believe it!' I could have said, but didn't.

This answered my question as to why the castle appeared familiar. The very French Château de Pierrefonds was, in the imaginary world of TV drama, the very English Camelot. My appetite was whetted and I was eager to explore. The castle was, however, about to close; I would need to come back in the morning. If only there was a handy local campsite... 800 metres down the road I found Camping de la Forêt, checked in and made camp.

Shortly before 9.30 a.m. the following morning I watched as the employees of the castle arrived for work and then set about opening up. I formed an orderly queue of one. The contrast with the noise, bustle and enforced herding I had experienced at Fontainebleau was welcome. After the first half-hour, I was joined by perhaps half a dozen other visitors. One turret per person – a perfect castle-wandering ratio.

In Pierrefonds we were back to Napoléon and the Bonaparte dynasty. In 1789, as I'm sure you are aware, France was revolting. *La Révolution* tore through the ranks of the aristocracy but, within 15 years, Napoléon Bonaparte had crowned himself emperor and set about defining modern day France. However, after his disastrous Russian campaign, the other European powers forced him to abdicate and sent him into exile on the island of Elba. Ever the restless general, he escaped and marched on the French capital to regain power.

Louis XVIII had been installed as the new head of state only to be overthrown by Napoléon on his return to Paris. In June 1815 the action moved to Waterloo – much more of that later – where Napoléon was defeated once and for all and eventually sent to distant Saint Helena where he died in 1821. Louis XVIII was restored to power. Was that the end of the Bonapartes? Not quite…

Over the course of what remained of the first half of the nineteenth century, things got a little messy in France, as democracy and monarchy fought for supremacy. Louis was succeeded by Charles X, who in turn abdicated and was replaced by Louis-Philippe (keeping up?). Meanwhile, Napoléon I (that's Napoléon to you and me) had had a son who was (you guessed it) Napoléon II. He was never accepted as emperor of France but that didn't stop him from adopting the title. He died, in Vienna, at just 21 years of age, without leaving an heir. Was *that* the end of the Bonapartes? Not yet…

In 1848 civil war appeared imminent so Louis-Philippe did the courageous thing and fled to England. The Second Republic was declared, elections held and a certain Louis-Napoléon Bonaparte, nephew of Napoléon I, was elected as president. However, prevented by the constitution from running for election a second time, he did the next best thing, which was to orchestrate a *coup d'état*, instigate an empire, declare himself emperor and rule as Napoléon III. Job done.* Was *that* the end of the Bonapartes? Yes.**

Despite his lack of democratic credentials, Napoléon III wasn't all bad. He became famous for engaging Baron Haussmann to redesign the Paris that we know and love today. Bringing a little relevance to this long tale, I should now explain that he was also responsible for rebuilding the Château de Pierrefonds.

Inside the castle, several paintings and one very old photograph showed how the building appeared prior to 1857: much like you would expect a crumbling, derelict, medieval castle to look. The architect Eugène Viollet-le-Duc was instructed by Napoléon

---

* Until the Franco-Prussian War of 1870 when France was defeated. Napoléon III went off to England where, in 1873, he died. He is buried at St Michael's Abbey, which is sandwiched between a modern housing estate and a railway line about 400 metres from Farnborough station. A fitting resting place for France's longest serving post-Revolution head of state?

** Actually, no. They are currently on Napoléon VII but there is some dispute as to who should hold this title. Napoléon VI considered his son, Prince Charles Napoléon, to have a (brace yourself) 'dangerous belief in democracy'. When he died in 1997, he stipulated in his will that the title should pass directly to his grandson, Prince Jean-Christophe. At this point, I give up.

III to start the renovations. He came with a good CV, having already set about restoring Notre-Dame Cathedral in Paris and the fortifications of Carcassonne in the south of France. The restorations were never completed but what Viollet-le-Duc created was a wonderfully fanciful version of how a medieval castle 'should' look. The interiors were as colourful as the exteriors were pristine. Indeed, it was easy to see why, when the TV executives were looking for a Camelot for Merlin and his mates at the court of King Arthur, they came knocking. I loved it.

I had been wrong to be so dismissive of what Picardy had to offer and, as I continued my cycle north, looked forward to discovering other places. I was again setting off with only a vague direction in mind and certainly no fixed route. I would cycle where my whim was telling me to cycle, albeit within the parameters of a ride that would hopefully have me in Maubeuge by the end of the following day.

—

It was almost impossible to travel through this part of Europe without regular reminders of the two world wars. I was heading in the rough direction of Saint-Quentin, picking out a route that kept me well away from any of the busy roads. Many of the little towns and villages sported quaint, almost poetic three-barrelled names: Cuise-la-Motte, Berneuil-sur-Aisne, Moulin-sous-Touvent, Tracy-le-Mont… It was difficult to imagine this area as one large battlefield. I smiled at the uncharacteristically short sign to the village of 'Cuts' but my mood was to change as I approached the town of Nampcel.

Initially, I thought the dark posts in a field behind some trees to my right were agricultural, supporting a crop that had yet to grow. But then I realised my error, parked the bike by the side of the deserted road and walked towards the entrance. The sign read:

Deutscher Soldatenfriedhof
1914–1918
MOULIN-SOUS-TOUVENT
Cimetière Militaire Allemand

It was a World War One German military cemetery containing the remains of 1,903 soldiers.

I had experienced German war cemeteries before on school trips to Belgium and found them to be sombre places, much more so than those of the victors – even more moving, even more thought-provoking. The cause for which these soldiers had been fighting was, rightly, defeated, thus making their deaths even more futile than those of the Allies. I noted with interest the handful of Jewish gravestones; they had given their lives to a country which would shortly turn its back upon them in the most brutal manner imaginable.

I was the only visitor and, rather fittingly, the sun had decided to shine on this portion of the day. I sat on the steps and thought for a few moments about life, war and death. I was reminded of the old school friend who had passed away the previous week. He too had died tragically young. I shed a tear for them all.

My delayed departure from Pierrefonds was inevitably going to make this cycling day a short one. When I arrived at Camping du Vivier aux Carpes, in Seraucourt-le-Grand, in the early evening, my mood was subdued, although I was not unhappy. I felt satisfied with my decision to take time to discover the story of a quirky historic monument. I felt equally satisfied at having devoted time to reflect upon the more important things in life. Yes, travelling by bicycle across a continent was a feat of physical endurance but such a journey was just as much about the people and places that I encountered as I pedalled. As I neared the end of my second country, I wouldn't have wanted it any other way.

PART 3

BELGIUM, THE NETHERLANDS AND GERMANY

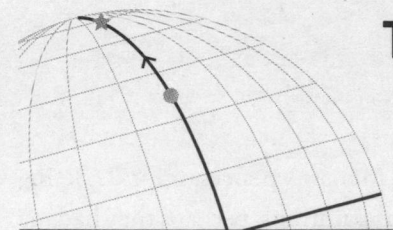

THE FIFTEENTH DEGREE
50°–51° NORTH

21–28 May

*'Maintenant, tu ne feras que ce qui te plaît sans
penser à ce que les autres exigent de toi.'*

That was Henri Matisse telling himself he would do whatever pleased him without thinking about what others demanded of him, and I liked where he was coming from. He'd just survived a tricky surgical procedure when he said it; I was on the cusp of having survived the rigours of cycling across two countries. I could sympathise, kind of.

I was in the town of Le Cateau-Cambrésis. Henri had been born there on New Year's Eve 1869 but, after a stint in Paris, spent much of his life on the French Riviera, where he died in 1954. He clearly had a soft spot for Le Cateau-Cambrésis, however, as he established a museum in the town with a donation of 82 of his works. It was a pity he never saw fit to establish a campsite. The polite lady in the tourist office broke the news gently.

'I'd have liked to visit the museum but with all my luggage on the bike, I don't want to leave it out in the street,' I pined.

'You can leave your bike here if you like,' she suggested.

Now that's customer service.

The museum was somewhat livelier than your average art museum. Groups of primary school children were on their end-of-year outing. They gave me bemused looks as I wandered amongst them in my cycling apparel. With Matisse's penchant for depicting large expanses of human flesh in his paintings, perhaps they had me down as one of his models. It may even have been one of the tasks on their clipboard: 'Locate and stare for a few seconds at someone who could feasibly have been painted by the artist.' Tick.

Next up was Maubeuge. I had stayed at Le Grand Hôtel in Maubeuge in 2010 as I cycled to southern Italy and had likened the experience to spending the night at the Moulin Rouge nightclub in Paris. Before you get too excited, this was entirely down to the decor rather than any form of entertainment on offer. Opposite the hotel, I found the bar where I had stopped for a beer nearly five years previously. Should I opt for a second night at Le Grand?

Ten minutes later I was at the reception desk of the Ibis hotel down the road, where I hoped that the colour scheme wouldn't keep me awake at night.

'I don't have a booking in your name, *monsieur*,' the hotel employee informed me.

'I have it here on my phone,' I offered.

'I can't deal with you until we have received the reservation email,' she retorted, sternly.

'So, what shall I do?' I asked, wanting to be annoying and knowing full well that in Maubeuge there weren't that many options.

'You can wait here,' she snapped.

'Will there be a place to store my bike?'

'Your bike?'

'Yes, it's a non-motorised vehicle with two wheels,' I quipped.

The receptionist, perhaps justifiably, ignored me.

The email did eventually arrive and I had the pleasure of overpaying for a bog-standard room in a hotel with a dubious level of cycle friendliness. But who cared? I was sure that however much cycling displeasure the Ibis corporation could muster, it would be more than compensated for by Belgium, now just a few kilometres away and home to the one and only European Cyclists' Federation (ECF), the people in charge of the EuroVelos.

Several years previously, I had contacted the organisation to request information and was put in touch with Kevin Mayne, their development director. He was once the chief executive of Britain's CTC, the Cyclists' Touring Club – or, as it has now been rebranded, Cycling UK. Knowing that I would be passing near Brussels, I contacted Kevin again and asked if he would be interested in meeting up. He was, and not only did he agree to cycle with me for some of my route through Belgium, but he also offered to put me up for a couple of nights. A guided visit to the nearby battlefield of Waterloo was also on the cards for the next rest day. It was good to have friends in reasonably high places.

Kevin had told me that after following the River Sambre over the unmarked Belgian border, I should follow a series of RAVeL paths. These were *randonnée-vélo* or 'walking-cycling' routes and within a few minutes of arriving in what I assumed to be Belgium, I started to notice the distinctive numbered RAVeL signs. A combination of RAVeLs 101 and 108 got me as far as Binche and thereafter it was the 422 to my meeting point with Kevin in the centre of the town of La Louvière.

My mobile phone hadn't rung once since leaving Tarifa so when it did, I assumed that the unrecognised number was that of Kevin.

'I'm in the main square. Look out for a red-brick church,' he explained.

This being Belgium, there were plenty of red-brick buildings to choose from but I quickly located a church – red brick, of course – in a square. A few homeless people were gathered near the entrance. Unless the ECF had hit bad times rather abruptly, I guessed he wasn't one of them. Nearby, a man with a bright orange armband was escorting a group of children across the road.

'Excuse me,' I said, 'is this the main square in La Louvière?'

'This isn't La Louvière,' he replied.

I put the man down as Belgium's leading pedant as, in fairness, when I did find Kevin in a similar square outside a similar red-brick church a few minutes later, I hadn't cycled that far.

Our common love of all things cycling on a European level made for easy conversation with Kevin over a coffee. We had 45 km to cycle but this was an area that he knew well, and he was familiar with all the twists and turns of the cycle paths. I cycled in his wake and was afforded the time to enjoy the pretty views along the canals, rivers and country lanes of Wallonia, the French-speaking lower half of Belgium. The route wasn't devoid of hills or indeed cobbles but by early evening, as the warm sun of late spring was on its final trundle towards the horizon, we arrived at Kevin's house in Chapelle-Saint-Lambert, about 25 km south of Brussels.

My own credentials to claim to be a 'proper' cyclist were somewhat dubious. My lack of technical knowledge, my inability to name men who have won the Tour de France but aren't called Bradley or Chris, my fading desire to wear black Lycra: none of these worked in my favour. Neither did my ownership of (give me a moment to count...) just one bicycle. Yes, one.

I regularly meet people who have more than one bike, usually two – one for racing, one for everything else – but often three (a mountain bike) and sometimes four (a rusting 'project' bike perhaps). Kevin had 12. The milking parlour next to the house he shared with his Kiwi wife, Cheryl, wasn't so much a bike shed as a bike archive. According to his biography on the ECF website, his collection consisted of 'two city/hybrids for daily use, two MTBs, two road bikes, two touring bikes, two fixies and a Chinese Flying Pigeon'.* That was only 11. Kevin had clearly put into practice the old cycling adage that if *n* is the number of bikes that you own, *n* + 1 is the number of bikes that you need.

In the morning it was rest day number six and it was time to catch up again, perhaps for the last time, with Napoléon – the original one, not his nephew of phoney-castle fame – at the place where he met his Waterloo at, err... Waterloo. When Monsieur B. escaped from Elba in February 1815, marched through France to Paris, overthrew the government and regained power, the rest of Europe wasn't best pleased. The issue was brought to a climax in June 1815 just south of the town of Waterloo, in modern-day Belgium. Napoléon and his armies were defeated; he tried but failed to escape to the United States and ended up as a prisoner on Saint Helena. And didn't escape.

---

* The traditional Flying Pigeon bicycle from China, despite having its origins in the 1930s and based upon the Raleigh Roadster of 1932, can still be bought today. It has sold in its hundreds of millions and, according to the company's website, in Maoist China '... was a symbol of an egalitarian social system that promised little comfort but a reliable ride through life'. They are, also according to the manufacturer, 'indestructible'.

My arrival in Belgium in late May 2015 was 199 years and 11 months after Napoléon's. Big commemorations were being planned for the two-hundredth anniversary of the battle on 18 June and, as Kevin and I approached the site on our bikes, large stands were being erected around the wide dip in the land where the event had taken place. High-level dignitaries were expected to attend a large-scale re-enactment. One of the stands appeared to be facing in the wrong direction.

'Is that for the French delegation?' I enquired. Kevin wasn't sure.

At the end of the day, a field is a field. Of more interest were the attractions on the north-western side of the battlefield. There were three and they each represented a different approach to telling the story of Waterloo.

First up was the Lion's Mound, built by the Dutch a decade after the battle and standing 43 m above ground. On top of the mound was an iron statue of a lion, symbol of the monarchy of the Netherlands. It was on this spot that William II fell from his horse after having been shot. Poor bloke. A fitting tribute. But hang on... He wasn't killed. It was a mere flesh wound. He wasn't even king at the time. I wondered how much bigger the mound might have been if he hadn't survived. That said, the view from the top was worth the climb of 225 steps. If you had been a visitor when the mound was finished in 1826, I dare say there would have still been a good number of people around who could have provided a first-hand account of the battle. Where better to listen to their recollections than on top of a man-made hill looking down upon the battlefield?

By the time of the first centenary of the battle, in 1915, Europe was once again at war. The decision to paint a panoramic fresco of the battle and house it in a rotunda at the base of the mound in 1912 was a timely one. If it had been left for a few more years, priorities may have been elsewhere.

But the sensory-hungry child of the twenty-first century demands more: 3D video, multimedia walls, buttons that can be pushed... Which is why, to commemorate the bicentenary of Waterloo, a third attraction has now been added. It's no longer de rigueur to build mounds or rotundas next to famous battlefields, so the Memorial 1815 is buried underground. Over 1,815 square metres (can you see what they'd done there?), it '... allows you to experience one of the most turbulent times in our history... as if you were there.' And it did. Indeed, the combination of mound, panorama and 'multi-sensory experience' sets a mighty challenge for the museum curators and architects of the early twenty-second century in the run-up to the tri-centenary.

Kevin and I cycled back to his house via Hougoumont Farm – a key point of the fighting – and what remained of the day was spent relaxing, eating, drinking and doing a little shopping. With his superior technical knowledge, Kevin gave Reggie the once-over and everything seemed fine. Over the course of the cycle through northern France, the annoying click had returned. It hadn't been the bottom bracket after all but as to what was causing the noise, both Kevin and I remained ignorant.

My original plan had been to cycle through southern Belgium and over the border to Germany. Kevin's house, however, was a little further north than I had envisaged. I sat with my host to discuss route options over breakfast and he suggested that I cycle to Leuven and then head east to Maastricht. This wasn't a problem, far from it. Maastricht was in the Netherlands and my continental journey had just been elevated from a seven- to an eight-country odyssey.

Kevin supplied me with a couple of maps and explained the system of nodes, which is popular across the Low Countries. Whenever two cycle paths – of which there were many – crossed, the junction was attributed a two- or three-digit number. My cycle between Leuven and Borgloon could be summarised as follows: 33, 73, 87, 86, 92, 91, 34, 35, 13, 64, 60, 59, 58, 50, 21, 51, 187, 188, 135, 189, 168, 169, 161, 151, 154, 152. How wonderful was that? Following the numbers was easy and, aside from one slight hiccup when crossing the town of Sint-Truiden (between 189 and 168), I was able to follow good-quality off-road cycle paths for almost all of the day.

I'd planned to stay overnight in Sint-Truiden but I wasn't able to locate a campsite or a reasonably priced hotel. I might have bitten the financial bullet and stayed put had it not been for the drunks inside the bar where I stopped. One customer was ranting at the counter, the woman serving me laughed mockingly when I asked if she spoke English and then a drinker, who did, proceeded to tell me that 'British beer is crap.'

I searched online accommodation options further along the line and at 152 was a nice-looking B&B called the Huis Van Loon. The house of the Loons? It sounded like the bar I had been sitting in but I was willing to give it the benefit of the doubt. It was an excellent call as not only was the B&B rather wonderful, but so was the cycle in the early evening sun through the fruit farms to the west of Borgloon. I celebrated the end of my final full day of cycling in Belgium with an 8 per cent blonde beer at the Goede Ogenblik – 'good moment' – bar. A good moment indeed.

Cycling day 41 was brought to you by *knooppunts* (that's 'nodes' to you and me) 136, 139, 128, 129, 107, 111, 112, 113 and 86.

The downside of node following was that I didn't need to refer to the map every few minutes and the towns and villages passed by anonymously. The upside was that I had more opportunity to appreciate the land and townscapes around me, and in the case of Dutch-speaking Flanders, there was much to appreciate.

After Belgium node 86 I *was* required to consult the map. The pencil-straight N79 would take me to Maastricht in the Netherlands quicker than a Eurosceptic with a blowtorch. Fuelled by a large bag of *Engelse drop* (liquorice allsorts), within half an hour I had arrived at a high bridge over the Meuse Canal where a small memorial was dedicated to British and Belgian soldiers who had died fighting here. Although a very modern construction, the foundations of the bridge were distinctly 1940s, with the bunker on one side having been converted into a swish restaurant. A 'World Peace Flame' was burning behind the reinforced glass of a display cabinet. Everything pointed to me having arrived at an international border but, according to my online map, I would have to cycle for another 250 metres on the other side of the canal to arrive at the point where Belgium became the Netherlands. When it arrived, the border was indicated only by a small sign noting that I was now in Maastricht. It was almost *too* understated.

Cycling along what had now been renamed the N278 was the stuff of dreams. For the first time in my life, I, a cyclist, really did feel as though I was being treated as an equal to the motorist. The 3 km stretch of road from the border to the centre of the city contained all the features that British councils like to list in their glossy *'Cycling Strategy for the Twenty-first Century'*-type brochures but never seem to get around to implementing. Segregation and space. Traffic signals for those on two wheels. Separate outer roundabouts with clearly marked priority to bicycles. Cycle lanes clear of street furniture. Two-way cycling on otherwise one-way streets. Hectares of secure bicycle storage. And guess what, petrolheads? Not one cyclist ignoring a red light. No helmet cams recording evidence of bad driving. Just two forms of transport functioning harmoniously side by side. It was as delightful to witness as it was frustrating to reflect upon just how far the British have yet to travel.

Maastricht was more modern than I had imagined. The city had much that *was* old but also much that was very new. This included a large shopping centre where I stocked up on food for the evening before completing the day's cycle by heading south along the banks of the Meuse to Camping De Oosterdriessen, where I settled in for the evening. Another tent had already been erected in the free camping area. Its occupant returned on his bike a little later. He seemed familiar and appeared to recognise me too: 'Weren't you at the campsite in Orléans?' he asked in what sounded like a Spanish accent. It turned out that he was the guy with whom I had exchanged brief nods on the morning of my departure.

Javier was from Argentina; he was also the first cyclist I had met who was heading to Nordkapp. We had much to discuss.

Javier's approach to cycling to the northernmost point of Europe – from Madrid – was a little more laid-back than my own. He'd picked up his bike second-hand and quite cheaply in Spain, equipped himself with eBay-purchased kit, and had no apparent time limit to his adventure. With a Spanish passport courtesy of a grandparent, he had no Schengen-limited visa, and explained that he was stopping to work and earn money from time to time. Back in Argentina he had been a chef for several years so, along with a decent level of English, he certainly had a skill that would find him work almost anywhere he went. I envied his Laurie Lee approach to travelling.

The following morning, an hour or so into the cycle across this most southerly and narrowest part of the Netherlands, I started to notice signs for a nearby American war cemetery. When I spotted the entrance, I decided to investigate and, set back a few hundred metres from the road, I found 8,301 headstones of American soldiers killed in action.

My mind immediately returned to the sombre atmosphere of the German cemetery I had visited in France. Despite the grand buildings in marble, there was nothing triumphal about what I could see here. There was, however, an uplifting and hopeful atmosphere that had been absent from the German cemetery. I gazed along the geometrically perfect lines of crosses. The men in the graves before me died in ignorance of the ultimate demise of the Third Reich, and the downfall of Hitler and the Nazis. They died hoping but not knowing. It was a strange, disconcerting thought.

Something rather special was about to happen. No, it wasn't that I was able to buy a punnet of strawberries from a vending machine beside the road (although I did have fun doing so). It was that, for the first time since leaving Gibraltar – now over 3,000 km of cycling to the south – an international border was being signposted and celebrated.

Bundesrepublik Deutschland

The celebration came in the form of a bush with the black eagle of the Federal Republic of Germany embedded neatly into its side.

If all this wasn't sufficient to excite me, 500 metres further down the road was a second sign welcoming me to Aachen. Alongside the multilingual welcomes was a list of eight *Partnerstädte*, or twin towns: Arlington in Virginia, Kostroma in Russia, Montebourg in France, Naumburg in Germany (presumably a hangover from the DDR days), Ningbo in China, Reims in France (another one? Was that allowed?), Toledo in Spain and *Halifax/Calderdale*, my hometown in the United Kingdom.

I hadn't been aware of Aachen's twinning infidelities across the globe but I had always known of the Aachen–Halifax connection. Indeed, one of the first foreigners I ever met was a German Boy Scout called Karsten who stayed with my family for a weekend back in the late 1970s. He was taking part in an exchange between Scouts in Halifax and Aachen, spoke good English and was very tall. This latter aspect of Karsten's physique formed a lasting impression on a small boy from the Calder Valley of Yorkshire. He will now be in his fifties and must, without a doubt, be in charge of something important in North Rhine-Westphalia.

Ten minutes later, after pausing to take a picture of *Halifaxstraße*, I was in the city centre. Four countries in five days was good going, although admittedly the jigsaw geography of this corner of Western Europe was aiding me somewhat. However, I wouldn't be crossing another border for probably a couple of weeks. The plan was to cycle over to the Rhine at Cologne and then head north to Düsseldorf. Keeping towards the western side of the country, I envisaged passing through Münster and Bremen before visiting friends in Hamburg. The final portion of Germany would be through Schleswig-Holstein.

Aachen's campsite, I was informed by the formal woman in the tourist office, didn't allow camping. Well, not my kind of camping – just 'camping' in a motorhome. Which isn't, can I say, camping. I'm glad I've got that off my chest. I booked into the central Hotel Klenkes instead and was allocated a room that would have given the proverbial cat severe head injuries. I escaped the cramped conditions and went to explore the rather more spacious cathedral.

Its ordinary exterior belied extraordinariness within. Built for Charlemagne in the eighth century, it contained not only the first domed church to be built north of the Alps, but enough shimmering gold leaf to keep Hatton Garden supplied for decades. Byzantine was the style: exotic domes, tall rounded arches and rich mosaics. Especially impressive when you consider that it had survived for such a long time. The building had been host to coronations for six centuries, the final one being that of Ferdinand I in 1531, after which point the centre of gravity of the Holy Roman Empire moved east towards what is now Austria.

Along similar lines, my own centre of gravity also needed to move east. Cycling day 43 consisted of an 80 km descent into the Rhine valley that dominated this part of Germany and which I would follow north until at least Düsseldorf.

My arrival in the centre of Cologne coincided with the discovery of another visitor from Britain. My compatriot had been in hiding for over 70 years and had just been discovered near the Mülheim Bridge. The BBC website broke the news thus:

Some 20,000 people in the German city of Cologne have been forced to leave their homes as authorities defuse a one-tonne bomb from World War Two. Schools and kindergartens – as well as the zoo – remained closed during the city's largest post-war evacuation.

I would need to cycle near the Mülheim Bridge the following morning so I could only hope that things had been sorted out by then. There was no sign of any form of panic in central Cologne, however. Indeed, when I met with my friend Janina, a former language assistant from the school in Henley, and mentioned the news to her, it was the first she had heard of the event.

I had initially suggested that we go out for a meal in the evening but Janina explained that she had to go to a concert. I had always considered her to be an educated, cultured woman and assumed that whatever event she was attending, it would involve classical music or perhaps even opera. I wouldn't have been at all surprised if she herself had been one of the performers.

'Sorry about tonight,' she explained, 'but I've had these Olly Murs tickets for ages.'

Turned down for Olly Murs. That put me in my place.

The campsite in Cologne was a few kilometres to the south of the city, on the other side of the river. It consisted of an open patch of land where a good number of independent travellers, many on two wheels, were enjoying the fresh air. The noise from the nearby bridge was a touch distracting but at least it wasn't at risk of being blown up by an RAF bomb, or so I assumed.

The combination of a day off, two short cycling days and a predominantly eastward shift had made the fifteenth degree the longest yet in terms of time. But now that I had reached the Rhine, there would be an abrupt change of direction and I would again be able to make more significant progress north. The next section of cycling would be easy, as it was simply a case of following the Rhine Cycle Route, otherwise known as EuroVelo 15 to Düsseldorf. I had already seen several signs for the route, as it passed outside the gates of the campsite. I saddled up and, via a short detour back into the centre of Cologne for breakfast and to take in the cathedral, I was off. *Einfach!*[*]

---

[*] Easy!

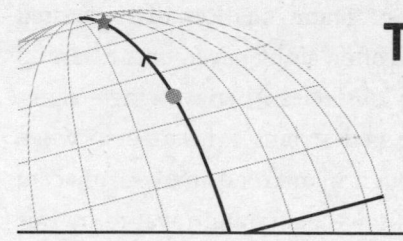

THE SIXTEENTH DEGREE
51°–52° NORTH

28–31 May

Through hard work, dedication, patience and perseverance, from a nation that lay in ruins after the war, the Germans have recreated a country that is envied by many, including me. When I think of cities that have been destroyed beyond recognition in my own lifetime – Beirut, Sarajevo, Kabul and, more recently, Aleppo in Syria – I take crumbs of comfort from places such as Berlin and Hamburg, which have rebuilt themselves from the rubble. And not just rebuilt themselves as second-rate versions of what they used to be; the German cities of today may lack the historical vistas of Paris or Rome, but they have been reborn as vibrant examples of economic success and cultural diversity equal to any other European city of the twenty-first century.

However... from the perspective of a touring cyclist, Germany was suffering from not being either Belgium or the Netherlands. I had become accustomed to good quality segregated cycling paths and signage that was so easy to follow it could have been designed by cyclists themselves (and probably was). Germany was a lurch back towards how cycling could often be back in Britain. Only a moderate lurch, but discernible nevertheless. There was lots of segregated cycling but in urban areas this was often along pavements where all of the obstacles that weren't really obstacles when walking – signs, flowerpots, curbs, as well as the pedestrians – became so when cycling. In the countryside, although many roads had an adjacent cycle path, this was frequently of low quality and ravaged by tree roots or simply by time. If I chose not to use the facilities on offer, this would incite some motorists (older men in Mercedes usually) to point out my 'mistake' in no uncertain Teutonic terms.

As for the Rhine Cycle Route signage, it was sporadic and confusing. When it appeared, it was a marvel to behold, with small blue squares clearly pointing in the direction of the Rheinradweg 15, but then it wouldn't appear for several kilometres and I was left with just the occasional red arrow. Was that my cycle path or one of the many others? My love of all things Germanic was being severely tested. In the kilometres north of Cologne I had to contend with large building developments requiring complicated detours, two long flights of steps, poor quality cycling paths and, to cap it all off, a group of mocking primary school kids. You know you are at a low ebb when you have become the victim of pillory by seven-year-olds.

I stopped to sit on a dilapidated bench at the southern limit of a large Bayer chemical complex. Its position sucking water from the Rhine might have been for the greater benefit of the German economy but it would mean another diversion away from the river for me. On the ground below my feet was a discarded bicycle stand and stuck to a nearby post was a home-made for sale poster for an '*Alu City Star Like*' bicycle. By ringing the number listed and paying

€150, it could be mine. I wondered if it made annoying noises like Reggie. Above my head was an inexplicable triangular green warning sign: *'Geschützter Landschaftsbestandteil'* it stated next to an image of a black eagle, wings fully extended, gliding and looking fearsome. Was I at risk of becoming someone's lunch? Behind me was an Aldi supermarket and above everything was a slate-grey sky.

Cycling across continents wasn't meant to be like this. I remained on the bench for about half an hour. I could have wept for no good reason but lots of little bad ones. I sensed a Mercedes day approaching. Was I beginning to feel drained by the whole Tarifa to Nordkapp experience? Had the enormity of the task only just become apparent? Did the prospect of perspiring my way north for another 50 plus days no longer fill me with unbridled enthusiasm?

North of the chemical complex, I rejoined the path beside the Rhine and, for the first time, the urban tentacles of Cologne loosened. The banks of the river were covered in spring flowers and pretty houses jostled for the best view over the wide expanse of water. I stopped once again about an hour after my earlier melancholic moment on the bench, but this time my view couldn't have been more different. I was sitting in a tiny café that had been built inside the control box of a disused riverside crane. It was called, unsurprisingly, the Kran Café.

I ordered a drink from the woman in charge; our lack of a common language prevented conversation, but she smiled and I reciprocated. That simple gesture seemed to say many things, none of which I could list but all of which seemed perfect for that moment. I stared out of the windows of the crane café and watched the large barges ply their trade on the river. Those heading upstream moved slowly against the prevailing direction of the water, whilst those heading downstream did so at speed. My morning had so far been very 'upstream', fighting against the obstacles of the urban world and the wind but also against my own mid-journey malaise. I *was* feeling somewhat drained and my enthusiasm *was* somewhat diminished.

But did I question my chances of completing the cycle from Tarifa to Nordkapp and reaching my objective? No. I knew that there was no chance of me abandoning the cycle to Nordkapp voluntarily. That said, I did need to focus on short-term objectives that would boost my enthusiasm for life on two wheels. There were, after all, plenty to choose from – including Hamburg, where I planned to take a short break from cycling to stay with friends Dominic and Annet.

—

The unkempt suburbs of Düsseldorf had lowered expectations for what I would find at its centre, but then I turned a corner and the long curve of an impressive waterfront was revealed. At each end of the cityscape were two almost identical suspension bridges and on the far side of the river was a broad area of parkland. Things were looking up.

Following mixed results, I had been staying clear of the accommodation sharing website WarmShowers but now, in Germany, I was willing to give it a second chance. I had contacted a woman in Düsseldorf and a man in Münster, and had high hopes of using someone's garden in Schleswig-Holstein. The woman in Düsseldorf was called Andrea and she lived with her husband Matthias somewhere beyond the green parkland. After such a mentally tortuous day, however, I didn't want to rush over there immediately. I needed a beer and, rather fortuitously, a beer festival of sorts was taking place along the banks of the Rhine. As I drained a couple of bottles of the local *altbier* and my stomach filled with a lip-smacking *currywurst*, my love of most things German began to return. I cast aside thoughts of sub-standard cycling infrastructure and focussed upon what really mattered in life: good German beer, good German food and the prospect of good German hospitality over the days to come.

I would have to cycle another 10 km before arriving at Andrea's sprawling and fashionably ramshackle house in the suburb of Meerbusch. Both she and her husband were lawyers, and they took anglophilism to a new level. Not only were they both fluent speakers of English, but also great fans of most things British to such a point that I wondered whether they'd never visited the country, just observed it from afar via *Downton Abbey*.

All four of their children – very evenly spaced out and in strict rotation of boy, girl, boy, girl (that's taking German organisation to a whole new level) – had spent the final two years of their secondary education at a private sixth form college in Lincolnshire. When the kids had been younger, however, Andrea and Matthias had taken the family cycling in Denmark, Sweden and Norway, and this was clearly a mine of information for me to plunder. The evening was spent consulting maps, looking at old photos and trying to remember their top tips.

Come the morning, I felt somewhat better prepared for cycling north of the German border. That was still more than a week away. In the meantime, I would continue to cycle along the Rhine as far as Duisburg and then head in a north-easterly direction towards Münster, hoping to stumble upon somewhere convenient to stop over on the way. And in terms of the cycling infrastructure, North Rhine-Westphalia was about to show me her better side.

This started almost immediately, just north of Meerbusch, where I was able to cycle along the levees of the Rhine, before ascending to a high bridge via a corkscrew incline that was for the exclusive use of bicycles (and the unicycle which overtook me mid-screw). It was impressive stuff for the first 30 minutes of the day.

Once back on the eastern side of the river, I continued to follow the Rheinradweg 15 signs until they started to escape from view near central Duisburg and I began my search for the Ruhr. I knew that as soon as I crossed it, I needed to make a right turn towards Münster but was conscious that the Ruhr itself headed south rather abruptly. I was pinning my hopes upon finding a cycle route adjacent to the Rhine–Herne Canal. The canal and the river ran shoulder to shoulder for a few kilometres after splitting from the Rhine but in such an industrialised urban area it was far from easy to decide which bit of water belonged to which river or canal and after which bridge I should start heading east.

I crossed an unmarked waterway near Oberhausen but then for 10 km didn't spot so much as a puddle. It wasn't until after nearly 40 km that I found what was unmistakably a canal – the Rhine–Herne Canal – and was able to descend from one of its high bridges, and move away from the road and onto the cycling-friendly towpath. I knew that the canal continued as far as Münster and that if I followed it, I would get there too.

Such was the apparent modernity of the canal that, for a few moments, I laboured under the rather delusional impression that it might have been built to celebrate my arrival. Alas, it hadn't (it had been built between 1906 and 1914, and widened in the 1980s) but even taking German engineering standards into consideration, it was impossible not to be impressed by its new bridges, smart pumping stations and one section that had been raised majestically above the farmland which it spanned.

Eventually, I was required to break away from the canal and head in the direction of some accommodation. Mention of the Ruhr valley conjured up images of a bleak post-industrial landscape but with gas holders painted with bright red polka dots here, not unattractive public spaces created around disused mine workings there and a former railway line converted into a high-quality greenway linking much of everything together, I was beginning to redefine my preconceptions.

The campsite that I had discovered via an internet search was near the town of Datteln and I asked Google Maps to direct me. I was a little suspicious at being led along ever darker and more remote forest tracks but then I spotted the unmistakable signs of a campsite. The owner, as cheerful as he was youthful, broke the bad news that it was full – there was a music festival taking place nearby – but that wasn't a problem for one small tent. *Ich liebe Deutschland!* That said, there was little evidence of the festival taking place and my night of slumber was only interrupted by the usual suspects – notably the lack of a sprung mattress – rather than anything musical.

The following morning I continued my cycle along the canals. Despite some comically dreadful weather that nearly blew me into the water, I arrived in Münster after a modest 55 km of cycling, chose a city-centre café, ordered a coffee, and watched the hailstones fire down upon Reggie and the rather alarmed population of the city.

Münster would be the second German night of WarmShowers accommodation, albeit with a twist. I met Dirk outside the hospital where he worked as a lab technician. We had exchanged several messages and he had explained that I would be staying in 'the house in the large garden'. I had wondered what this might be. A palatial granny annexe surrounded by lush vegetation and sumptuously furnished, albeit to the tastes of an octogenarian? I could live with the decor for just one night.

It turned out that the Germans like their allotments just as much as the British and Dirk had one close to the hospital. I was given a guided tour of the plants, the rabbit-proof fencing, the ornaments… I could sense where this might be going… the shed.

The interior of the shed was comfortable, with a chair, table, wardrobe... break it to me gently, Dirk… and a sofa bed.

'So Andrew, you will sleep here,' announced Dirk.

'Fantastic,' I lied.

The prospect of sleeping in a shed on an allotment was made somewhat more appealing by Dirk's fondness for beer. He lived nearby with his girlfriend Anita and en route back to his flat we paused at the local supermarket to fill up the trailer of his bike with bottles of the local Münster brew.

It was to be a relaxed evening of light-hearted, congenial conversation that only confirmed just how similar the British and the Germans are in terms of their outlooks on life. It was interesting listening to Dirk and Anita talk about their own big cycle trip from Alaska to Panama, a ride of more than 10,000 km over ten months. I couldn't help but feel envious that they had been able to spread the journey across such a long period of time.

At the end of the evening, Dirk escorted me back to 'the house in the large garden'. You would think that spending the night in a shed was far preferable to spending a night in a tent, and in terms of comfort, it was. Alas, my ears were on edge, listening for the tell-tale scratchings of mice (or worse) and although I never heard them, the worry did keep my mind far too active for sleep to kick in in any meaningful way. In the tent, as long as I didn't suspect that the scratchings were man-made, it was comforting to hear the gentle movements of wildlife outside. Whatever creature was out there, it was unlikely that gnawing through the material of my tent was the most appealing option for dinner.

Dirk had given clear instructions for the morning. It was a Sunday and I was happy to get going without him needing to travel down to the allotment. Locking up behind me and leaving the key under a gnome, I headed back into the centre of Münster to pay homage to a famous poster.

The poster in question was created in 1991 by the municipal council of Münster in an attempt to boost public support for increased spending on cycling facilities and public transport. It consisted of three photographs of the same city street and became rather iconic. Each photograph had been taken from a high vantage point and showed how much space was taken up by 60 people when they travel. In the first, the street was crammed with 60 cars; in the second a bus was the only vehicle and in the third, the 60 people were each on a bicycle. The message was clear but, for those who were struggling, above the photographs it stated: 'Space required to transport 60 people.' Its beauty was in its simplicity.

The distinctive shape of the buildings along the street and its cobbled surface were sufficient clues for me to correctly identify the location used as the Prinzipalmarkt. I found the spot from which the images had been taken but my position lacked one thing: height. Behind me was the tower of the Lambertikirche and the photographs must have been taken from somewhere in its steeple.

The experience reminded me of visiting the site of the Battle of Waterloo; I was there because of what it represented rather than what I could see. It was just another pretty cobbled street, in the same way that back in Belgium it had been just another pretty field of corn. How strange the human condition that we find satisfaction in visiting places not for what they are now but for what took place there many years before.

THE SEVENTEENTH DEGREE
52°–53° NORTH

31 May–1 June

For most of the first 15 km of the cycle from Münster I cycled alongside the Dortmund–Ems Canal, another industrial giant of a waterway with Victorian (well, Wilhelm II for the pedants) origins and not a quaint hand-operated lock or flower-decorated narrow barge in sight. Just as the Rhine–Herne Canal on the previous day, this was a very twenty-first-century canal, capable of feeding the inland industrial requirements of the mighty German economy and then transporting its not inconsiderable output back to the container ships on the coast.

Dirk, however, had recommended that I take in Tecklenburg, a small town at the top of a hill en route to Osnabrück, so I peeled away from the towpath to find it. After such a long period of cycling on the flat, the required steep climb to 200 metres was sufficient to provoke mild altitude sickness, but the recommendation had been well placed. Tecklenburg delivered in most respects as a small German hilltop town: higgledy-piggledy timber-framed houses clustered around a cobbled square with a fountain and freshly hoisted *Maibaum* at its centre. There was a relaxed Sunday morning atmosphere and for an hour or so I drank coffee and listened to a succession of traditional Germanic tunes, courtesy of the local brass band and its generously lunged operatic singer. The musicians of the Noorkerländer Kapel were smartly co-ordinated in their black trousers, white shirts and bright red waistcoats, but they weren't the only ones to have dressed up to coincide with my arrival.

I was surrounded in the square by several cycling groups. Each consisted of about four or five men and although they all had different expensive-looking racing bikes, every member of each group was wearing a perfectly co-ordinated cycling outfit: the same shoes, socks, Lycra leggings and tight-fitting shirt emblazoned with the name of a company who probably wasn't sponsoring them. There were no suggestions of any race taking place; they were simply weekend enthusiasts out for a ride. But the care and attention each group must have taken to decide upon a distinctive 'look' for its members was commendable. There was no inter-group fraternisation and as I watched the various huddles sip their espressos, I wondered if I had inadvertently stumbled upon a stand-off of rival Münsterland cycling gangs. One false move of a pump and it might all kick off. As the Noorkerländer Kapel's vocalist hit some alarmingly high notes for a Sunday morning, this stranger in town shuffled off over the cobbles, lest he be hit in the crossfire of compressed air. My own 'look' was decidedly less co-ordinated, the cold morning requiring functionality over fashion.

The first large town in Lower Saxony was Osnabrück. It was now mid-Sunday afternoon and the streets were quiet, the shops closed, the traffic approaching non-existent and the people at home being happy. I knew this, as my guidebook told me that in a nationwide poll, the citizens of Osnabrück had been declared the most content with their lives. How did you measure such a thing?

'Excuse me. Are you content with life?'

'Yes.'

'Thanks.'

I stared intently at the few people who passed by. They didn't appear to be deliriously happy with their lot in life but neither did they look particularly hard done by. Further research into the minds of the Osnabrückers was required and perhaps I could conduct it at the out-of-town campsite.

Campingplatz Niedersachsenhof was deserted; I wondered whether another RAF-induced evacuation had taken place. I loitered around the reception area for a while, pondering my options. Much of the site was hidden beyond hedges and trees but from what I could see, it had many of the unwelcoming charms of the Montargis 'wild camping' place back in France, albeit with fewer prostitutes or dodgy young men.

I went online and discovered a reasonably priced hotel option a few kilometres further north but as my finger hovered over the 'book now' button, a man appeared and asked if I was planning to stay the night. He wasn't one of the happy folk of Osnabrück; my finger touched the screen, I made my excuses and cycled off in the direction of the Landgasthaus Kortlüke.

The employees of the *Gasthaus* were a happiness researcher's dream. Even the prospect of washing my somewhat soiled clothes didn't faze them in the slightest and, once laundered, they were delivered to my room with a smile. In the meantime, I had been lying on the floor, somewhat minimally dressed, perusing the map and my onward journey to Bremen. It being a large city that I had never previously visited, I planned to take a day off and explore on Tuesday. Monday would be spent cycling the 100 plus kilometres to the campsite to the north of the centre of Bremen. My eyes scanned the towns and villages through which I might pass: Venne, Diepholz, Twistringen, Bassum... Syke. Syke! There was a town in Germany only one consonant short of being my surname. Goodness.

Syke. Home to the Syke people, or the Sykes? I was a little unsure of the linguistics but I wasn't going to let that prevent me from cycling into town, seeking out the *Rathaus* and announcing that I had returned home.

Suddenly, a suspected day of inconsequential cycling across lower Lower Saxony had been transformed. The following morning I was up early and eagerly demolished the buffet breakfast. I wondered if the other guests could sense my excitement.

'Excuse me. Are you excited?'

'Yes!'

The flat terrain allowed me to pick up considerable speed and by midday I was in Diepholz. It was interesting to note on a roadside information panel that the D7 cycling route also passed through the town. The D7 was subtitled the *Pilgerroute*, or the 'pilgrims' route'. There was no mention of EuroVelo 3, the long-distance route I had been following in my idiosyncratic way since northern Spain, but that too was called 'the pilgrims' route'. I could only guess that I was indeed following the European route as it continued to piggyback upon national and regional ones in the direction of Trondheim in Norway. And to think my ancestral home was on that very same route! Amazing.

The path continued to be as flat as a Wiener Schnitzel and I was soon starting to see unnecessarily precise cycling signage for Syke: 40.9 km, 24.3 km, 7.9 km... And then the moment itself, on the Bassumer Landstraße, a blue sign:

SYKE
Partner in Europa

It was good to see that my 'hometown' had also embraced all things European. Yet another thing to bind us together.

With a smile on my face, I slowly cycled into the centre of Syke; every mention of the name made me grin even more broadly. '*Herzlich willkommen in Syke*', '*Stadt Syke*', '*Gymnasium Syke*'... And then into the town centre itself. '*Syker Mangelstube*', '*Syker Bierhaus*'... I was desperate to find a reference to '*Sykes*'. Never had I regretted more not having a black marker pen in my pocket.

Alas, the real Syke wasn't meeting my high expectations and the smile on my face was beginning to wither a little. This was no Tecklenburg. The streets weren't as well kept; the buildings looked somewhat less photogenic and the shops a tad more functional... My ancestral home appeared to be home to a large number of €1 outlets, although TEDi Top Euro Discount had expanded into the 5€ market with its range of colourful 'Tupperware' and plastic sandals.

Where was the magnificent central *Marktplatz*, medieval *Rathaus* and my ancestral coat of arms?

I eventually found the central square but it displayed all the architectural merits of the 1970s rather than the fifteenth century. At its heart was an interactive steel water feature that wouldn't have looked out of place in a children's playground. It had been built upon modern cobbles that were now home to a collection of weeds and fag ends. No town hall that I could see. No coat of arms that I could adopt.

Undeterred, I was keen to find someone in authority to whom I could report my arrival. I continued to cycle through the centre and towards the western edge of the town. I wondered how the people of Syke might have fared in the great German survey of happiness.

'Excuse me. Are you content with life?'

'Well, I stack fake five euro Tupperware at T€Di Top Euro Discount and I wish my kids would keep away from that filthy water feature in the main square...'

Then, leaning on a railing beside the smart McDonald's McCafé and McDrive (by far the most impressive building I had seen in Syke up to that point), I spotted two police officers. Both looked very authoritative in their all-black uniforms. They would have to do.

'Excuse me. Are you content with life?'

Sorry... Wrong question.

'Excuse me. I wonder if you could help me...'

It had seemed like a good idea up until the moment I opened my mouth. How would they interpret my decision to visit Syke based simply upon the similarity of my surname? They *were* armed.

'My name is Sykes... It's Syke, with an s on the end.'

'OK,' the female officer responded, hesitantly. Her name was Sandra and she spoke good English. Her colleague Olaf didn't.

'I thought perhaps there might be a connection.'

'OK, interesting. I don't know,' replied a rather bemused-looking Sandra before she turned to Olaf and told him to get back-up, quick.

'I don't come from Syke – it's pronounced *Zyke* in German – but Olaf does. He was born here.'

At this point a short exchange took place between Sandra and Olaf.

'Look Sandra, love, just get rid of him. I've met these Sykes idiots from England before. They come over here with their permanent marker pens and cause all kinds of damage. "Syke" refers to the bottom of a valley I think,' explained Olaf, perhaps, in German.

'Olaf says that "Syke" refers to the bottom of a valley,' explained Sandra.

What about the rest?

'What can you tell me about the town?' I asked.

'Well, about forty-five thousand people live here; there's not much industry and most people work in Bremen,' she went on.

'Where can I buy a permanent marker pen?'

I took their photograph just to prove that I had spoken to someone in authority in my ancestral home. Whatever its lack of physical beauty, I guessed that Syke wasn't a hotbed of criminality in Lower Saxony and that I hadn't distracted them too much from their crime-fighting duties. I left them to continue the vital job of leaning against the railing and looking important.

I thought that that would be that with Syke, but not quite. My conversation with Sandra and Olaf had taken place beside the main road to Bremen and, after a wander around a bike shop for no good reason other than it being a bike shop, I set off north. Within a few minutes, I noticed a monument by the side of the road under some trees. Written beneath the bronze silhouette of a soldier were the following words:

HIER
LAGERTEN DIE SCHWARZEN
UNTER
FRIED. WILHELM
v. BRAUNSCHWEIG_OELS
AM 5. AUGUST 1809

'Here camped the Blacks of Frederick William of Brunswick and Oels.' 'The Blacks' referred to his soldiers, the Black Brunswickers, famous for wearing all-black uniforms. Perhaps Sandra and Olaf hadn't been in the police after all.

There was also a small plaque on the ground. One word caught my eye: *Großbritannien* or Great Britain. A connection between Syke and Sykes after all? I carefully pieced together the meaning of the rest of the text.

On 5 August the Duke and his troops rested here... The fight against Napoleon's troops... had failed. When the troops reached Syke safely, they only had one aim: escape to secure Britain.

Could it be that they had taken a small brethren of locals to Great Britain with them and a colony of these people had created the dynasty of Sykes?

Of course not. Onwards...

THE EIGHTEENTH DEGREE
53°–54° NORTH

1–7 June

No one has ever made a movie called *The Hanseatic League*, but they should. Conflict, intrigue, espionage, adventure... A Hans Zimmer score? It has Oscar success written all over it. Mr Spielberg?

I was now in deep Hanseatic League territory. With its capital in Lübeck on the Baltic coast, the League was an international superpower of medieval times, whose sphere of influence grew over four centuries to encompass independent territories from London in the west to Russia in the east. Created to facilitate trade between its member city states, its emergence as a political and military force led it into conflict with the other superpowers of the age, notably England and Holland, and towards its ultimate demise in the latter half of the seventeenth century.

The most obvious twenty-first-century hangovers from the Hanseatic League are the Free Hanseatic Cities of Bremen and Hamburg. They are the two smallest regions of the German state but home to the richest Germans by some distance. According to Eurostat, the EU's statistical agency, per capita incomes for Bremen and Hamburg in 2014 were €46,000 and €59,000 respectively. The next richest German region was Bavaria, with average incomes of 'just' €41,400. The only other places within the EU with more affluent residents than Hamburg were Luxembourg, Brussels and London.

It was now Tuesday, rest day seven and Bremen was my chosen spot to relax. I had stayed at the *Campingplatz* the previous evening but after a 5 km ride I was in the centre, pondering the day ahead. I knew little about the city but I had an entire day during which to plug the holes in my knowledge. I sought out the tourist office, picked up a map and signed up for a guided tour.

'Do we have any non-German speakers?' asked Thomas, the softly spoken guide, in crystal clear English.

I sensed my fellow tourists were holding their breaths in the hope that everything wouldn't have to be translated. I raised my hand and a few words of polite disappointment rippled across the group.

'*Entschuldigung*,' I said, apologetically, causing a minor level of confusion.

Thomas knew his stuff and, as we wandered between the curiosities of the city centre, after each mini speech in German, he turned to me with a hint of linguistic pity and gave me a shortened summary. I limited my questions so as not to further stoke the ire of the others in the group.

The centre of Bremen, sandwiched between the River Weser and a comical zigzag moat, was a mixture of the quite old, the very old and the quite new that looked quite old. Most of it was located within a very short walk of the central *Markt*. The 600-year-old *Rathaus* ticked the 'very old' box, with its neighbour – the two-towered *Dom* – doing likewise for the one marked 'quite old'. The

Böttcherstraße was my favourite, however; constructed during the 1920s at the behest of Ludwig Roselius as the home for his Kaffee Hag coffee company, it was a narrow street flanked on either side by ornate brick buildings and made to look as something from a much earlier age.

Roselius wanted to be a Nazi but they didn't let him join the party; his artistic preferences, as displayed in the architecture of the Böttcherstraße, were considered 'degenerate' – so much so that Hitler and his cronies decided to protect the buildings for future generations as a classic example of such heinous art. Thanks, Adolf. A variety of artistic ventures and fine restaurants have now taken up residence and it was all rather pleasant. Between two of the façades, at 12, 3 and 6 p.m., a *Glockenspiel* banged out a traditional tune. Or rather, it used to do. Following the purchase of the Böttcherstraße by a local bank, the traditional tune was, according to Thomas, that of a TV advert.

The Hanseatic League was mentioned on numerous occasions, but nowhere near as often as the donkey, the dog, the cat and the cockerel. Were they ever out of sight? I doubted it. The animals were the main protagonists in a Bremen-based story by the Brothers Grimm* and were to be found standing one on top of the

---

* The animals are old and destined for the slaughterhouse so they escape to Bremen to find a better future as street musicians. En route they find a house to stay in but it is occupied by thieves. By standing on each other's backs and making a cacophonous noise, they scare off the crooks and take up residence. When the thieves return after dark, they are attacked by the animals but, unable to see what they really are, the villains assume them to be a witch, an ogre, a giant and a judge. The thieves never return and the animals live, as is said, happily ever after...

other in statues, children's puzzles and colourful works of art, as well as filling most of the shelf space in souvenir shops. The image of the small tower of animals has even been adopted as the official symbol of Bremen; although the animals have certainly found their own fame (courtesy of the Grimms), the purveyors of tourist merchandise have been the ones reaping their fortune ever since.

Come Wednesday morning I found the signs for the HH–HB (Hamburg to Bremen) cycle route and started cycling north. Sort of. The area to the north of Bremen was a vast swathe of Lower Saxon farmland and, in its quest to get to Hamburg, the HH–HB route clearly had ambitions of visiting every single farm and field. Although my direction of movement was undeniably towards the north-east, I had the distinct feeling that just as much time was being spent cycling south and west.

The reward for all the toing and froing was the quaint villages and hamlets through which I cycled. It was difficult to imagine how their inhabitants led anything other than a thoroughly enjoyable existence. Decidedly Midsomer, with subtitles but without all the murders. But I couldn't to and fro all day. So, when my lateral movement reached its climax near the town of Zeven in an act of award-winning toing and froing several times along the same stretch of cycle path in search of the next HH–HB sign, I decided to take a more direct route to Harsefeld by following the road instead.

Distance-wise, it had been a good day: 95 km cycled dragged my daily average comfortably above target at 75.5 km. Admittedly, many of these 95 km had not been in a particularly helpful direction but let's not quibble. And when it came to quibbling, the woman running Campingparc Harsefeld was in no mood for that.

'*Sprechen Sie Englisch?*' I asked politely.

'*Nein,*' she shouted back. She was rather elderly so I put her volume down to hearing issues rather than disgust at me not being able to speak German.

'*Eins, eins, eins,*' I explained, pointing first at me, then the bike and then the rolled-up tent.

'*Eine Nacht?*'

'*Ja. Eine Nacht.*'

Considering I spoke only a few words of German and she was approaching a state of total deafness, this was going rather well. What's more, it was cheap: €6.50 plus 50 cents for the shower.

'*Drei Minuten,*' she bellowed before handing me a token.

'*Schnell, schnell, schnell!*' I responded, referring to the speed that would be required to get washed whilst at the same time trying to inject a little humour into our exchange, but she didn't smile. Did she think I had told her to get a move on?

Instead, she directed her lungs towards her younger sidekick – himself of pensionable age – and shouted instructions. He duly ushered me away to a pitch out of earshot of his boss/mother.

As I packed up the tent on Thursday morning, I was excited: I was nearly halfway to Nordkapp and there was blue sky above me. It had been absent for some time and I was looking forward to cycling again in the sun. As the crow flies, the centre of Hamburg was only 30 km away. Factor in the twists and turns of the HH–HB cycle route, as well as the increasingly urban environment through which I was travelling, and that would certainly increase. At least I would have the sun on my back as I cycled.

Within a couple of hours of setting off, I could see the great cranes of Hamburg in the distance and, if nothing else, they gave me something to aim for. I knew that the port of Hamburg was on the southern side of the Elbe and that the city centre was on the opposite bank. Cycling in the direction of the cranes would have me knocking back a celebratory beer in the centre of Hamburg quicker than a man showering at the campsite in Harsefeld.

Rather than detour to the east of the city to cross the river by bridge, my plan was to make use of the St Pauli Tunnel, which, since 1911, had been linking the docks on the south with the commercial centre on the north. Deep shafts had been dug on either bank of the river and two 400-metre tunnels bored between each shaft. Nowadays, the tunnel was just as much a tourist attraction as a vital piece of urban infrastructure but it was clearly still being used by many Hamburgers to travel to and from work.

It was 12.51 p.m. on Thursday 4 June when I pulled on Reggie's brakes and we ground to a halt in front of the imposing façade of Hamburg's *Rathaus*. I had cycled halfway to Nordkapp: 3,750 km. Yippee! The realisation was as exciting as it was frightening. I had 3,750 km still to cycle. Yippee? With a bench upon which to sit and a view upon which to feast, I sat, feasted and reflected.

Leaving Tarifa two months previously was starting to become a distant memory. I traced a line in my mind across western and northern Spain, along the coast of France, up the Loire to Paris, onwards to Belgium, then the Netherlands and finally through Germany to the point where I was sitting. Holes were beginning to develop. Where did I sleep on that first night after the youth hostel in Jerez? Had it taken one day or two to cycle from St-Jean-Pied-de-Port to the coast? Was it Matisse's museum I had visited or Monet's? The string of events, people and places was no longer immediately recollectable, simply because it was now so long – and the memories tied to it were beginning to fall off, as they fought for space amongst all the others. A glance in my diary could answer all my questions. Of course... Dos Hermanas, the place where I had chatted with 'Mercedes day' Paul; just the one day to the coast via the Portakabin tourist office in Bayonne; and it was Matisse, not Monet. The noise of those kids!

I stared at the colourful clock of the *Rathaus*. It struck 1 p.m. and I wondered what memories I would be looking back upon when (or even if) I arrived at Nordkapp. Whatever they turned out to be, my record keeping – diary, online posts, photographs, etc. – would clearly be essential in supplementing my memory. Without them, I might have to make things up at a later date. A travel writer who makes things up? Surely not...

On a physical level, with potentially 50 per cent of the cycling completed, I seemed to be holding up just fine. It is, perhaps, one of the great misconceptions of long-distance cycling that it must be physically challenging for most of the time. It certainly can be, especially when geography or meteorology is working against you. However, as much time is spent sitting on a saddle doing very little, it's a method of long-distance travel that is *usually* at the less strenuous end of the spectrum. In addition, the more pedalling that takes place, the more your body gets used to the daily activity and only grumbles on rare occasions. For me the left knee was usually the one to cause trouble and, at times, ache for a few hours, before the pain faded away and it returned to working without complaint. Indeed, it would be fair to say that I had felt more knackered after some of the 'rest' days than I had on most of the cycling ones. Wandering around a city, actively seeking out interesting things to see and do can be utterly exhausting. Pleasurable but knackering nevertheless. My mind, however, could play tricks. When I know that the end of a long journey is nigh, my brain seems to send messages to the limbs, saying: 'Relax... It's nearly over...' When that happens, even the flattest of rides can become torture and in the back of my mind I was expecting the mind games to start somewhere in northern Norway. Time would tell.

—

My English friend Dominic lived in the northern suburbs of Hamburg and that meant that my cycling day was not yet at an end. I remounted the bike, switched on Google Maps and started to follow the directions. Since I had last visited Hamburg some ten years previously, much had changed in Dominic's life. He had got married to his long-term girlfriend Annet, they had moved to the house in the suburbs towards which I was now cycling, he had retrained to work as a secondary school teacher in Germany and had become father to a second child. Leni, his daughter, was ten and I had met her when she was just a baby. Nick was five and, as I approached their front door, he was crying.

On occasions, my departures may have provoked tears (although don't press me for exact details...), but this was a first. I was relieved to hear that I wasn't directly to blame for the upset. So excited was Nick at the prospect of my arrival that he had decided to run around the first floor of the house in frenzied anticipation. When the doorbell rang, he had forgotten that the stairs were in their usual place and promptly fell down them.

The initial plan had been to stay with Dominic and Annet for two nights, Thursday and Friday, but when they offered me a bed for three nights, I struggled to turn them down. I had just completed half of my journey so I deserved a proper break from the cycling. What's more, there was much to do. Reggie needed repairing, I needed reclothing for Scandinavia and the beer in Dominic's cellar wasn't going to drink itself. It would have been rude to say no, so I didn't.

Top priority was Reggie's annoying click, which still hadn't gone away. If anything, it had got worse but I was determined to eradicate it once and for all. Fortunately, the closest bike shop was only a few minutes away from the house so we formed a five-person, ten-wheeled convoy and set off. Upon arrival, Dominic and Annet translated my concerns to the mechanic, Wilhelm, and Reggie was left in his very large and hopefully safe hands overnight. Perhaps where the French had failed, a far-from-chatty German would succeed.

The next 48 hours turned out to be an elongated period of doing nothing, interspersed with short periods of doing something: a perfect combination of recuperation and relaxation without boredom being allowed to rear its ugly head. Later on Friday afternoon we strolled back to see how Wilhelm had got on with the bike.

'I always try to work out what the maximum charge might be so as to avoid heart failure when presented with the bill,' I explained to Dominic, 'and this time I reckon no more than a hundred and twenty-five euros.'

'I'll go for a hundred and fifty euros,' he added rather ominously. He did, after all, have much more experience of getting a bike repaired in Germany.

At the shop, Wilhelm spent much time pointing at (and presumably referring to) the rear hub of the bike. The spokes and rim looked very clean and shiny.

'Has he changed the entire wheel?'

'Yes. He says that's where the clicking was coming from.'

A short test ride outside suggested that the noise had gone so we returned to the counter and I was presented with the bill.

'Quick, ask him to find the defibrillator.'

'How much?' asked Dominic.

'Two hundred and twenty-four euros and seventy-five cents.'

'I'll phone for an ambulance.'

Dominic's stock of beer took a particularly severe dent that evening.

Saturday was spent 'investing' more money: a thick fleece for those chilly Scandinavian evenings, a new pair of heavy-duty trainers to replace the cycling sandals I had been wearing up until that point and a second backup battery pack. Hamburg had prepared me well for life north of the German border; my body would be warm, my feet would stay dry, my phone wouldn't run out of power and, crucially, I was getting used to paying through the nose.

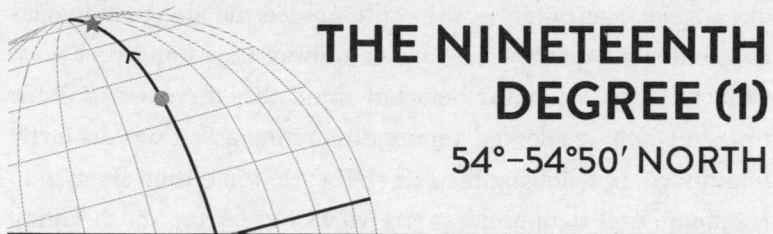

THE NINETEENTH DEGREE (1)
54°–54°50′ NORTH

7–10 June

The good news as I cycled through the northern suburbs of the city towards the border with Schleswig-Holstein was that Reggie was being uncharacteristically quiet. There was the purring of a cleaned chain passing smoothly over the rear cogs but nothing else. No clicking. I was once again riding a bicycle that was only making the noises it was designed to make, and that made me a very happy cyclist.

The Vía de la Plata that I had followed in Spain had been built by the Romans, making it about 2,000 years old. Schleswig-Holstein (and Jutland in Denmark) could beat that by some margin with the *Ochsenweg*, or the 'oxen way', an ancient cattle track. It claimed heritage going back some 6,000 years. That was a lot of resurfacing. Of more relevance here is that the EuroVelo 3 – the route to Trondheim in Norway – chose to follow the Ochsenweg cycle path from Hamburg to northern Jutland. My plan was to cycle along it until Flensburg, the last town in Germany, and then head east across the islands of Denmark to Copenhagen and beyond.

I found my first Ochsenweg cycle path sign in the small town of Langeln. Thereafter, as the route guided me along its angular course down country lanes, across railway tracks and past great wind turbines, I couldn't help but think that the cows of olden times might have adopted a more direct itinerary. It was distinctly reminiscent of following the HH–HB cycle route from Bremen to Hamburg: well signposted, pretty views but far too much faffing about.

After a lengthy cycle approaching 100 km, I arrived at a campsite by a lake near Borgdorf-Seedorf. It had been a chilly day, with a strong wind from the north removing any hint of warmth from the sunlight. As I waited for the campsite reception to open, I looked forward to pitching the tent in the large patch of empty ground beside the water, pulling on my newly purchased thermal jacket, sinking into my camping chair, putting on my slippers and smoking my pipe. Well, some of those things anyway, but it was that kind of evening and that kind of view.

However, it wasn't to be. When the reception opened, I was processed in a manner akin to being admitted to a remand facility. The man was polite but formal and extremely to the point. I was handed half a roll of toilet paper, although no criminal charges were read out and, after paying a deposit for the shower smart card, I was free to go. My allocated pitch had a view of lots of caravans but, alas, no lake.

—

Until mid-afternoon, cycling day 52 was very much a repeat of cycling day 51. The Ochsenweg was just as angular, the wind turbines just as majestic and my ability to follow the signs successfully for an entire day just as poor. I learnt a little more about the cattle route; it had first been used in the Bronze Age and later considered part of the Way of St James to Compostela, although I doubted the cows ever got that far. I even came across another surviving transporter bridge, one of the remaining 13. Just 11 to go.

After 65 km, I arrived in the pretty town of Schleswig – where quaint, one-storey houses surrounded an unbelievably well-kept graveyard and white church – with the intention of finding a local campsite and bedding down for the night. Schleswig was situated on the banks of what my guidebook referred to as a fjord – the term was clearly not exclusively Norwegian – and suggested a ferry might be required to get to the campsite, so I sought out the tourist office to check.

The two affable girls running the place lacked the essential skill that tourist office employees require: local knowledge.

'Can I catch the ferry to the campsite after 4 p.m.?' I asked.

The girls exchanged blank looks and there ensued a scramble of searching activity. This only ended when I picked up a leaflet with a picture of a ferry on the front marked *Fähren* and asked for translations. The last ferry had gone.

'There's another one tomorrow,' one of the girls suggested in good faith, but ultimately unhelpfully.

There was a second camping option but this was further along the fjord. *Did I have the energy?* Here too a ferry would be required to cross a narrow channel feeding the fjord. Was it still running late in the afternoon? A second frenzy of searching activity started until one of the girls had the brainwave of googling the question.

'Yes. It leaves at 9 a.m.'

'I've missed that too then.'

'No. It goes…'

The girl started to move her finger backwards and forwards.

'…all day. I think.'

To make them feel a little better about our encounter I asked one final, easy question. In all but one key respect they had been model ambassadors for their town. It would be good to end on a high.

'Is there a supermarket on the road to Missunde?'

I left the building none the wiser but with a smile on my face.

Via a wrong turn into an industrial estate, 10 km of winding country roads, a ferry attached to a chain and even a small supermarket, I arrived close to Camping Haithabu. Things were looking up. *Now, where was the site?* Online search… Err… 10 km back near the centre of Schleswig. This level of incompetence would surely get me a job at the tourist office. There was, however, a third site marked on the map, where I thought Camping Haithabu had been. I would at least check it out before setting off again. Camping Haithabu had sounded perfect…

But so was Campingplatz Wees am Ostseefjord Schlei. Indeed, I seemed to have stumbled rather inadvertently on a campsite that was about to rocket itself into my top five of the trip so far. It had everything that the previous night's site hadn't had: friendly welcome, free (and untimed) shower and a stupendous view over a wide lake upon which a handful of small yachts bobbed beside a band of yellow reeds. Magnificent. But it was cold so I wrapped up, sat down next to the tent and heated a can of beans to a temperature that began to compensate for the lack of warmth in my body.

Early the following morning I crawled from the tent as soon as I could detect sunshine streaming over the horizon. I took up a meerkat-like position and stood for perhaps ten minutes to allow my body to warm up. Despite the lack of heat, I couldn't have wished for a better location in which to spend the first hour or so of my final full day in Germany.

I fell into conversation with my neighbour, William from South Africa. He was 70 and explained he was spending the summer renovating a sailing boat moored nearby. I recounted my own mid-life summer adventure.

'You're doing the right thing. My children are forty and forty-five; they're burnt out with the stress of their jobs. I can't understand it,' he explained, adding that the elder of the two had already suffered a heart attack.

William had moved to Germany with a new partner and had an eight-year-old son, although he no longer lived with the mother.

'I think here in Germany he has a much greater chance of living a better-quality life than his brothers in South Africa.'

It was difficult to disagree with him. I was coming towards the end of my two-week journey across Germany and had found it to be a land where the hard edge of Anglo-Saxon capitalism had yet to tread. Yes, they worked hard and, yes, they liked to make money but they managed to balance things out with a quality of living that so many in the English-speaking world seem to have cast aside as inconsequential. When my knees are knackered and my work finished, I too want to come and spend my summers renovating boats in an out-of-the-way place like Campingplatz Wees am Ostseefjord Schlei. Perhaps one day I'll be back.

—

It would be a short but hilly cycle to Flensburg, on the Danish border. The Danish influence was increasingly evident, and I passed many houses flying the Danish flag and numerous Danish schools. Here was the Schleswig-Holstein Question on display for all to see. '*Only three people,*' said Lord Palmerston, British prime minister to Queen Victoria, '*have ever really understood the Schleswig-Holstein business— the Prince Consort, who is dead— a German professor, who has gone mad— and I, who have forgotten all about it.*'

That doesn't give me much of a chance but basically… it was a dispute over what belonged to whom: the Danes, the Austrians or the Prussians. In the end, they had several fights about it. The long-term outcome was that Northern Schleswig is now in Denmark and Southern Schleswig combines with Holstein to form the German region of Schleswig-Holstein – the one through which I was about to finish cycling.

By cycling the 15 km along the fjord to Missunde, I had moved away from the Ochsenweg. So, rather than double back to Schleswig to find it, I decided to make up my own cross-country route by cycling from small town to small town along country roads. It was a strategy that worked well and I arrived in Flensburg before the clocks struck 12 after just 40 km of cycling. I was now only 5 km from the Danish border but would not be leaving Germany until the following morning, as I had arranged via WarmShowers to camp in the garden of Franziska and her retired Lutheran priest husband Klaus.

I needed to be at Franziska's house at around 5 p.m. This gave me plenty of time to explore the city centre, although much of it was spent sitting beside the harbour and simply watching the world go by. As harbours go, it was a good one and, from my position at the southern end of the fjord, there was much to see. On my left was a wide promenade and beyond that the pretty harbour-front buildings. To my right was a hill smothered in greenery and large houses. In the near distance was a sharp steeple. I wondered if this was where Klaus had tended his flock. Immediately in front of me, on the water, was an eclectic mix of small boats: pleasure cruisers, sailing boats, yachts and colourful fishing boats. None were vulgarly large and it all appeared to be rather, well… Scandinavian. I could say with confidence that I was now in Scandinavia in every respect apart from actually having arrived there.

The cold night in Missunde had got me thinking about how suitable my sleeping bag would be further north, so when I finally dragged myself away from the thoroughly relaxing position by the harbour, I was on the lookout for an outdoor shop. I found one in the Große Strasse and went in for a browse. Before I could make it anywhere near the sleeping bags, I noticed a familiar face: Javier, the Argentinian who was also cycling to Nordkapp.

Our routes since Maastricht had been remarkably similar but they were about to diverge, with Javier continuing north through Jutland and me heading east to Copenhagen. Putting aside our respective purchasing plans, we found a café and sat outside in the sun, chewing over the trials and tribulations of our journeys to Nordkapp. Although I didn't know it as we chatted, it would be the last time I would see him. Upon arrival in Norway he decided to find work and delayed the final push for Nordkapp until later in the summer. I left the search for a replacement sleeping bag until another day.

I found Franziska and Klaus's house not far from the spire I had noticed. It had indeed been the church where he had been the

Lutheran pastor prior to retirement. They were both keen touring cyclists and able to pass on a considerable amount of good advice about cycling to Copenhagen. From what they told me, travelling by bike in Denmark couldn't be faulted. I did hope that it would live up to all my expectations.

We continued to sit, sip wine, eat Scandinavian chocolate and chat long into the evening. Klaus talked about his experiences growing up in post-war Germany and he certainly had a tale to tell. He was born in 1945 in an area along the Baltic coast that subsequently became part of East Germany. At the end of the war, his parents became refugees but the family was taken in by a local aristocrat who lived in a large house, where they shared two rooms for six years. Despite the tragedy of the situation, Klaus explained that, from the perspective of a young boy and with many other refugee families also living in the house, it had been great fun. I suspected that this kindness shown to him during his formative years had been instrumental in his choice of career.

The following morning Franziska escorted me on a short tour of her favourite local places, including the nearby Sankt-Jürgen Straße: a row of now-much-gentrified fishermen's cottages painted pale yellow, green or blue and many with flowers tumbling from the boxes beneath their tall windows. We then cycled the short distance to the meticulously restored merchants' courtyards in the centre of Flensburg. Here, as we stood in a narrow alley beneath black timber-framed houses, Franziska explained that the cattle being herded along the Ochsenweg would rest overnight before continuing their journeys to the markets further south. It seemed as fitting place as any at which to end my own journey along the route.

All that remained of the *Bundesrepublik* was a climb up a hill to a supermarket, where eager Danes were filling their cars with cheap beer, and then a freewheel cycle back down to the border. A large expanse of tarmac, once home to border guards and sniffer dogs, was now only host to a small collection of flags and one solitary sign reading: *Danmark*.

PART 4

DENMARK AND SWEDEN

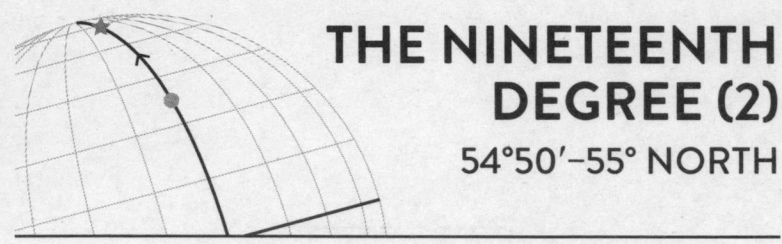

THE NINETEENTH DEGREE (2)
54°50'–55° NORTH

10–15 June

Close your eyes and imagine the shape of Denmark. The image in your mind is probably along these lines: a big bit that sits on top of Germany and then a handful of islands on the right. But you've missed the detail…

The big bit on top of Germany is Jutland, of course, and quite straightforward. That said, you probably placed the border with Germany a tad further south than where it actually is. I'll forgive you but the Germans might not appreciate you reigniting the Schleswig-Holstein problem. As for the islands on the right, there are, in fact, about 400. My job over the next few days would be to fathom a route across them as far as distant Copenhagen. Rather fortuitously, the ability of the natural world to fragment a country into islands is directly proportional to that country's ability to buy ferries and build bridges, or so it seems. Denmark had lots of them and I would be using many to hop from Jutland to Als to Funen to Tåsinge to Siø to Langeland to Lolland to Falster to Bogø to Møn and, finally, to the biggest of the lot: Zealand. Geography lesson over; let's get on with the cycling.

Remember how, at the supermarket on the German side of the border, the Danish had been filling their boots with cheap alcohol? The first thing I encountered on the Danish side of the border was a sex shop. What could the Germans be filling their boots with in there that they couldn't get back in the Fatherland? I had always considered both the Germans and the Danes to be very liberal when it came to such things but clearly the Danes were even more broad-minded than I had imagined. I could be in for an interesting week.

Spurning the opportunity to go inside and have my question answered definitively, I cycled on, and almost immediately turned right and headed east. My journey over the next few days would see me make almost no progress north but, as that – now knackered – crow would fly, 200 km along a line of latitude to the most easterly point of Denmark at Møns Klint. The plan on this first day was to follow a route along the northern edge of the Flensburg Fjord and over a couple of islands to the town of Fynshav, where I would stay overnight before catching the ferry to Funen the following morning.

Initial impressions of Denmark weren't great; they were exceptional. A long, straight road guided me down to the fjord and presented me with sublime views over a large expanse of clear blue water. Short wooden piers poked out from the shore with a few rudimentary boats tethered to their vertical supports. The road hugged the coastline and large, well-maintained houses with enviable views were scattered across the slope to my left. The gardens came in many shapes and sizes but, almost without exception, they all had a flagpole. Hanging from each one was a thin strip of material sporting the white cross and red background of the Danish flag. It was a sign of national pride with which I would grow increasingly familiar as I made my way through Scandinavia.

I had decided to follow Danish cycling route 8, the *Sydhavsruten*, or 'south sea route'. It stretched from Rudbøl near the west coast of Jutland to Møns Klint in the east and was signposted, somewhat sporadically, with blue-and-red panels. The lack of signs, however, didn't concern me. Why would it? All the roads were of good quality, with a wide and clearly marked cycling band on the right. Where a segregated cycle path had been built, its surface was never ravaged by the roots of trees and, unlike in Germany, pavement cycling was almost non-existent.

Upon arrival in Sønderborg, I paused to change some euros into kroner (DK) and buy food. People had warned me of two things that would shock me in all three Scandinavian countries: the cost of food and, especially, the cost of alcohol. In the first supermarket I found, I purchased a can of beer for 10DK (almost exactly £1), a bag of crisps for 6DK and some digestive biscuits for just 5DK. Expensive? Hardly. It appeared that even the cost of keeping myself fed was not going to dent my growing appreciation for all things Danish.

The final 20 km of this first day in Denmark took me away from the shores of the fjord to the ferry port at Fynshav. From my pitch on the campsite – itself a shockingly modest 75DK – I could see the ferry come and go a couple of hundred metres away. After pitching the tent, I eased myself into the camping chair and toasted my good fortune at having found a country that delivered as promised on so many levels. Could it possibly continue to do so all the way to Helsingør? Irrespective, it had been a great way to spend my birthday, which I celebrated with an inexpensive crisp in one hand and a warm, inexpensive beer in the other.

When I emerged from the tent in the morning, Denmark had taken on a different feel; it was cold and the sky grey. The ferry – a large roll-on roll-off-type ship – edged its way to the side of the dock with its bow door wide open (I failed to cast aside memories of *The Herald of Free Enterprise*), and then deposited me, Reggie and the handful of other island hoppers at the end of a long causeway. One of the first signs I noticed was indicating cycle route 8 which, if nothing else, confirmed that the ferry captain had chosen the right island from the 400 on offer.

The landscape of Funen may have been flatter than that of Jutland and Als on the previous day but the pretty views were quintessentially Danish: modest, tidy and meticulously well-ordered. Much time was spent stopping, pausing, gazing and taking photographs, and as the afternoon progressed, the clouds began to break, allowing everything to be bathed in sporadic floods of Scandinavian sunshine. The signs – often sporting directionally challenged arrows and almost always absent in urban areas – weren't playing ball, but as most of my route hugged the southern coastline of Funen, the reassuring presence of the sea more than compensated for any frustrations.

Perhaps the cycling signs in and around Faaborg and Svendborg – the two main towns – had simply been hidden beneath the hundreds of political posters. It was election time in Denmark, a fact that was hard to ignore. The general election was due to take place on 18 June and Denmark's first woman prime minister, Helle Thorning-Schmidt, was hoping to lead her Social Democratic party to a 'red' coalition victory against a tide of 'blue' Conservative opposition*. I wouldn't like to cast aspersions upon the morals of the Danish political elite but from the perspective of this casual observer, bringing the voters over to your way of thinking appeared to rely significantly upon the distribution of free pens and bottles of water. As a cycling writer, these were most welcome and as I pushed Reggie through the pedestrian precincts, I built up a small collection of both items, despite my initial protestations that I wasn't eligible to vote.

Notwithstanding the best efforts of a series of roadworks, I eventually managed to work out the complex algorithm preventing all but the most determined of cyclists from crossing the high bridge to the island of Tåsinge. Upon arrival, a short climb through Vindeby brought me to a T-junction. It was that time in the mid- to late afternoon when I was beginning to fight the temptation of following the main road – especially tempting in Denmark, where I knew that a good quality cycle path would be provided for me. But no, I would persist with route 8, so I turned left along a longer route via the coast.

I was immediately rewarded with a cycle along country lanes and past quaint, single-storey thatched cottages with colourful front doors and gardens that wouldn't have looked out of place at the Chelsea Flower Show. But an even greater delight was in store. For several kilometres I had been noticing signs for Valdemars Slot – a Gothic-sounding castle, Danish style? Frankenstein meets Hogwarts meets Lego?

---

* The Conservative 'blue' coalition went on to win and Lars Løkke Rasmussen replaced Helle Thorning-Schmidt as prime minister, allowing her to go off and spend more time with her family. In her case this meant her husband, British politician Stephen Kinnock, son of Neil and Glenys...

'What is it?' I asked the only person I could find upon arrival at the large red-brick (and decidedly un-Gothic) building. She was running a canoe hire shop incongruously located in the gatehouse to what was clearly a stately home. Perhaps my question should have been more specific.

'It's a stately home,' she explained. 'It belonged to the wife of the nephew of the man who wrote the Sherlock Holmes books.'

'Conan Doyle?' I suggested.

'No...'

'Arthur Conan Doyle?'

'No, he's not the author. He's the nephew of the author.'

This was getting comical. Then she had a brainwave: 'Fleming!'

'James Bond?'

'Yes, James Bond – not Sherlock Holmes.'

It can be so easy to confuse your British literary superheroes. By this point, I'd forgotten my original question so I let her continue.

'It was owned by the wife of Rory Fleming, the nephew of Ian Fleming.'

It turned out that the person who now owned the *slot* was an aristocrat who had given the place to his daughter when she married the lucky Rory. When they divorced, he promptly bought it back from her and she went to live in divorced bliss in London. The 'baron', as the canoe shop woman described him, was still alive and lived in a modest house close to the *slot*, which was now a museum dedicated to big-game hunting.

Over the course of the next hour, I managed to turn an 8 km end-of-day cycle from the western side of Langeland to its eastern coast at Spodsbjerg into a 20 km obstacle course. This involved a 5 km cycling loop that brought me back to where I started ('Mmm...

That's a very familiar bridge…'), hauling poor Reggie over deserted roadworks that blocked the entire width of the road and pavement, narrow paths completely encased in small trees but which finished at dead ends, and to cap it all, coming close to running over a man and his snarling dog, who both insisted on maintaining their statuesque positions in the middle of the cycle lane. I hoped he wasn't fluent in Chaucer but, following a colourful outburst from me, I cycled a little faster just in case he was. With over 400 islands to civilise, the Danish had a job on their hands and I could only surmise that Langeland was still on the work-in-progress list. It had been an odd, out-of-character place.

Cycling day 55 passed in a very similar vein to that of cycling day 54 but with one added attraction: the return of a cloudless sky. The view from the shore where I chose to sit as I waited for the ferry to Lolland was beyond stunning: crystal clear water lapping the rocks beneath me, a horizon that almost imperceptibly melted into the sky and trees tumbling into the water on the other side of the cove, softening the sharp edges of the roofs of the red-and-white houses nearby.

It would turn out to be a long day, stretching to nearly 110 km, but although my calves may have been straining, in most other respects I was increasingly at ease with my surroundings. Perhaps there was something comfortingly familiar about this country and its people that I hadn't experienced in any other place since leaving Tarifa. Even in the parts of France where I had lived for many years, as a passing cyclist, I was an outsider. Here in Denmark, however, where I was just as much an outsider as anywhere else, there were hints of home, especially when I watched the people and pointlessly eavesdropped on their conversations. In Maribo, where I had stopped to buy food from a small supermarket, I ate my mid-afternoon snack whilst listening to a group of teenagers who had gathered around the trolley park. I had no idea what they were talking about but I was struck by how similar they were to their British counterparts: spitting, ignoring old people who dared to collect a trolley, swigging high-energy drinks and subsequently burping loudly. It was all quite endearing.

My initial plan had been to stay overnight in a campsite near the busy coastal town of Marielyst and when I arrived, there were certainly plenty to choose from. Alas, there were also plenty of families with their screaming kids – I preferred those who hung around in supermarket car parks, snarling at old folk – so I continued north along the coast and eventually stopped at an idyllic clifftop site near Ulslev run by a woman who had the financial acumen of campsite owner Josh Fiddler in *Carry On Camping*.

'That'll be a hundred and ten kroner for the pitch.' Not bad.

'But also thirty-five kroner for a Danish camping card – it's compulsory.' Ah… (Why hadn't it been compulsory on the previous two Danish sites?)

'Showers are five kroner for four minutes.' All of four minutes? Luxury!

'Washing machine twenty-five kroner.' It had been at least a week so going without was not an option.

'Dryer is twenty kroner.' Nothing worse than damp clothes.

'Two beers? That'll be one krone deposit for each bottle.' At least I would get the money back.

Just like Mr Fiddler, she smiled as she detailed the charges and I was happy to hand over the cash. Had I known at the time that I would fall asleep to the soporific noise of waves gently caressing the beach just a few metres from my tent, I would have probably offered to pay double.

The stretch of coastline north of Ulslev was considerably more wooded than anything I had so far encountered in Denmark. However pretty the countryside had been up until this point, I appreciated the subtle change from wide-open farmland to a more enclosed environment for no other reason than variety being very much my thing.

Touring cyclists, who had been all but absent since my arrival in Denmark, also began to appear again. A naked wild camper waved most of what he could from his pitch near the water, a small train of four young women nodded seriously as our paths crossed (apart from the one at the back who smiled broadly and shouted a warm greeting; I suspected her cheeriness might have been wearing thin on the others) and when I arrived at the ferry docking point at Stubbekobing, numerous cyclists were milling around on the quay.

By the time the boat arrived, most had disappeared, leaving just me, a couple of colourfully clad racing cyclists and a man in his Toyota to board and cross the 2 km wide stretch of water to the small island of Bogø. I say 'ferry' but it was more of a floating platform with sides attached to stop people, their cars or their bicycles, from falling over the edge. In that respect, it did a marvellous job.

My journey across Bogø was never going to be a long one and, within a few minutes of arrival, Reggie and I were crossing a long causeway that linked it to my penultimate Danish island, Møn. At this point it was very much a return to how the cycling had been up until the end of the previous day: gone were the woods, allowing the ever-strengthening gusts of wind to pick up speed across the empty and ever-so-slightly hillier terrain. In a country whose highest point above sea level is just 171 metres (at a place called Møllehøj on the eastern side of Jutland), everything topographical was on a different scale, so cast aside images of great peaks and valleys. This was a landscape upon which giants could have happily played croquet. But after so many days of horizontal travel, it was a discernible climb towards the high cliffs at Møns Klint.

I was doing myself no favours in travelling this far east. It would have been much easier to cycle the dozen or so kilometres to the bridge between Møn and Zealand than to deviate the 40 km to Møns Klint. But as I knew it to be the easternmost point of Denmark, I felt the urge to include it on my itinerary for the same superlative reason that I had wanted the entire trip to start in Tarifa and end at Nordkapp: I liked points at which thousands of years of geology had cut off the option of onward travel.

It was late afternoon by the time I arrived at the large Møns Klint campsite a couple of kilometres from the cliffs. The owners had gone out of their way to embrace environmentally friendly tourism and the site sported a subtitle: 'Powered by nature'. At its hub stood a large thatched barn, and all around were fields dotted with tents and motorhomes. Everything was in the open apart from the large free camping area set aside for the likes of me, which was in a clearing surrounded by tall trees. The most visible indication of the site's environmental credentials was in the communal facilities, which were shared not only with other campers but with high-speed swallows darting to and from their nests in the covered walkway. Somewhat distracting to begin with, but an arrangement between man and bird that seemed to be working well.

This was clearly no big city with a host of attractions; however, I had been yearning for a day off which didn't involve much effort, so I decided to stay for two nights and take Sunday as my tenth day of rest. For a sunny weekend in mid-June, the campsite and surrounding area were far from busy. Indeed, on the second night I was the only camper within the clearing in the trees; I could *almost* have imagined I was wild camping.

The cliffs, their wooded paths and walkways, and (according to the T-shirts that were on sale) the 994 steps down to the narrow pebble-strewn beach were marginally more populated but not in any way that could have been described as busy. It was simply a wonderful place in which to sink into nature, stroll, dip your feet in the sea, climb steps slowly, exchange smiles with others, think, take photographs and relax. I took great pleasure in indulging in each activity at length.

I might have been a little less relaxed had I been aware of the unsteady nature of the ground beneath my feet. I had seen the warning signs beside the paths:

ENTER AT YOUR OWN RISK
Landslides from the cliff occur most frequently in winter and spring but can occur all year

But, as with most people, I dismissed them as an excessive dollop of health and safety nonsense instigated by ever-cautious lawyers. There were, however, good reasons for the concern. In 2007, following the wettest winter on record, two of the area's 128 metre-tall cliffs crashed into the sea, taking with them some half a million tonnes of Denmark and creating a new 300-m long peninsula in the process. Wars have been fought over less. This all happened on the night of 27 January. On 29 May in the same year, a new

'GeoCenter', constructed through the course of the winter, was opened by Queen Margrethe only 200 metres from where the collapse had taken place. In order to minimise the visual impact of the visitor centre, most of it had been built underground. Now, I'm no architect, engineer or geologist but could there have been a connection? If so, the authorities were keeping very quiet about it.

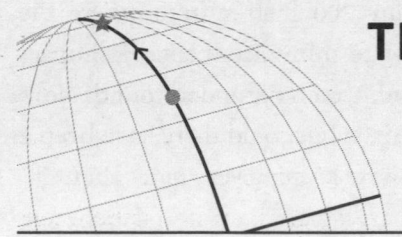

THE TWENTIETH DEGREE

55°–56° NORTH

15–18 June

Although the cyclist himself was bearing up well, after ten weeks on the road, various items of kit were beginning to show a little wear and tear. My laminated camping mat had developed an enormous blister that would have your average chiropodist sharpening a saw. It had the double whammy effect of reducing the often-slim chances of falling asleep, while at the same time increasing the chances of being woken when I did. The handlebar mount for my phone was no longer watertight due to a broken clasp. If the weather took a turn for the worse further north, this would cause problems in accessing online information whilst cycling. The extra battery pack purchased in Hamburg for use in the more remote areas of Norway was malfunctioning, making it as useful as a household brick. Of more immediate concern were my reading glasses; the old ones had a cracked lens so I threw them away as soon as I purchased a cheap replacement pair on a ferry. Perhaps, alas, the new glasses were *too* cheap, as the frame had already broken and they were held together with Sellotape.

It detracted somewhat from the suave adventurer look that I had been trying, but failing, to foster.

As for the bike, although he too was faring well after his lavish upgrade in Hamburg, I had become concerned by the lack of tread on the tyres, the rear one especially. I wasn't sure how poor the terrain might become in the final third leg of the ride but I *was* sure that bike shops would be increasingly few and far between. This thought motivated me to pull into a branch of Fri Bikeshop during my final few kilometres on Møn, in order to have both tyres replaced.

It was thus with a little more traction that, after nearly a week of easterly movement, I was once again heading north in the direction of Copenhagen on my final Danish island of Zealand. The capital would hopefully be the perfect place to solve my equipment issues before I set foot on Swedish soil later in the week.

Cycling route 8 had now finished and was replaced with route 9, which followed the eastern seaboard of Zealand as far as Helsingør. I knuckled down to the job of cycling into a headwind on an unseasonably cold day. I couldn't remember if any of the previous 57 cycling days had been so decidedly chilly. Despite it being late June, the combination of a north wind and a clear blue sky had the temperature plunging to the lower teens and me wrapped up like an onion. On a scale of 1 to 5 – with 1 being T-shirt, shorts and factor 50, and 5 being Captain Oates with a bit less fur – I had started the day at 3 and upgraded to 3.5 whilst Reggie's tyres were being replaced. As is often the case, I was put to shame by other cyclists, in this case three Germans – grandfather, father and daughter – who had paused beside the road. They were cycling from Berlin to Copenhagen and all dressed at number 1 on the scale. Perhaps they were putting more effort into their cycling.

Then again, perhaps not. I realised that the older man and the woman were both cycling electric bikes. Although increasingly commonplace in towns and cities, this was the first time I had seen them used for cycle touring.

According to the Confederation of the European Bicycle Industry, 20 million bicycles were purchased in the European Union in 2014, a figure that has been stable for much of the twenty-first century. When it comes to electric power-assisted cycles (EPACs), however, the picture is much less static. In 2006 only 98,000 EPACs were purchased across Europe. By 2014, that figure had grown to over 1.1 million, with Germany, the Netherlands and Belgium purchasing nearly three-quarters of all electric bikes sold.

When I had met Kevin Mayne of the European Cyclists' Federation in Belgium, he told me that such was the popularity of e-bikes in some countries that many governments were grappling with appropriate legislation. How fast should an e-bike be allowed to go? Should they be permitted to use cycle paths? Is it just cheating for lazy people? (Sorry, I made that one up…). In British law, the following rules apply: an e-bike must weigh 40 kg or less, be no more powerful than 200 watts, not exceed 15 mph and have working pedals, and the rider must be 14 or over.

It looks like the e-bike's day is coming and that in Germany, where there are now over 2.5 million of them on the road, it has already arrived.

'How often do you have to charge them?' I asked the woman.

'We plug them in overnight but that's enough for the following day,' she explained.

I was beginning to see their merit, although I remained sceptical as to quite how long they would have lasted climbing the hills back in Spain.

Powered only by human energy, I found a campsite close to Faxe Ladeplads, a town that should surely have had a character in *The Hitchhiker's Guide to the Galaxy* named after it. The campsite was a large, anonymous place populated with empty caravans and only a handful of people. Its saving grace was the nearby beach, which made for a wonderfully peaceful place to sit and watch the evening fade into night.

The following day's cycle to Copenhagen involved me chopping off a chunk of coastline to shorten my journey to the capital but not before I had been given the low-down on the Danish thatching industry, courtesy of a female thatcher called Petina. Along with her boss, she was in the process of roofing another excessively pretty cottage but was more than happy to break off for a chat.

'A thatched roof will last for about forty years so, although it costs around four hundred thousand kroner [forty thousand pounds] per roof, it's worth the money,' she explained.

'Are there many female thatchers?'

'I think there's just me. It takes four years to learn the trade and there are only three or four who train each year. I'm going to England next month to see how British thatchers do their job.'

Shut down the mines, introduce a poll tax and ignore any opposition? I didn't want to spoil the surprise for Petina so refrained from comment and, after spending a few more minutes admiring her work, cycled on.

—

Copenhagen was on the horizon and, as I cycled around the long curve of the Køge Bay to the south of the city, I was beginning to encounter the urban environment again. I was now following a busy dual carriageway but there was, naturally, a segregated cycle path to use. As I neared the centre and as the red-brick buildings grew steadily from three to four and then five storeys, my mind was alert. I had read and heard much about Copenhagen, with its top-level credentials as a city of cycling, and I was keen to experience it first-hand.

'Cycling is not a goal in itself but rather a highly prioritised political tool for creating a more liveable city,' wrote Ayfer Baykal, the Technical and Environmental Mayor of the city. The city's current '*Bicycle Strategy*' covers not just a two-, three- or even five-year period, but 14 years – 2011 to 2025 – and the document is littered with practical, costed plans that would make your average UK cyclist weep.

The goal is 3 lanes in each direction on 80 per cent of the network…
In 2025, most one-way streets for cyclists have been eliminated…
Funding has been allocated to intelligent traffic system solutions
for cyclists. Pilot projects with LED lights embedded in the asphalt,
perhaps with alternating use of space like virtual bus stop islands…

I don't even know what a 'virtual bus stop island' is. But I'm convinced that someone at Copenhagen city hall is busy making sure they build one.

The northern part of Copenhagen was a far cry from the industrialised and commercial southern side of the city through which I had cycled earlier in the day. We British would label it as 'gentrified', although I suspected that, this being Scandinavia, it had never been anything other than genteel. The best camping option appeared to be 7 km to the north, in a coastal suburb called Charlottenlund. It was either that or pay a small fortune for one of the few remaining hotel rooms available online.

Camping Charlottenlund Fort turned out to be a real find. Located within a small decommissioned military base dating back to 1887, it came complete with 12 cannons and was surrounded on all sides by a functioning moat. With that level of security, who needed a D-lock? It had once been a small cog in a ring of steel surrounding the Danish capital and helped to keep the inhabitants of Copenhagen safe during the fractious years of the late nineteenth and early twentieth centuries. Alas, even wide moats and thick stone walls provided little defence in an era of air bombardment, and the network of fortresses, batteries, ramparts and floodable plains became somewhat redundant. In the long run, Copenhagen's loss turned out to be its gain, as many of the fortifications were now dedicated to the peaceful pursuits of leisure and tourism.

It was only a couple of days after my rest day at Møns Klint but that wasn't going to prevent me from taking time out to explore Copenhagen. Without the panniers and tent, I felt more at one with the 'normal' cyclists of the city as I pedalled back along the road leading into the centre. As I cycled, I counted the bicycle shops – there were 18, one every 400 metres – and watched the cyclists carefully. It struck me that, despite what I had assumed, many did wear bright Lycra and a sizeable minority were wearing helmets. Some even ignored red lights.

However, the most surprising thing of all was the number of cars. In a place so renowned for its cycle-friendliness I had always imagined them to be few and far between. But the roads were just as busy as in any other large town through which I had cycled. Copenhagen appeared to have found a way of building a transport infrastructure that provided for all rather than persecuting the carbon-producing drivers. More carrot than stick; there is a more environmentally friendly, healthier and perhaps even quicker way to get to work – come join us! But if you insist on taking the car, so be it. Was this the real secret of the Danish capital's cycling success story? Keeping everyone happy and on board, even those who weren't yet prepared to embrace the two-wheeled revolution?

Aside from stalking my fellow cyclists, the bulk of the day was spent wandering the streets with a large group of fellow tourists. Several competing 'free' tours of the city had their starting points in front of the town hall at 11 a.m. With price not being a factor – each guide earned money through tips – it was tricky to choose between them. The decision as to which group to join was based entirely upon a snap judgement about how engaging the guide might be. Those who gave the merest hint that any forced hilarity or, God forbid, audience participation might be involved were swiftly cast aside. I opted for a woman in her early thirties who turned out to be Irish. Despite her lack of authentic Danishness, she was a wise choice.

Admittedly, like any northern European city, Copenhagen wasn't at its best under a grey sky and an occasional downpour. However, Maria, the guide, escorted us cheerfully from interesting nook to fascinating cranny, recounting tales of past and present Danes and their exploits: of Tivoli, the nineteenth-century city centre amusement park and Christiania, its liberal 1970s cousin. Of Hans Christian Andersen, his outstayed welcome at Charles Dickens's house in London and his charmingly diminutive, if somewhat disappointing, Little Mermaid. Of Tommy Sneum, a Danish aviator-turned-spy who, in 1941, planned but failed to assassinate Heinrich Himmler with a crossbow. And of kings and queens, their 1,000 years of rule and the Crown Princess*, a Tasmanian-born Aussie of Scottish parents who first met the Crown Prince in a pub in Sydney during the 2000 Olympic Games.

With the tour over, I wandered around the colourful harbour before seeking out various replacements for my damaged or defunct kit and cycling back to the campsite for a second night next to the cannons. All that remained of Denmark was a relatively short but rain-sodden 40 km cycle to the northern port of Helsingør along the self-styled Danish Riviera. At times it was the kind of rain that left me cowering under trees in a vain attempt to stay dry. It was, however, much appreciated by the slugs and snails who basked in the dampness in their thousands along the quiet, tree-lined cycle paths I was following. To the many orphaned slugs and snails of eastern Denmark, I can only apologise, but please take comfort in the knowledge that your parents were squashed by a brand-new set of high-quality puncture-resistant tyres and I for one didn't feel a thing.

---

* Born Mary Donaldson in 1972, she is now Her Royal Highness The Crown Princess of Denmark, Countess of Monpezat and Knight Grand of the Order of the Elephant. Now that's successful social climbing.

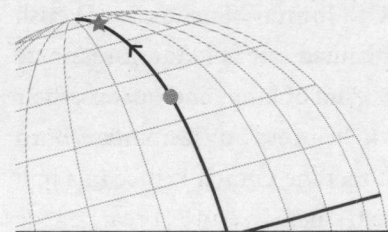

THE TWENTY-FIRST DEGREE
56°–57° NORTH

18–21 June

In the summer of 2014, a year prior to setting off on the cycle from Tarifa to Nordkapp, I had caught the overnight sleeper train from London to Inverness with Reggie by my side. More trains and rail replacement buses took us as far as Thurso and we camped beside the beautiful beach at Dunnet, before setting off on an eight-day adventure along the northern and western coasts of Scotland. It was all in aid of research. I had never before spent a prolonged period of time cycling along isolated, windswept coastlines and didn't want to be too surprised by what I found upon arrival in Sweden and Norway. The magnificent Scottish Highlands had prepared me well, throwing weather in my direction that would have had even Bear Grylls wincing, but I hadn't expected my research to be of much use prior to setting foot on the Scandinavian Peninsula.

The rain and blustery conditions weren't helping but Helsingør in Denmark had the appearance and feel of a distant outpost: a dead-end railway terminus, wrapped-up inhabitants and a squat, defensive castle. It reminded me instantly of the isolated towns along the remote Scottish coast through which I had cycled the previous summer. Perhaps I shouldn't have been surprised. I had, after all, now crossed the fifty-sixth degree of latitude, the point after which the Scottish Highlands and Islands start rising above the Lowlands and fragmenting into the Atlantic. Did such a thing as summer exist this far north?

At Camping Helsingør I was allocated a pitch and as I reached for my already sodden tent, the heavens opened yet again. I returned to the reception hut and promptly upgraded to a cosy wooden chalet. Inside the small square hut I had everything that I could possibly want to keep me (and potentially four friends) snug and warm. Very *hygge* indeed. It was tempting to stay for however long it took for the climatic depression to pass but I knew in my heart that come the morning I would be itching to catch the ferry and set foot in Sweden.

In the meantime, I had a castle to explore, and not just any castle. This was the Kronborg Slot, home to Danish royals of old and, as the castle of Elsinore – Helsingør, anglicised – Shakespeare's *Hamlet*. Built upon a cape protruding out into the Øresund strait, viewed from the town centre it had appeared somewhat sunken, with just its upper floor, roof and towers visible. Even after I crossed its angular moat, the *slot* was still partially hidden behind high walls. Only once inside its square courtyard was I able to appreciate all its three storeys of Renaissance splendour.

The current building was finished in 1585, although a castle had stood on the site since the 1420s. Its main function was to levy tolls on passing ships making their way into and out of the Baltic Sea. At the height of its power, a third of the national budget of the Kingdom of Denmark was generated through the castle's tolls. When the ships couldn't pay in hard cash, they did so in the commodities they were carrying, including precious salt and wine. As a result, the cellars of the Kronborg Slot became home to a collection of some of the finest tipples in all of Europe. Aside from cash, salt and booze, control of the Øresund helped to keep Denmark a main player in European politics for centuries.

Shakespeare was inspired by the tale of a legendary Danish prince called Amleth, so he moved the 'h' and created 'Hamlet'. It must have been something to do with Tudor copyright laws. The authorities had, quite justifiably, seized upon the fictitious connection between Kronborg Castle and *Hamlet*, so there were regular reminders around the site, helping to give this solid lump of Danish history an interesting twist.

Fine dining had never really been on the agenda since setting off from southern Spain but having explored the castle, I found myself passing a modern building of gleaming glass and red brick. It was called *Kulturværftet*, or 'culture yard', and inside I could see a swanky café. Perhaps this was my opportunity to gain an insight into the wonders of Danish cuisine. Noma, René Redzepi's Copenhagen restaurant dedicated to revitalising Nordic food, was crowned the World's Best Restaurant for three consecutive years from 2010 and then again in 2014. By 2015 it had fallen back to number 5 but that's still not bad. I could only hope that the café of the *Kulturværftet* had been inspired to greatness by these culinary triumphs down the road.

I chose a dish of marinated herring, beetroot and red onion salad, served with two slices of dense nutty bread, all washed down with a glass of vintage red wine from the cellars of the castle (or so I liked to imagine). A small pile of salt crystals completed the carefully arranged scene and it was so delicious I would have been tempted to lick the plate clean had the pretty ensemble not been served on a slate roof tile instead. Perhaps this new trend for fine Scandinavian dining was the real reason why so many of the houses had to be thatched.

—

It was now cycling day 61 and the red, white and blue 'HH' – presumably Helsingør–Helsingborg – ferry was spending its day as usual, chugging from Denmark to Sweden and back again. For a modest 31DK I joined my fellow passengers on deck to watch Denmark get smaller and Sweden get bigger. They fell into two categories: Swedes transporting cheaper alcohol back home (Helsingør had plenty of off-licences selling it to them) and Chinese tourists. I put this down to the *Hamlet* connection. But it was 9 a.m. on a Friday morning; where were the workers? Where were the lorry drivers? Shortly after arriving in Sweden, I was in the town centre of Helsingborg asking myself a similar, but more general, question. *Where was everyone?*

The tourist office, where I had hoped to pick up some maps, was located within the Dunkers Kulturhus, but it was shut. The notice on the window, half in English, half in Swedish, explained why:

CLOSED FOR MIDSOMMAR

I sat on the steps of the Kulturhus for a few moments, searching for 'midsummer' in my electronic Rough Guide. It explained that during the summer solstice, or the weekend closest to it, the towns emptied as everyone headed into the countryside, and 'an atmosphere akin to Mediterranean *joie de vivre* takes over Sweden'.

I was happy for the Swedes, but it meant a muted welcome to country number seven and, initially at least, I would be on my own.

I reached for my phone for some Google route-finding assistance, but it was refusing to connect to the data network. That was taking public holidays to a whole new level. After a few moments of electronic fiddling, I gave up and concluded that it probably wouldn't start working again without the intervention of a call centre in Mumbai. I would have to do this the old-fashioned way. Looking at my paper map of Sweden South, I could see a cluster of green campsite symbols near the coastal town of Båstad. I set off in the hope that when I arrived at my destination, the Båstad Internet would be working.

The first half of the journey as far as Ängelholm was pretty standard stuff as far as the cycling went. The suburban landscape was alarmingly similar to that of a British town and, with it being so quiet and sporadically so wet, it was reminiscent of going for a bike ride on Christmas Day back home, albeit without discarded Santa hats strewn here and there.

When the wind started to slow me down north of Ängelholm, however, I knew that it was also pushing the grey clouds south. Sure enough, by early afternoon the sky was indeed a bit brighter. The effort required to climb a modest 200 m hill was almost immediately rewarded by a fast descent towards my destination, and local signage guided me to the gate of Båstad Camping. Although I was enjoying the opportunities for endless jokes about Båstad this and Båstad that, my guidebook pointed out that the correct pronunciation was /*bow-sta*/. This didn't stop me gleefully snapping pictures of comical references to the Båstad Polis and the Båstad Skola. The Båstad Internet didn't make me smile, however; my phone remained as communicative as a toddler in a strop.

Come Saturday morning there was good news on several fronts: the weather looked half decent, the campsite owner – a keen cyclist himself – had filled me in on the Kattegattleden (more of that in a moment) and several employees of Vodafone in different call centres across the globe had managed to fix my phone issues. How wonderful it is that we live in a world where someone in an office on the Indian subcontinent can sort out my problems on a campsite in Sweden. Once we had eliminated the is-this-customer-an-idiot? questions (is mobile data switched on? Is roaming switched on? Is the phone switched on!?), it was determined that my 'APN settings' were wrong for Sweden. Quite what APN settings might be, and why the Swedes needed different ones to all the other countries through which I had cycled up to this point of the trip, I remained ignorant. But they did.

So, back to the Kattegattleden. Had I never spoken to the guy running the campsite, I might well have spent the next few days fathoming my own way along the western coast of Sweden. As it was, I didn't have to, thanks entirely to the Kattegattleden. The Kattegat Sea sits in the gap between the coasts of Jutland to the west, Zealand to the south and Sweden to the east. The Kattegattleden was a cycle route that started in Helsingborg, finished in Gothenburg and followed a route along the Swedish coast that was as near as possible to the sea without actually having to cycle along the beach. The discovery of this Swedish cycling marvel reminded me of stumbling upon La Vélo Francette back in France. At the tourist office in La Rochelle I was perhaps the first to receive a brochure of the route that had yet to open officially. Here in Sweden there can't have been many other cyclists who had cycled along the Kattegattleden since its inauguration just a few days earlier, on 6 June. This was at the cutting edge of adventure.

As I cycled north from Båstad, it was a godsend. Every twist and turn of the route was well signposted, even when there was only the merest hint of possible confusion. Much of the path had been recently resurfaced and almost all of it was either off-road or segregated. The few drivers who happened to pass me were accommodating in the extreme and I began to forget the last time I had felt in any way threatened by someone behind the wheel of a vehicle.

The ultimate accolade that I could bestow upon the Kattegattleden was that it allowed me to forget about the nitty-gritty of cycling, and concentrate instead upon the more important jobs of relaxing and watching the world go by. The landscape wasn't spectacular but it was undeniably attractive, in a similar vein to what I had experienced in Denmark. Bronze Age burial mounds competed for my attention with black wooden windmills, smart red-brick churches and captivating views across a calm and empty expanse of sea. This, it seemed, was a day when nothing could go wrong.

After 80 km of cycling along the Kattegattleden, I arrived, unplanned, at a campsite adjacent to a beach just north of curiously named Ugglarp. The site was the busiest I had yet to encounter since leaving Tarifa, which I put down to it being the midsummer weekend. Although my preference had always been for quieter places, it seemed unlikely that I would find anywhere that wasn't equally full of life. My main concern was whether they would be able to fit me in.

'Yes, we have spaces for tents,' explained the young receptionist. As with all of her colleagues, male and female, she could have walked out of an H&M catalogue. 'It's three hundred and fifty kronor per night.'

I wasn't yet comfortable with Swedish prices but I knew that 100 Swedish kronor equalled about £8, so 350SK would be… Goodness. For one night?

Earlier in the day I had chatted with a couple of German cyclists who had been bemoaning the high prices of the campsites in Sweden. Gulp. I asked the model/receptionist if I could see where I would be pitching the tent. In reality I wanted a few minutes to think and compare prices with other sites online.

The good news was that the area allocated for small tents was much quieter than elsewhere on the site and offered lots of luscious grass upon which to pitch the tent. Online, however, a horror story was unfolding. I found the price list of the next campsite north. It was charging only 240SK per night per tent – except for the midsummer weekend, when the cost would be (I hope you are sitting down) 1,140SK. That was over £90. I returned to the reception desk to give them the good news.

'Where are you cycling?' asked an older man standing behind the woman who was dealing with me. I assumed him to be the boss.

'I'm on my way to Nordkapp,' I explained. His eyebrows flicked upwards and a look of admiration pushed his bottom lip forward. He too was a cyclist and was impressed with my efforts to cycle across the continent from bottom to top. Our short conversation and my cycling efforts paid dividends.

'Just charge him two hundred kronor,' he instructed the woman.

The money saved was spent on food and a couple of cans of beer at the campsite shop. My modest investment in alcohol paled into insignificance compared to that of the other campers who, in their extended family groups, were knocking back beer and wine in a manner that implied Prohibition was only hours away. The downside of my somewhat secluded spot on the grass was that I received no invites to join in the festivities. Instead, I kept myself amused by entering full Desmond-Morris-people-watching mode. As they partied well into the midsummer evening, I questioned whether I would ever be able to cut it as a Swede. I didn't have the looks, I couldn't afford a Volvo and I was normally nodding off after a couple of glasses of red. I would have to content myself with a decent knowledge of the layout of IKEA and an ability (if pressed) to knock out a few Abba classics on the guitar. Not bad for a Brit.

The longest day of the year was now upon me: Sunday 21 June. It wouldn't be the longest one of the entire journey to Nordkapp, however, as the days would continue to lengthen as I travelled further north. There was still even a chance that I might arrive at my final destination in time to witness the fabled midnight sun. If nothing else, it would be a motivating thought to keep me pedalling. As I approached the fifty-seventh degree of latitude, I had Gothenburg in my sights and the final 200 km of the Kattegattleden would hopefully get me there as effortlessly as it had brought me to Ugglarp.

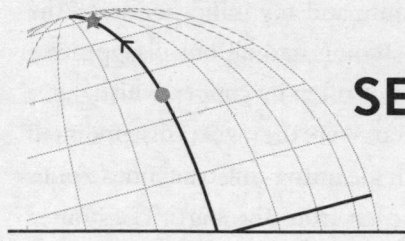

THE TWENTY-SECOND DEGREE
57°–58° NORTH

21–23 June

At some point close to the fifty-seventh degree of latitude I paused and stared at a tree. Its trunk stood at an angle of around 20 degrees from the vertical and most of the branches were arched towards the south. The tree had clearly grown in an environment where the wind was pushing it from the north. Constantly. It was a small yet sobering display of nature at work and, on a more personal level, visual evidence of what I would be fighting against in the coming weeks. I turned into the wind and continued cycling.

Food had been on my mind for much of the morning. Being Sunday of the midsummer weekend, I had struggled to find much to eat since leaving the gates of Ugglarp Camping. A newsagent in the main square of Falkenberg had supplied coffee and a couple of small pastries for breakfast but battling as I was against the northern gusts, their calorific value had been quickly expended and my stomach was again left bereft. This was never a day destined to be shortened by lack of light, but it could feasibly be curtailed by a lack of fuel.

The impeccable Kattegattleden continued to allow me to focus upon the sights rather than the route and my mind pondered the minutiae of Swedish life. Roof thatching had all but disappeared, replaced by more practical red tiles or often by copper, which, after years of weathering, had turned green. Were the owners disappointed that their houses had changed from gleaming constructions to ones of oxidised green or was that the plan from the start? The houses themselves had no letterboxes. Instead, at the end of most side roads was a long row of plastic bins, one for each household. All the postman had to do was drop the mail into the box. No dogs to fight off. No grannies with whom to pass the time of day. No Christmas tips? Postman Pat wouldn't have had many tales to tell if he had lived and worked in Sweden. And the cars. Yes, inevitably lots of Volvos, but also many old American cars parked up next to the houses. A little digging later revealed a Scandinavian subculture called *raggare*; its members, in the post-war years, had a penchant for buying old American cars and, even now, around 5,000 vintage American cars continue to be imported into Sweden every year.

In the early afternoon, far too many hours after the minimal breakfast in Falkenberg, I eventually found somewhere to buy a more substantial meal. It was a rudimentary but achingly pretty shack next to the picturesque bay at the excessively umlauted Träslövsläge. The sign on the shed read, in English, 'Taste of Sweden'. A couple of small blue-and-yellow Swedish flags had been attached to two corners of the hut, a fishing net strewn across its gable end, and a handful of wooden and metal chairs set up on the rough grass. I ordered a cold drink and a large shrimp sandwich, which I devoured within a minute before returning to the counter for a second.

Examining my CatEye cycling computer, I noticed that I had already cycled some 50 km. If this were to be a two-day journey to Gothenburg then I would need to be looking out for somewhere to stay within the next few hours. For a moment my mind lingered over the thought of continuing all the way to Gothenburg but, after a hearty lunch, lethargy was setting in so I remounted Reggie and continued my slow plod along the coast. Aside from the wind, the environment was perfect for cycling: predominantly flat, rural (but not isolated), a band of wild flowers blurring the transition from land to sea and a coastline as placid and unthreatening as a Swiss marriage guidance counsellor.

In Varberg the route was blocked by triathletes. I watched as they ran barefoot beside the high walls of a coastal fortification and entered the 'transition zone' before speeding off on their bikes for a long circuit around the town. Was I being subconsciously shamed by their speed and desire to get to the finishing line in good time? Perhaps, for as the kilometres stacked up, the thought of continuing to Gothenburg returned over and over. Most of my daily cycles since leaving Tarifa had been less than 100 km and I was continuing to maintain an average a whisker above 75 km per day. Cycling day ten from Plasencia to Salamanca, through the storms of Spain, had been the longest yet at 133 km but I had still to cycle a truly epic distance in one day. Could today be the day to rectify that?

I saw my first sign for Gothenburg near Kungsbacka. It told me that I would need to cycle another 61 km along the Kattegattleden to get there. It was 6 p.m. and that wasn't going to happen. However, from Kungsbacka I could see that the cycle route doubled back on itself to take in a small peninsula. The direct route to Gothenburg would be much shorter: 28 km according to Google Maps. That was tempting. The sky was dark with rain clouds that were yet to release their payload; it could be a very wet 28 km. On the other hand, the only campsites I had seen near Kungsbacka had been rammed with white motorhomes, with barely any visible green patches for even a small tent. Pushing on to Gothenburg and booking into a hotel for a couple of nights was too tempting. The decision had been made. I abandoned the cycle route and continued north along the road.

For the final two hours I chased the trains as they sped past me on the nearby track. The clouds were increasingly black but, whatever forces of nature were at work, they were doing a remarkable job of hanging on to their moisture. As the minutes passed and as the fields gave way to housing estates, factories, offices and shops, I approached the centre of Gothenburg, pulling up in the large square outside the train station a few moments before 8.30 p.m. I had been riding for most of the day and had covered 169 km at an average speed of 19 km/h. Not a bad midsummer's day's work.

The Ibis 'Styles' hotel had one attraction that outweighed it being an Ibis hotel in the first place: it was a boat. Well, I had my suspicions whether it had ever seen action on the high seas (think barge with hotel constructed on top), but its location on the river was perfect; to the south of the river Göta was the centre of Gothenburg and to the north the dock where the yachts of the Volvo Ocean Race were, in an act of breathtaking serendipity, about to arrive in town.

My first destination on Monday morning was the tourist office located inside the large Nordstan shopping centre. After nearly two weeks in Scandinavia I had yet to come into contact with anyone who didn't speak English, yet I remained reluctant to do away with the inevitable question.

'Excuse me. Do you speak English?' I asked the woman behind the desk.

According to a 2012 survey by the European Commission, 86 per cent of Swedish adults feel confident enough in English 'to be able to have a conversation'. The figure is identical in Denmark and only beaten by the Maltese (89 per cent) and, of course, the Dutch (90 per cent). The overall percentage of EU citizens who can speak English as a good second language is 38 per cent, with the Hungarians (20 per cent) and, interestingly, the Spanish (22 per cent) being the least enthusiastic. One country has failed utterly to embrace the joys of second language learning: the UK. Just 19 per cent of us speak French and a paltry 6 per cent German. Was it any wonder that 52 per cent of the country voted to turn their backs on the EU in the 2016 referendum when so many of us have never been able to engage with our fellow Europeans in their own language? I blame the teachers.

Not only do nearly nine out of ten Swedes speak English, but they do so exceedingly well. In its annual ranking of English language proficiency, Education First place Sweden in top position. And they are getting better; their score for 2015 was up by 3.14 points on the previous year. It will come as no great surprise to discover that Sweden is in the EU's top three when it comes to spending on education.

So the answer to my question in the tourist office in Gothenburg was, naturally: 'Of course,' delivered with a slightly bemused smile.

Armed with a brochure outlining a walking tour of Sweden's second city, I set off in the sun for a wander.

Away from the docks and the busy commercial centre around the station, there was much to admire in the quieter cobbled backstreets, although first impressions were a little subdued. The oldest building in Gothenburg was the *Kronhuset*, or 'old city hall', dating from 1654. It was a rather austere red-brick building with ageing copper shutters and a sharp green roof. Despite the surrounding craft shops and cafés, I couldn't help but think that the real action was elsewhere so I didn't hang around and instead decided to keep walking.

I crossed the zigzag canal – reminiscent of those I had seen in Bremen and Copenhagen – in the direction of the Skansen Kronan fortress but never got that far. Instead, the long Haga Nygata in a former working-class district of the city was more my style. The street was lined on either side with low-level buildings, many constructed from wood and most of them converted into shops, cafés and restaurants. The absence of traffic allowed for aimless strolling and – with its subtle pastel shades, good-looking people in sweaters and inclusive, relaxed atmosphere – it was altogether the most 'Scandinavian' thing I had yet encountered.

The busy commercial thoroughfare of the wide Kungsportsavenyen brought me back to where I had started in the square outside the main train station. I would have been happy if this relaxing day in Gothenburg, complete with its contrasting districts of considerable charm, had ended there. But this was Monday 22 June 2015 and exciting nautical things were happening elsewhere in town.

Cast your mind back to southern Spain. You will remember that my journey had started two days before setting off from Tarifa at the home of my uncle, Ron, in Estepona on the Costa del Sol. He had always been a keen sailor and, as his career as a petroleum engineer took him from one sun-drenched sailing paradise to another, he honed his skills as a competent seaman. Now retired, he was in the perfect location to continue his passion for sailing and had spoken to me about having seen the yachts of the Volvo Ocean Race depart on their round-the-world odysseys from Alicante in October 2014. It was a nine-leg race ending with the vessels returning to Gothenburg eight months later. By sheer coincidence, the boats and their crews had arrived in Gothenburg after their journeys of nearly 40,000 nautical miles on the very same day as mine of 3,003 miles on land. Admittedly, they had set off six months earlier, but let's not quibble. It was still a coincidence, of sorts.

The long, high Götaälvbron spanned the river and linked the commercial centre of the city with its docks where the boats had only that morning moored. As I crossed the bridge, my elevated position provided panoramic views of the complex of marquees and prefabricated 'pop up' buildings that had been arranged along what the organisers had named 'Main Street'. Champagne corks were popping, a TV helicopter was buzzing around overhead, beaming its pictures back to the big screen (and, probably, Ron in Estepona) and an enthusiastic English commentary was being blasted out of the speakers. It was distinctly bewildering but thoroughly good fun.

My knowledge of sailing was minimal to say the least, but as I examined them through the wall of rain, the yachts seemed remarkably similar. Their liveries were distinct but I couldn't tell their shapes apart. Had the yachting design fraternity finally agreed upon the ultimate hull that would keep the boats cutting through the seven seas like a dolphin fleeing from a Japanese fishing boat in search of tuna?

My question was answered by a nice chap from Volvo. He was no expert sailor himself but had volunteered to stand inside one of the main sponsor's marquees, guard the exhibit behind him and fend off questions from the uninitiated such as me. It was, perhaps, a nice change from designing the next generation of airbags.

'All the boats are identical. They are the Volvo Ocean 65,' he revealed.

He was now looking at the exhibit – a Volvo Ocean 65 – or rather half of one. The yacht had been sliced in two to give a cross-section view of everything inside the hull.

'This is the first time all the teams have used the same boat. It was to reduce costs and make the race fairer,' he explained. One of the 20 m yachts could be picked up for a mere €5 million.

Conditions on board were decidedly cramped for the crews of eight men, nine men/women or eleven women plus one 'on-board reporter'. This latter role seemed an attractive one: taking a few snaps and mucking around with a waterproof GoPro whilst everyone else laboured away on deck.

'Yes, but you'd need to be the cook and cleaner as well,' retorted Volvo airbag man.

I had done pretty well keeping myself going on the previous day with my emergency can of ravioli and a packet of digestive biscuits, but such culinary excellence might not go down so well with a crew of ravenous yachters. I decided to put my yachting career on hold.

I was to cross the Götaälvbron for a second time the following morning, as I restarted my quest to the north. Alas, the Kattegattleden had now finished and I was again required to put some thought into route planning. This wasn't helped by me entering the 'unmapped' zone. Having purchased 15 paper maps to cover the entire cycle from Tarifa to Nordkapp, I had discovered a gap. Between Marco Polo's 'Sweden South' and 'Norway South' maps was a 100 km slice of Scandinavia across which I had to travel without their assistance. It had started before Gothenburg but as the Kattegattleden had been so utterly faultless in its signage, I was rarely required to glance at a map in the first place. Now it was different. I did, of course, have Google Maps to consult but it would be a constant struggle to see the 'bigger picture' on the relatively small screen of an iPhone 6.

Several things came to my assistance: a long, easy-to-follow cycling motorway beside the real motorway for the first 10 km of the day, some sporadic signs for the very general *Cykelspåret*, or 'cycle track', a charmingly to-the-point Canadian cyclist whose abrupt opening words were: 'How far is Gothenburg?' but who rapidly morphed into an entertaining, chatting companion, and a newly appointed member of staff at the Kungälv tourist office who – despite trying to persuade me that the nearby castle had been built 400 years after the date given on the information board outside – provided me with a few general maps. And then there was OpenStreetMap.

I had known of OpenStreetMap's existence for some time but, up until this point of the cycle, had rarely used it. Over the remaining few weeks of the trip, it would prove invaluable. Run under the auspices of the OpenStreetMap Foundation, its aim is 'to create and provide free geographical data'. Think Wikipedia for map geeks like me.

In many places – the Netherlands for example – the cycle map layer of OpenStreetMap reveals an intricate lattice of routes linking the corner of almost every street. In other, less populated places, isolated red lines mark out the long-distance cycling routes of the EuroVelo network.

Swiping my finger down the screen of my phone, I followed the continuous red line north, not only across my cartographical gap but beyond and towards the border with Norway, to Oslo, to Trondheim, to Bodø, to Tromsø and to Nordkapp itself. For the first time since leaving Tarifa, the end of my journey was in sight. Just.

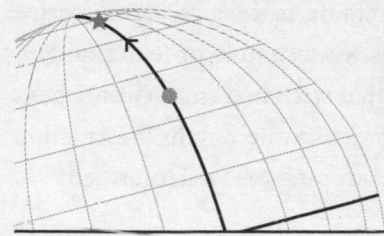

THE TWENTY-THIRD DEGREE
58°–59° NORTH

23–26 June

When the Almön Bridge – the third of three consecutive bridges linking the Swedish mainland to the country's sixth largest island of Tjörn – was opened in 1960 with a span of 278 metres, it was the longest arched bridge in the world. At 1.29 a.m. on Friday 18 January 1980, the Norwegian-owned bulk carrier MS *Star Clipper* struck the arch of the bridge. The roadway it was supporting collapsed, in its entirety, onto the ship below. Although no members of the crew were killed, the damage caused to the vessel knocked out radio communications. It was a foggy night and before traffic could be stopped, seven vehicles had driven into the empty void and eight people had been killed.

'Goodness,' I mumbled.

I never expected to discover such shocking news as I was pootling by bicycle along the picturesque coast. The authorities had wisely gone for a suspension-style bridge second time around, with no arches into which lost ships could crash. Moments earlier, I had crossed the Tjörnbron, which had taken just 22 months to design and construct.

I was now in Bohuslän, Sweden's westernmost province and an archipelago of some 3,000 islands that stretched from Gothenburg in the south to the Norwegian border in the north. Information boards next to the new bridge were keeping me well informed:

Bohuslän is synonymous with ocean, sunshine and swimming.

Naked swimming, according to my guidebook. But on that score there was good news. The boards again:

The Skagerrak is an extension of the Gulf Stream whose tempering waters give rise to one of Sweden's most unique maritime environments.

And you won't freeze your bits off when skinny-dipping. I continued to read and be enlightened:

A string of communities lie scattered along the coast with histories formed by fishing, shipping, the stone industry and the bathing era.

The 'bathing era'? We never studied that in history. The Bronze Age, the Iron Age, the Middle Ages, the Age of Steam, yes. But the Bathing Age? Ah, there was another board.

Tourists discovered Bohuslän in the 1800s. In the beginning they were upper-class folk who followed in the footsteps of King Oscar II. Today, Bohuslän is a holiday paradise for everyone.

From what I could see, it certainly was, with the banks of the fjords busy with hotels, summer houses and, fortunately for me, campsites. That said, I wasn't particularly tempted to dive into the water as Oscar had done all those years ago. It was still rather too chilly for that. Perhaps Swedish kings of old had been made of stronger stuff than me. Instead, I pitched the tent near a small jetty and settled in for the evening with the two towers of the suspension bridge popping up over a hill to my right. Sitting in my chair, I closed my eyes, emptied my mind and relaxed...

'*Hallo! Hallo? Deutsche?*'

I reopened my eyes and lifted my hand so I could block the sun and see who was speaking. It was a man in his sixties, sporting a distinctive white beard.

'Err... *Nein. Englisch,*' I replied.

Realising that perhaps my German was minimal, he switched language.

'To where are you travelling?' he enquired.

'To Nordkapp, in Norway.'

'That won't be very interesting. The scenery will never change.'

I guessed that the man in front of me hadn't just retired from working as a motivational speaker. I steered the conversation away from the controversial topic of how mundane my life over the next few weeks was to become. He was called Helmut – from Baden-Baden in southern Germany – and was cycling north in the direction of Oslo at which point he planned to head south again along the Norwegian coast. He was a retired engineer in the semiconductor business.

'But I hadn't worked since the factory was shut down in 2007.'

I could sense that something outside of Helmut's control was to blame.

'I blame the oil price,' he explained.

Yes, just as I had thought.

Packing up the tent in the morning, I waved and smiled to nearby Helmut but refrained from conversation so as to minimise the chances of me throwing myself off the end of the jetty and ending it there and then.

Good news was around the corner in the small town of Myggenäs, though. Not only was the place *not* infested by midges (Helmut, unsurprisingly, had pointed out the etymology of the name the previous evening), but the local supermarket provided me with an excellent breakfast of chocolate muffins and good coffee.

As I queued to pay for yet another pair of replacement reading glasses, I glanced down at the screaming headline on the *Aftonbladet* newspaper:

HÅLL UT! DÅ KOMMER VÄRMEN

Beside the headline was a graphic consisting of the sun, an orange-coloured Sweden and a thermometer with its mercury at maximum level. '*Kommer värmen*'? It's going to get hot!

As of 11 a.m., the heatwave had yet to kick in. The sky was overcast and it remained quite cold but I had great hopes of splashing on the factor 50 by the end of the week. In the meantime, I had a few islands over which to hop. The red line of the *cykelspåret* on OpenStreetMap adopted a zigzag approach to crossing the archipelago. I was aiming to cycle as far as Fiskebäckskil, a town that, from the photographs I had seen, seemed to encapsulate everything that was coastal Sweden. To get there I needed first to cross the islands of Tjörn, Orust, Malö and Flatön, before returning briefly to the mainland and then over the water again to Skaftö.

The weaving road linking the small settlements that were strewn across the rocky yet green landscape was a joy. The cycling was Goldilocks in nature: not too easy, not too difficult, just right. The traffic was light, the views were picture-perfect and my mood was high. If this was the price to be paid for travelling between two points only 30 km from each other on the map but nearly 70 km along the road, so be it.

Small ferries that resembled toy aircraft carriers plied their trade linking Orust with Malö and then Flatön with the mainland. As I queued for the first of these, a fellow cyclist pulled up behind me. I turned around in nervous anticipation of seeing Helmut and having my good mood smashed to smithereens but was delighted instead to see a woman. Her name was Klara and she explained that she was cycling from Gothenburg, where she worked at the university as a professor of 'environmental impact', to meet up with her partner further north to do some kayaking.

'Do you know how much the ferry costs?' I asked, as I hadn't been able to see a sign.

'It's free,' she explained. 'They are considered part of the road network so we don't pay.'

Could this day get any better?

Upon arrival on Malö, we cycled together and chatted. For some time, one question had been on my mind and this chance meeting with an environmental professor might provide the perfect opportunity to get it answered.

'Klara, what makes a fjord a fjord?'

'That's a very good question,' she replied, smiling. 'A fjord needs to have been created by a glacier but the glacier should have left a deposit of moraine at the mouth of the fjord, giving it a much shallower inlet channel than the fjord itself.'

I wondered if Slartibartfast* had been aware of this when he had designed them.

—

There wasn't a great deal to do in Fiskebäckskil apart from wander around the narrow cobbled lanes, admire the pretty wooden buildings and gaze across the fjord (or was it?) to similarly picturesque Östersidan. But this was precisely the delight in being there: wandering, admiring, gazing. I was an expert in all three. The buildings had been scattered across the shallow incline of a hill in an organic fashion and painted yellow, blue or green in a random order, which only added to the harmonious coming together of civilisation and nature.

After indulging in an ice cream, I caught the ten-minute ferry to Lysekil, where I found a deserted campsite, pitched the tent and sat back in my chair. I closed my eyes, emptied my mind and relaxed...

'*Hallo! Hallo?* Andrew?' Helmut seemed pleased to see me.

I tried to keep conversation with my new German friend away from anything that might give him cause to express a negative opinion but it wasn't easy. In the morning, I repeated my goodbyes

---

* Slartibartfast, designer of planets, who won (according to Douglas Adams in *The Hitchhiker's Guide to the Galaxy*) an award for his design of the Norwegian coastline.

from the previous day but within a couple of hours I was with him again at a café on the main road north, nodding out of politeness rather than agreement.

'Norway is too hilly, the roads are bad and the weather is awful…' he moaned before getting his teeth into the Swedes: 'They are poor cyclists. Their bikes only have three gears and you will never find a bike shop to repair your bike properly.'

What had I done to have this man inflicted upon me? His oratory then took a surreal twist: 'Cycle touring only became possible after 1990 when the technology allowed for proper gears to be used.'

'Did you say 1990? One, nine, nine, zero?' I questioned, checking he hadn't confused his numbers.

'Yes, 1990. *Eins, neun, neun, null.*' I sensed he was annoyed by me questioning his facts.

I was tempted to cite the case of an American, Maximilian J. St George, who, in the years following World War One embarked upon a 26,000 km bicycle tour of Europe. He ventured to most parts of the Continent and upon his return to the US wrote a book entitled *Traveling Light or Cycling Europe on Fifty Cents a Day*. I had tried but failed to find a copy, but mentioned Maximilian, his adventure and his book on my website shortly before setting off to cycle from Greece to Portugal in 2013. Then, on the day I left my job as a teacher in Henley-on-Thames, my colleagues presented me with a package wrapped in tissue paper. Carefully unfolding the wrapping, I found a copy of the book. It was a touching moment.

With Norway now just a day away and with a wallet of unused Swedish notes, I decided to treat myself to a slap-up lunch. A nice plate of fish perhaps? At Hjalmars restaurant on the quayside in Hamburgsund I ordered a herring salad followed by grilled cod on a base of new potatoes and shrimp. The bill? A not-so-hefty 127SK, or around £10. Yet again, the cost of life on the road in Scandinavia was proving to be far from expensive. With the midsummer weekend now several days ago, the campsites were charging no more than £15 per night. A bottle of notoriously pricey sun protection spray had cost me a mere £8 and even the alcohol, when purchased from the supermarket, was only what I was used to paying back in Britain.

Just wait until you get to Norway chuckled the voice in my head with an accent reminiscent of Helmut's, but I remained hopeful.

My day ended with a short, sharp climb from the coast at Grebbestad to a campsite close to the Tanum UNESCO World Heritage Site, famous for its Bronze Age rock carvings. Opposite the quiet campsite was a deserted reconstructed mud hut village. I wandered around, making comparisons between the simple life of the Bronze Age folk and my own life on the road. I concluded that although they might not have had the option of booking a decent hotel online when needed, their camp beds of straw were somewhat more appealing than my laminated camping mat. I was tempted to stay in the abandoned barn overnight but then figured that by doing so, I may well have had to share my bed with the local rodent population. Better off in the tent.

Back across the road, I sat in my chair, closed my eyes, emptied my mind and relaxed… Silence. Helmut was elsewhere.

Post-Gothenburg, the days had developed into a routine of pack-up, breakfast in a local supermarket, a good day of cycling, new campsite and relax. My final day in Sweden was to be no different but I wasn't quite expecting the first encounter of the day to be along these lines: 'Are you Andrew Sykes?'

Gulp. Had that European arrest warrant been issued already? Minor traffic offences flashed through my mind as I turned to see a young cyclist.

'You're Andrew Sykes, aren't you?' he asked, in an accent from the English Midlands.

'Err... yes,' I confirmed, a touch confused. Was I *that* famous? No.

'It's Nick. I stayed with Steve in Trondheim. You've exchanged messages with him.'

So I had. I would hopefully meet up with Steve in Norway and, yes, he had mentioned someone called Nick who was heading in the opposite direction.

'Hi. I'm Saskia from the Netherlands,' interjected Saskia, from the Netherlands.

This was rapidly turning into a conference. Three touring cyclists all descending upon the local supermarket for their breakfast. We sat down together to eat and exchange stories.

We all had a different approach to cycling. Nick's asset was his willingness to go with the flow. He had started his ride in Bergen with the intention of cycling to Nordkapp but the weather hadn't been great so, after Trondheim, he'd headed south over the mountains to Oslo and now Sweden. He was wild camping – he'd just spent the night in the local recreation ground – and was using an inexpensive mountain bike.

Saskia's forte was her speed. She too was cycling from Tarifa to Nordkapp – the first person I had met who was doing so (Javier, the Argentinian cyclist, had started in Madrid) – but on a more easterly route that had included Switzerland. What's more, she was an osteopath and every few weeks she was stopping, flying back to see her patients and then, a week or so later, returning to the point where she had paused before continuing. She was covering considerable distances every day and had a bike that would allow her to do just that.

Route details were exchanged, locations of campsites noted and anecdotes swapped. Helmut, I reflected, wouldn't have felt comfortable in the little bubble of cycling positivity that we had created.

I excused myself for a few moments to use the facilities inside the building, before returning to the table to say my goodbyes. During my short absence, our conference had welcomed a new delegate: 'Cycling along the coast towards Norway today will be suicide with all the Swedish people driving to their holiday homes. Suicide!'

Helmut. I shrugged my shoulders. We all said farewell, Nick set off south towards Gothenburg, Saskia and I – at different speeds – headed north towards our impending deaths at the hands of holidaying Swedes, and Helmut... who knows? I never saw him again.

PART 5

NORWAY

THE TWENTY-FOURTH DEGREE
59°–60° NORTH

26–29 June

Thanks to European integration and, more specifically, the Schengen Agreement, border posts across the Continent have been abandoned for the benefit of free movement of goods and people. The free movement of people from Norway into Sweden had been evident for all to see at the large Nordby supermarket a few kilometres south of the border. Almost every car in the car park sported a Norwegian plate. The free movement of goods was evident in their trolleys, stacked high with food and drink. I stopped there myself, with the intention of stocking up on things that I imagined might be excessively expensive in the land of the fjords. Examining the shopping trolleys of my fellow shoppers, that appeared to be everything.

There was, however, good news ahead. Although the posts had indeed been abandoned long ago, geography was still able to make this final border crossing a memorable one. Sweden met Norway not on land but on water. More precisely, in the middle of the Svinesund, a dog-leg sound near the Norwegian town of Halden. A bridge, 80 m above the sound and almost as empty as the deserted customs buildings on either bank, carried Reggie and me out of the European Union and into Norway. I paused in the middle of the bridge. On the carriageway to my left a thick white line had been painted and, in large capitals, the word *Sverige* painted on one side and *Norge* on the other. Now, that's how you do borders.

Among the nicest things about arriving in a new country are the changes that accompany it. Here in Norway, the roads signs were yellow, reminiscent of Germany, the cycling signs brown and the middle of the road was marked with a continuous yellow line. On this side of the Svinesund, the trees seemed a little taller, the forests a tad deeper and the buildings slightly more run-down than those in Sweden and Denmark. If I were to squint, my new surroundings could have doubled for a distant outpost in the northern United States where camouflaged men sit defending their Second Amendment rights whilst growing their beards and narrowing their minds. It was ever so slightly discombobulating.

The cycling signs told me that I was following route 1, the coastal route. That was OK for the time being, although it wouldn't take me as far as Oslo. For that I would need route 7, the pilgrims' route. I could see from OpenStreetMap that the latter branched off where route 1 turned west to follow the coast in the direction of Kristiansand. I would need to look out for this junction the following morning.

The American-themed introduction to Norway was to continue an hour or so across the border at Høysand Camping. The reception building was a white-painted wooden lodge in an architectural style not dissimilar to that of Southfork Ranch in *Dallas*. I opened the door, went inside, and the two people in the room turned and stared. On the right, sitting on a bench, was a young woman in her late teens. On the left, behind a desk, was a man of similar age, wearing a white suit complete with white waistcoat and white tie, clearly under the impression that he was managing Caesar's Palace in Las Vegas rather than a three-star campsite in southern Norway.

Their body language suggested that I was interrupting something, although, bearing in mind the distance between them, I wasn't quite sure what that might be.

'Hi,' I said, a little uneasily. 'Do you speak English?'

At this point the man started to speak Norwegian, at speed, and the girl giggled, uncontrollably. His intonation and tone implied that I was the butt of his words.

'Just joking,' he then said.

The subsequent few hours were a frustrating struggle. The camping area was in the shade, boggy and on a slope. The washing machine system was a costly, time-consuming palaver. And Boss Hogg and his girlfriend could be seen outside their ranch, flirting. Oh dear… Had Helmut's take on life on the road now rubbed off on me?

—

It was a cold, bright start to Saturday and cycling day 68. I hadn't slept well due to the incline of the pitch, but I was eager to try to put the bad experiences behind me and move on to new, preferably flatter, pastures. Oslo was my destination for the day, and I intended to take the following day off in order to explore the capital.

Cycling route 1 sent me off in the direction of a town called Sarpsborg where, according to the electronic sign, I was the thirty-third person to have arrived by bike that morning. Quite impressive for 8.30 a.m. The sign also reminded me that the Norwegian for 'cyclist' was *syklist*, a word sufficiently close to my surname that it would surely have the Norwegians crying with laughter.

In recent days, Reggie's gears had been slipping and the brakes were looking decidedly worn, so my main preoccupation in Sarpsborg was to find a mechanic. Dodging the roadworks along the main street, I quickly found a bike shop and a bearded mechanic called Petter who was up for the challenge. He needed to finish the job he was doing so asked me to return in a couple of hours when the work would hopefully be completed.

'What's your name?' he enquired. This was my chance; prepare yourself, Petter, for an attack of mirth.

'Andrew Sykes,' I replied. 'Sykes, as in *syklist*.'

'S-Y-K...' he clarified.

'... E-S,' I completed.

Not even a smirk.

Leaving Reggie to have his mechanical worries tended by Petter, I wandered further into the centre of town. Unsure as to how much I might have to pay for the work to be done, my own concerns were financial. I found a cash machine and withdrew 2,000 Norwegian kroner (NOK), or around £160. I hoped that this would keep me going for a few days at least, even after having paid for the repairs. I then found the main square, ordered a coffee and started to read up on all things Norwegian. Up until then, Norway had been, for me, a bit of a blank canvas. My guidebook did its best to fill me in on the tourist stuff but I needed some hard facts so went online to consult the CIA Factbook. First up was a bit of background information:

History: *Vikings... Union with Denmark... Swedish invasion... Twentieth-century independence... Neutrality in WW1 and WW2...*

But invaded by the Nazis anyway... Discovery of oil and gas... Rejection of EU membership.

Geography: *Slightly larger than New Mexico...* (How big is New Mexico?*)... *Rainy year-round on west coast...* (Bugger.)... *Highest point 2,469 m... One of the most rugged coastlines in the world...* (Double bugger.)

Then came the financial stuff.

Economy: *GDP per capita: $68,400...*

At this point I looked up the CIA Factbook entry for the United Kingdom.

Economy: *GDP per capita: $41,200...*

A difference of around £20,000. It seemed logical to assume that a higher GDP would equate to higher prices but as I scanned through the data, there were no further clues. Finally came confirmation about the source of the country's wealth.

'Norway saves state revenue from petroleum sector activities in the world's largest sovereign wealth fund, valued at over $800 billion,' explained the CIA spies.

That was a lot of rollmop herring.

Mindful of the financial situation, I refrained from ordering a second coffee and opted instead to go for a haircut. The trim was courtesy of Mohammed, an Iraqi refugee who had arrived in Norway in 1995 after the first Gulf War.

'Why did you choose Norway?' I asked.

'I didn't. I wanted to go to Canada or Australia but Norway chose me [CIA Factbook: 'Net migration to Norway in 2015 was 7.25 per 1,000 people; net migration to the United Kingdom in 2015 was

---

* Since you ask... 315,194 km², or 15 times the size of Wales.

2.54 per 1,000 people.'] so I couldn't go elsewhere,' he explained. 'Life in Norway is so boring compared to Baghdad. Everyone spends so much time inside. And Ramadan is a real problem in the summer, as the days are so long.'

He did have a point. For a Muslim in Norway in 2015, not only had the holy month been in the summer, but it had also straddled the longest day of the year. Mohammed still had another three weeks of daylight fasting ahead of him.

'How much for the haircut?'

'It's normally a hundred and seventy kroner but you're a foreigner so just a hundred.'

Perhaps Mohammed had been reading the CIA Factbook too.

I returned to the bike shop and chatted with Petter as I watched him finish working on Reggie.

'How much for the repairs?'

'Five hundred and fifty-eight kroner.'

Fifty pounds. No discount for foreigners. It could, on reflection, have been a lot worse.

As I had also found elsewhere in Scandinavia, good-quality segregated cycle paths beside most roads were the norm in Norway and I made full use of them whenever possible. I picked up the signs for the pilgrims' route near a small town called Halmstad and followed them for much of the day. It was turning out to be a gentle introduction to Norway. The unseen Oslofjord was gradually narrowing a few kilometres to my left, leaving me to cycle through a green landscape dominated by arable farms. Yet in no way did the area feel remote. Aside from the many red barns strewn across the land, it was difficult to travel more than a few hundred metres without passing another substantial – and usually white – house, an out-of-town shop or a small factory. Between the road and the fjord was a railway line and to my right a major highway; there was even a sizeable airport in the small town of Rygge. This was countryside that was trying its best to be part of the urban club but, thankfully for me, repeatedly failing to gain full membership.

As the sun made progress towards the west, I continued to make progress north. In the mid-afternoon I paused in Moss, where I sat on the sloping banks of a short, narrow canal and watched as small boats took a shortcut to the northern reaches of the fjord. There would be no shortcut for me, but I didn't mind. North of Moss, the increasingly deep blue sky created a wonderful backdrop for the landscape of small towns, villages and lakes beside which I was now passing. There was no wind to speak of and no good reason to stop. Occasional pauses to fuel up on chocolate kept my energy levels high and there was little chance of my enthusiasm waning. By early evening, I was increasingly confident that I would arrive somewhere near Oslo by the end of the day.

Then, as the road I was following emerged from the trees to coalesce with the shore of the Oslofjord, I found Camping Oslofjord. The facilities weren't great and the noise from two roads on either side of the hill where it was located was inescapable. However, the welcome from the twenty-somethings running the place was cheerful – they didn't ridicule me for my lack of Norwegian – and it would be my home for two nights, as I took time out to explore Oslo, some 10 km further north.

Reading through the list of things I could possibly do in the Norwegian capital, I decided to focus my attention on just one. This didn't mean I had to neglect my customary wander: impressive new opera house, oversized bronze tiger in front of the station, lots of plaques about playwright Ibsen, walk around the perimeter of the Royal Palace, receive ticking-off from guard for taking photographs of his sentry box... I then caught a ferry across the fjord to my chosen destination of in-depth tourism, the Fram Museum.

I was on a cycling quest to the polar north, stopping in Nordkapp only because Slartibartfast had seen fit to stop designing fjords and put a sea there. Most people I met who had visited Nordkapp had cruised there on a luxury ship. Few had travelled overland and even fewer had cycled. I was beginning to consider myself as a polar explorer, of sorts. So when I noticed in my guidebook that the Fram Museum was dedicated to err... people like me, and even contained 'the world's most famous polar ship' – the 400-ton, 40 m long *Fram* – I was on my way.

Back in the late nineteenth century, if you were an explorer who wanted to explore the Arctic Ocean in winter, you had a problem. The boat that you were planning on using would become encased in ice and crushed. Adventure over – back home to the wife and kids. (Sorry, it did seem to be a male-only profession back in those days.) Chances are, however, that you weren't Fridtjof Nansen, described as 'one of the greatest men Norway has ever nurtured... and a legend in his own lifetime'. Nansen proposed a solution: design and construct a ship – the *Fram* – that when surrounded by ice would be pushed up and float with the ice pack itself. By doing

---

* I could go on. According to the Fram Museum: 'He was the personification of a great hero; the first among sportsmen, explorers, research workers, statesmen and humanitarians. Long after his death millions continued to remember him as the foremost exponent of human compassion.' What's betting he was also a sensitive lover, changed nappies more efficiently than Mary Poppins and tossed a mean *salade niçoise*?

so he would be able to prove the theory that there was an ocean current and drift of sea ice from Siberia towards Greenland via the North Pole.

The *Fram* set off in June 1893 and by September it had indeed become encased in ice off Siberia. It wasn't crushed and over the course of the next three years the ship drifted, as predicted, across the Arctic Ocean. However, when he realised that it wasn't going to cross the North Pole itself, Nansen and fellow explorer Hjalmar Johansen decided to set off on dog sledges to try to do it themselves. They left the *Fram* at 84 degrees north in March 1895 and started walking in the knowledge that they would never be able to find the boat again. By this point I was beginning to see where the 'legend' epitaph came from. After only a month, battling extreme cold, Nansen realised that it would be impossible to reach the Pole so at 86°14' – the furthest north anyone had ever travelled – they turned around, heading for home. It would take them over a year to get there and their journey involved fighting off polar bears, shooting walruses for their skins, blubber and meat, and sitting out the long winter in their 'den', a stone hut that they built with their own bare hands.

Back in Norway, the *Fram* and its crew were presumed lost so it must have been a bit of a surprise when Nansen and Johansen rocked up on the boat of British explorer Frederick G. Jackson who had bumped into them in June 1896 on Franz Josef Land. As for the *Fram*, she drifted with the ice and arrived back in Norway just five days after Fridtjof and Hjalmar.

All this explorer stuff left me feeling somewhat inadequate. The museum was full of tales such as the one of Nansen and his chums. The *Fram* itself went on to escort Otto Sverdrup to the Canadian

Arctic and then, perhaps most famously for a Briton brought up on tales of heroism on the part of Captains Scott and Oates, Roald Amundsen to the shores of Antarctica.

More than a century after all these events had taken place, I returned to the campsite to contemplate my own quest to the north. It was unlikely that I would have to battle extreme cold, resort to killing the local wildlife to feed and clothe myself or build a hut to sit out the dark winter months. It might get a little nippy from time to time, my emergency can of ravioli (now replenished after Sweden's 'emergency') could well see another outing and I might have to be prepared to slum it occasionally in a hotel if my tent got a bit too damp… But a quest it was and as I set off in the direction of Nordkapp, I could feel the spirits of Nansen, Sverdrup and Amundsen willing me, a plucky Englishman, on. *I may be some time.*

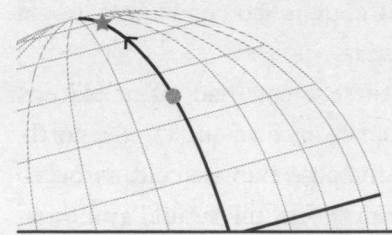

THE TWENTY-FIFTH DEGREE
60°–61° NORTH

29 June–1 July

It had been a slightly bizarre night of post-midnight comings and goings on the campsite south of Oslo.

Excuse me, madam, it's now past midnight and I'm curious. Why do you keep moving your car?

And you, sir, why did your friends turn up with two more caravans and then disappear?

The woman over there with the short leather skirt? Why are you cleaning your van with a vacuum cleaner at 2 a.m.?

These were all questions I asked, but not within earshot of anyone who might be in a position to give me an answer. I was reminded of the 'business activities' of the women of the Bois de Boulogne in Paris and on the campsite in Montargis. But here? Near Oslo? Surely not.

I headed back into the centre of Oslo. The grey sky and rain of the previous day had been replaced by bright sunshine – perfect weather for the fjordside opera house of gleaming white marble and glass to look its best. Its architecturally obtuse angles gave it the look of a stealth bomber, albeit one painted white, and its influence on the old port district nearby was clear to see. Around a dozen gleaming towers had only just been completed on the opposite side of the road to the opera house. Each tower had been built in a distinct style and was a different shade of white, black or brown. There was no hint of any nods to the past; they had clearly been designed and built looking unashamedly to the future, and they looked wonderful against the backdrop of a blue sky and mirrored in the water of the harbour.

The plan had been to pick up some cycling/camping/polar explorer (?) brochures at *Den Norske Turistforening*, or DNT – the national tourist office – located in a more traditional street in the centre of Oslo. It is a sign of our times that the world has moved so far online that all the nice woman who served me could do was to point me in the direction of various websites, many of which I had already visited. Every now and again I yearned to live in the world of Fridtjof Nansen and his explorer chums where the question 'Have you looked online?' had yet to be uttered by anyone ever.

It was a long, steep climb out of Oslo through smart, well-kept suburbs. In the centre of the capital I had been struck by the extent to which certain areas were being rebuilt, seemingly for the twenty-second century, never mind the twenty-first. In the residential areas, however, the penchant was for covering the buildings with large, colourful murals. It reminded me of the Albanian capital Tirana, through which I had cycled in 2013. There, the city's former mayor Edi Rama had encouraged a policy of painting the drab communist era buildings so as to cheer the place up and the strategy had worked a treat. I wondered what the motivation had been for doing a similar thing in architecturally interesting Oslo.

After 20 km of almost continuous climbing, there was a short descent towards the small town of Lillestrøm and it was there that I found my first sign for cycle route 7, the pilgrims' route. This would be the cycle path that would hopefully take me as far as Trondheim, at which point I would again hook up with the coastal route, number 1, as far as Nordkapp.

It was a liquorice allsorts of a day on the bike. I had already cycled through a city and its suburbs but ahead of me was open countryside. The terrain was equally mixed: ups and downs of varying lengths separated by longish stretches of flat riding. Even the weather wanted to show me just how wonderfully eclectic it could be: predominantly sunny in the morning but later in the afternoon a storm to rival the one I had endured on the approach to Salamanca, in Spain. On this occasion, I was caught out and drenched before I decided to cower under a bush. When the rain kept falling, however, I came to the conclusion that I couldn't possibly get any wetter so re-entered the tank of water and continued cycling. If Fred Astaire could sing and dance happily in the rain, I was up for the challenge of cycling in the rain and having fun doing it. I may even have broken out into song.

In the early afternoon, the sun was shining again and I was happily pedalling my way along the cycle path when I noticed a horse a few metres from the track on my right. *What big ears you have* was the thought that passed through my mind before I slowed down and took a better look. That was no horse. From what I assumed to be a safe distance, I quickly took a photograph. When I reached a nearby petrol station, I stopped again to examine the photo in more detail but before I could do so, I was approached by a Norwegian woman, also on a bicycle, speaking excitedly in her native tongue. I held up my hands in an attempt to slow her down.

'Sorry. I don't speak Norwegian,' I explained.

Her English wasn't great but markedly better than my Norwegian which, after only a few days in the country, was still limited to '*hei*', '*ja*', '*nei*' and '*Jeg vet at jeg ligner Fridtjof Nansen, men jeg er faktisk bare en syklist fra England*'.'

'Did you see the… elk?' she asked, unsure that she had used the correct word.

'The moose?' I replied.

'*Ja*. But in Norway it is an elk,' she clarified.

'Yes, I did. Should I have been worried?'

'They're only dangerous if you are between them and their babies.'

It all sounded quite cute. An elk and 'their babies'.

'But I've never seen one so close to Oslo,' she went on.

It was, perhaps, a sign of things to come. Wildlife had yet to become a major feature of this trip. It had, however, been one of my main concerns about cycling through Norway and thus, prior to setting off, I had done a little digging as to what I might find.

Reindeer, of course. Elk, clearly. My main preoccupation, however, had been bears. The Norwegian Environment Agency noted five species of 'large carnivore': the brown bear, the lynx, the wolf, the wolverine and the golden eagle. It was reassuring to know that the elk wasn't likely to try to eat me, although with a weight of upwards of 300 kg, your average elk could most certainly knock me off my bike and trample me to death.

I had met a pack of wolves whilst cycling in southern Italy a few years previously. They had been more interested in the food

---

* 'I know I look like Fridtjof Nansen but I'm just a cyclist from England.'

waste left by tourists than in sinking their gnashers into my succulent thighs. I cycled straight past them, albeit carefully. In Scandinavia there were around 430 'registered' wolves but the vast majority of these had chosen to live in Sweden. Perhaps over there the registration form was simpler for them to fill in. The risk of bumping into one in Norway seemed slight.

I had only ever associated the word 'wolverine' with a Hollywood film so to discover that it existed in the real world was somewhat of a revelation. However, with only 340 animals in Norway, it again seemed unlikely I would encounter any. That said, their distribution along the long border with Sweden meant that they were never too far away. Lynxes – of which there were 310 in 2015 – were probably more afraid of me than I was of them. They were similarly distributed along the spine of Scandinavia.

With their penchant for small animals such as grouse, ducks and hares rather than large cyclists, it appeared that I wasn't at risk of being carried away by a golden eagle. The Environment Agency estimated the number of breeding pairs to be between 700 and 1,100. Bearing in mind the eagle's ability to fly some distance from the nest, I was hopeful that I would spot some of them high in the sky as I cycled north.

Which brings us to the bears…

Around 150 years ago, there were 4,000–5,000 brown bears in Scandinavia, roughly 3,000 of them in Norway. Bears were ruthlessly hunted in both Norway and Sweden in the early twentieth century, and almost exterminated. Today, the stronghold of bears in Norway is along the border with Sweden, Finland and Russia.

So said the Environment Agency. They went on to admit that it wasn't easy to count bears, as they spent much of the winter in hibernation. However, the *Altposten* newspaper reported that walkers were being encouraged to collect bear scat (yes, that's bear shit to you and me, presumably found in the woods) for DNA analysis. The important thing was not to contaminate it and to freeze it as soon as possible, before sending it off to the authorities for checking. This research had revealed there to be at least 128 bears in Norway in 2015, of which 53 were females and 75 males.

So, my chances of coming face to face with a brown bear were also slim. But the burning question – was the brown bear dangerous? – had yet to be answered. It was thus useful to discover a publication written by a certain Jan-Erik Olson for the Scandinavian Brown Bear Research Project, handily entitled *Is The Brown Bear Dangerous?*

The good news was that the last reported death by bear in Norway was way back in 1906 when a 13-year-old boy surprised a bear that was in the process of munching away at a carcass. The boy didn't quite provide dessert but he was seriously injured and succumbed to meningitis a month later in hospital. The most recent death in Scandinavia had been in Finland, in 1998, when a jogger again surprised a bear. It was suggested that the surprise might have been due to the jogger's almost silent approach into a headwind. It could be argued that a cyclist's approach in similar conditions might also provoke alarm in a bear. This I could understand. Whilst commuting to work in the open countryside of South Oxfordshire, I would often surprise the local deer population and as a result get a little too up close and personal with the fleeing animals.

Although the report by Mr Olson said that the Scandinavian brown bear was not dangerous, he did go on to state that many people had been 'hurt, scratched and bitten by bears'. I suppose it depends upon your definition of danger. In fairness, I could see where he was coming from. I have fallen off my bike on many occasions over the years and hurt myself but I don't consider cycling to be a dangerous activity.

The publication rounded off with some useful advice about encounters with bears: signal your peaceful intentions, no uncontrolled movements, don't run and retire cautiously. I'm sure I was given similar advice at teacher training college about dealing with 15-year-old boys. If the bear stood on its hind legs, it was doing so not to scare the living daylights out of you but in order to see or smell better. If the bear roared, snorted or uttered 'sounds reminding of murmurs or whistles', it *was* trying to scare the living daylights out of you so run like hell. No, sorry, forgot… Don't run. And you shouldn't shoot: 'A wounded bear is a dangerous bear!'

If you were attacked, the choice was between climbing a tree (best option) and playing dead (worst option). Although this latter strategy has been proven to be successful, bears have learnt to associate human scent with food either left as refuse or as bait placed by hunters and photographers. They smell you and think food…

Mr Olson concluded his pamphlet thus: 'If you treat him with respect and do not threaten or hurt him, he returns his respect by withdrawing.'

Wise advice indeed and just as applicable to teaching teenagers as confronting bears in a Norwegian forest.

That evening, not yet close to the mountainous border between Norway and Sweden further north, I slept on what I assumed to be a bear-free campsite at the southern tip of Lake Mjøsa, near the small town of Langset, although it wasn't quite as idyllic as it sounded. The noise of the traffic at the campsite near Oslo had been replaced by the noise of trains trundling across the nearby bridge and planes on their final approach to Oslo airport.

In the morning, I chose to cycle along the western shore of Lake Mjøsa. For much of the day the road hugged the edge of the lake with only a narrow forested strip of land between me and the water, and where gaps in the trees existed, beautiful views across the wide lake and towards the low, green hills in the east were revealed.

In the early afternoon, the road climbed temporarily away from the lake, only to return close to it at the town of Gjovik, where I paused to stock up on provisions before continuing the few kilometres to Sveastranda Camping. The welcome was friendly and the free camping area idyllically positioned next to the water. The site was busy but such was its spaciousness that I had plenty of ground to call my own; any conversation with a neighbour would have required us both to shout. A number of tall trees beside the lake provided shade from a sun that was now not setting until very late indeed.

That evening I made good use of my camping chair and my increasingly proficient ability to sit and, with a contented smile on my face, stare across a placid lake to the mountains beyond. This was the Norway I had been dreaming about for so long and, to cap it all off, there wasn't a bear in sight.

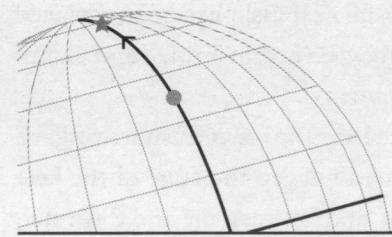

THE TWENTY-SIXTH DEGREE

61°–62° NORTH

1–2 July

The first couple of hours of cycling day 71 were a physical struggle but I was unsure why. Between the campsite and Lillehammer – a journey of around 30 km – there was little climbing to be done and yet my legs were aching. Cycling day 70 hadn't been particularly taxing, with only one small climb of around 100 metres. Accumulated fatigue? Perhaps. That said, I'd had seven rest days in June, as opposed to only six in April and May combined. It seemed more likely that my body was having a tantrum to match the one taking place in my brain.

So why was my brain disgruntled? That I *could* figure out and it was all down to a road. Up until this point, I had managed to avoid much of the busy E6 either by following cycle routes 1 and 7 or by choosing alternative quieter roads. However, 5 km north of Sveastranda Camping, the E6 joined me on the western side of Lake Mjøsa. Unfortunately, it was being upgraded and, for long stretches, the traffic had been shunted onto my minor road. It made for unpleasant cycling.

Lillehammer was on the eastern side of the lake and, thankfully, the E6 skirted around the town rather than ploughing straight through the centre. As with most people who were alive at the time to watch it on TV in 1994, I associated the town with the Winter Olympics. Nowadays, some might immediately think of *The Sopranos* spin-off television drama *Lilyhammer*, which was filmed there. A small, unassuming place, it hung onto its Olympic heritage: a sign to the *Olympiaparken* here, a colourful Olympic-themed manhole cover there.

The arrival of the Olympics must have been a shock for a town with a population of only 25,000. In several ways, however, 1994 was a turning point for the Winter Games. They were the first not to be held in the same year as the Summer Games and, perhaps as a result of the noble yet ultimately flawed efforts of Eddie 'The Eagle' Edwards two years earlier, they were the first Winter Olympics where competitors needed to (brace yourself) prove that they were half decent before turning up with their skis. In 1992, when the Games had taken place in Albertville, France, the British team had consisted of 49 athletes. In 1994 the number dropped to 32. So much for Pierre de Coubertin's words of comfort to all those who fail miserably: 'It's not the winning but the taking part.' Time would tell whether I would be one of them. I still had over 2,000 km to cycle.

My journey continued along the snaking valley north of Lillehammer, in the direction of some rather large, snow-capped mountains. But enthusiasm was lacking and after barely one more hour in the saddle, I had found a campsite near the town of Granrudmoen, where I sat on the steps of the wash block feeling rather sorry for myself.

I couldn't blame the E6 for my malaise this time, as I had been able to follow a secondary road since Lillehammer. Feeling disgruntled with life on the road was one thing but feeling disgruntled for no good reason was quite another. That only made me feel *more* disgruntled. Where was that Eddie 'The Eagle' spirit in me that could propel me forward against the adversity of feeling a bit grumpy? I was sure Eddie must have had his off days, when he spent far too much time wondering, 'Why bother?'

It was only 2 p.m. The small reception office was closed and the rest of the one-field site was all but abandoned. The wash block was open and there were signs that at some point in the afternoon someone might arrive: clothes hanging up to dry, and a table and chairs set up next to one of the few campervans. I closed my eyes and ignored my aching limbs. For perhaps 15 minutes I didn't move; I listened to the distant sounds of rural Norway – the river, the wind, the traffic on the E6 – and tried to relax.

This was crazy. I jumped to my feet, got back on the bike and cycled up the short, rough track in the direction of the road. It was going to be a case of mind over matter. My map showed a good number of other campsites strung along the valley; one of *those* would be my home for the night.

Within a few minutes of pulling myself together, I was standing on a bridge spanning the wide river, admiring the view of blue sky, pristine farmland hugging the valley bottom and increasingly tall mountains in the distance… Fantastic. The morning's gripes were a distant memory – no! They were gone, not even a memory. My mood was high and my legs… Where had the aches gone? Ha! 'It's not the winning but the taking part.' Piffle! I wasn't there just to take part, just to observe as life passed me by. I was there to succeed, to vanquish, to win!

Too much Olympic spirit?

I was now back on the eastern side of the water and campsites began to appear thick and fast. *Nah, too near the road… Too busy… Too quiet… Just look at that view… What a pretty chalet with a turfed roof… And we are beginning to climb away from the road… Can you hear that? No, me neither!* The E6 had disappeared from earshot.

As the road had now climbed modestly above the valley floor, I paused again to take in the view. While I gazed, I was approached by a woman dressed for a strenuous hike. She was from Germany and on a pilgrimage from Oslo to Trondheim.

'That's amazing,' she cooed when I explained where my own final destination would be. She then called over her much younger male friend to join in on the admiration.

How had I managed to transform an early afternoon of aches, pains and mental malaise into an early evening of feeling as high as an errant drone and even receiving plaudits from an athletic elderly German and her toy boy? An achievement worthy of an Olympic medal in itself.

Even when I was required to rejoin the busy E6 for the final few kilometres of the cycling day, my mood could not be dimmed. It wasn't long before I had set up camp and, from my position in my camping chair on the manicured lawn of Elstad Camping, near the town of Ringebu, I watched as the sun slid slowly down the side of the shallow hill opposite me. I had expected it to disappear soon after my arrival, but no. Such was my northerly latitude that the movement of the sun was now much more horizontal than vertical, and it kept the campsite bathed in sunshine for much of the evening. I pondered the astrophysics that allowed me to witness the spectacle in the first place. Late in the evening, when finally the sun had disappeared on its short journey below the horizon, I crawled into the tent and slept well.

—

I was making real progress in my journey from the southern to western coastline of Norway. Point-to-point, from Oslo to Trondheim, was almost exactly 400 km. From Oslo to Ringebu it was almost exactly 200 km. However, I was still languishing at only 200 metres above sea level. Looking on my map at the peaks to the north of Ringebu, there were some substantial mountains ahead of me: Høggia 1,641, Gravskardhøgda 1,767 and Store Sølnkletten 1,827. There was never any risk of me having to climb to any of those heights, as I would be weaving a path along the roads between the mountains, but they were indicative of what was to come. The path north to Trondheim was littered with dozens of peaks significantly higher than anything Britain could have thrown in my way. I had a challenging day ahead of me.

The good news was that I would be leaving the E6 to fathom its own way to Trondheim on a route further to the west. Cycle route 7 was a more adventurous beast and so was I. Fortifying myself with a strong black coffee and breakfast in the centre of Ringebu, I set off for the mountains, assuming that I would have a few kilometres of respite before the real climbing kicked in. How wrong I was. Within metres of leaving the pretty wooden buildings on the main street of the town, the climbing started abruptly and, over the next two hours, the gradient never relinquished its grip on the side of the mountain.

Great joy can be found in climbing a mountain using only the power of the human body and the determination of the human mind, knowing that in a relatively short period of time, a point will be reached from which you can look down, think *Yes, I did that* and smile, a little smugly. It's exactly what I had done on a wet and windy day in 2009 after a 60-minute plod through the 300 m of ascent from Alston to Hartside Top during my first long-distance cycle along the Pennine Cycleway in Britain. It's exactly what I had done on a cold morning in 2010 after a two-hour shakedown over the cobbles from Andermatt to the Gotthard Pass in Switzerland. And it's exactly what I had done under the blue sky and sun of Provence in 2013 after an uninterrupted three-hour crawl up 1,600 m to the summit of Mont Ventoux. It's also exactly what I used to do upon reaching the 'summit' of the 500 m long Chalk Hill from Harpsden village to the eighth green of Henley Golf Club on my way home every day after work. All 39 vertical metres of it. Not once did I approach the foot of that hill and wish I was in a car, for I knew that gratification awaited me at the top. I had done the training and I had the experience to know that it was never a race. Find the granny cog, slow down, sit down and let the thighs do the work. Hartside Top, the Gotthard Pass, Mont Ventoux, Chalk Hill – the same strategy worked every time.

Only two things stopped me in my tracks as I nudged forward from 200 to 1,000 m: a woman and a church. The former was in her twenties and dressed lightly. She needed to be, as she was powering herself up the mountain on long roller skis. With her long blonde hair, tall, athletic build and tanned skin, the woman fitted the Scandinavian stereotype quite well. She had stopped to rest – this was a challenging hill for even young, fit Norwegians – at a point where there was a break in the trees and subsequently a satisfying view down into the valley. I had seen numerous people speeding along the cycle paths using roller skis – think normal skis with a small wheel at either end – but this was the first time I had seen anyone attempt such a steep incline.

'It keeps me in shape for the cross-country skiing season,' she told me before going on to explain that she worked in a hotel at the ski station at the top.

'Do we have far to go?' I enquired, tentatively.

'Only a couple more hours,' she replied, smiling.

As for the church, I initially stopped only to take a photograph. The building, in the village of Venabygd, was small and simple, with wood-panelled walls, a tiled roof and a tall wooden spire. The walls and the spire were painted white and stood out in sharp contrast against an almost cloudless sky. Then, as I was packing away my camera and about to remount Reggie, I noticed a small green plaque attached to the wall by the church gate.

Commonwealth Krigsgraver
Commonwealth War Graves

I abandoned what I was doing and went to investigate. In a corner of the well-kept graveyard I found five graves in a row. The stones were identical to those found in the cemeteries of northern France and Belgium. My initial thoughts were that they must have been killed in an airplane crash en route to bomb Germany. But none of the five men were in the RAF. The first grave was that of a signalman aged 19 attached to the Royal Corps of Signals. The next three were of privates in the Sherwood Foresters aged 22, 20 and 21. The final grave was for a 38-year-old sergeant from the same regiment.

Norway remained neutral during World War Two but that hadn't prevented the Nazis from invading anyway. The Norwegian government called upon the British for help in repelling the Germans and a brigade consisting of two Territorial Army battalions, the 8th Sherwood Foresters and the 5th Leicesters, was dispatched. The troops disembarked at Andalsnes, 170 km south-west of Trondheim, on 18 April 1940 on an 'ill-fated' mission. The merchant ship carrying their equipment had been torpedoed and sunk. This included their means of transport so the soldiers did the next best thing and caught the train south instead. First contact with the German forces was made near Lillehammer on 19 April but it seems likely that the soldiers in the graveyard at Venabygd were killed at the Battle of Tretten on 23 April. The remnants of the brigade retreated to the coast and were transported home to Britain.

Four of the five men buried in Venabygd were barely even 20 years old at the time of their death. They had all been born around 1920. The previous evening, whilst watching the sun slide down the mountainside, I had received a phone call from home. My step-grandmother had just died. She was 95 years old. She too had been born in 1920. Walter Summersgill, the 19-year-old royal signalman, came from Hunslet, Leeds. My step-grandmother had been brought up 10 miles down the road, in Rawdon. It seemed entirely possible that at some point during the 1920s or 1930s they had unknowingly walked past each other whilst out shopping in Leeds, had perhaps sat a few rows apart from each other in the Hyde Park Picture House or even swum together in the Roundhay Park Lido. Who knows? Walter was soon to die. Connie would live well beyond the end of the century. Life is fragile and can be cruelly unfair but it was somehow satisfying and poignant to have made a connection between two children of pre-war Leeds after all those years.

—

After another hour of toil, I had climbed to 1,000 m and the hard work of the day had been done. In terms of distance, however, there was much more cycling to be completed. It would be another 50 km before I crossed the sixty-second degree of latitude and 80 km before I stopped at the next campsite. The environment had now changed dramatically. Predominantly flat, it was a treeless plateau of low, hardy vegetation and rock. Some of the lower peaks were within a couple of kilometres of the road, but in the distance the larger mountains, dusted with snow, kept silent vigil over the high land I was crossing. This wasn't, however, a deserted place. Many people had chosen to either live here or at least have a summer house and grassy turf was being put to good use as insulation on the roofs.

Had the weather been poor, it would have been a hellish place across which to cycle, but it wasn't and high, wispy clouds drifted across the sky. The good conditions had attracted a few other adventurers on two wheels and a good number of campervans whose drivers had mastered the art of placing their stark white boxes in just the right place to ruin a good view. This was, alas, a feature of life that I would have to become accustomed to on my way to Nordkapp. For a few kilometres the road fell back into the valley before finding a comfort level of around 700 m, where it remained for the second half of the day. The physical high point had now passed and, I imagined, the visual high point too. I hadn't, however, counted on discovering the Sohlbergplassen.

THE TWENTY-SEVENTH DEGREE
62°–63° NORTH

2–4 July

Architects have become adept at hiding things so as not to detract from the beauty of their surroundings. Think of the recently constructed buildings I had seen at Waterloo and Møns Klint, where the infrastructure had, at least partially, been buried into the ground. Is it possible, however, not simply to minimise the impact that a construction may have, but to build it in such a way that it improves the visual quality of the surrounding area?

I think it is. And I cite as evidence the infrastructure that has been designed and built by the government of Norway to provide for the needs of those travelling along the 18 *Nasjonale Turistveger*, or National Tourist Routes. I knew nothing about them until I arrived at the Sohlbergplassen viewing platform next to Lake Atnsjøen.

In 1914, celebrated Norwegian painter Harald Sohlberg came to Lake Atnsjøen, looked up towards the sky and painted *Winter Night in The Mountains*, one of Norway's most famous pictures. I learned this from a woman who had brought her elderly mother to look at that same view. The reason why all three of us had stopped at an identical point along the route was courtesy of the location of the viewing platform.

Now, if, in your mind, you have an image of scaffolding and a few wooden planks, think again. If you have an image of a perfectly smart, functional platform with a railing at one end to stop you from falling into the water, think again. If, however, you have an image of a long walkway, whose sides have been beautifully crafted from thin pieces of vertical concrete curving gently around the slender pine trees of the surrounding forest and which, at its farthest point, opens wider and descends slightly to reveal one of the most stunning views in Norway... you are probably nearer to the reality.

The architect was a certain Carl-Viggo Holmebakk and the platform was built in 2006.

> *He constructed a concrete platform that virtually hovers in the air... The steel-lattice floor provides water and light to the soft forest floor covered in moss and lichen... By placing the foundations on slender pillars, the forest floor could be preserved in near-pristine condition, and only one single tree had to be felled during the construction project.*

So said the information panel. It was stunning and I formally submit the construction as exhibit A in my argument as set out in the first paragraph of this chapter. As for the view itself, it was epic yet simple. Beyond a band of lakeside conifers next to the platform, a broad stretch of water snaked into the distance. The banks of the lake – carpeted without interruption by more trees – sloped gently away, but the eye was drawn magnetically towards the Rondslottet mountain in the distance. At nearly 2,200 m, it was Norway's third tallest peak. Six more peaks clustered around the Rondslottet, their summits all capped with snow. I stood and stared for quite some time.

I later looked up the Nasjonale Turistveger online and was delighted to discover that, as I continued my journey north, I could, potentially, be following five more of the routes: the Helgelandskysten, the Lofoten, the Andøya, the Senja and the Havøysund. If they were to deliver jaw-dropping spectacles half as good as the one I had seen earlier, I was going to be in for a treat. By the time I arrived in Nordkapp, I could have a clutch of exhibits with which to argue my case, or so I hoped.

Møns Klint, way back in Denmark, had been a turning point, literally. Shortly after leaving the high cliffs at the easternmost point of the kingdom, I had passed through the fifty-fifth degree of latitude. Since then, with my journey heading predominantly to the north, the subsequent lines of latitude were being crossed at an almost alarming rate. It had taken me only 15 cycling days to travel through the seven degrees since Møns Klint. By contrast, it had taken me 24 cycling days to cross the seven degrees prior to Møns Klint. Although I was now regularly putting in a cycling day in excess of my desired average of 75 km, I had geography to thank just as much as my own physical effort. From Paris to Møns Klint there had been ten degrees of eastward movement; from Møns Klint to the end of cycling day 71 there had been just two degrees of westward movement. However, my progress was about to slow. As soon as I arrived on the northwestern coast of Norway, I would again begin to move in an easterly direction; despite only eight degrees of latitude separating me from Nordkapp, I needed to cycle through 16 degrees of longitude. There were still several weeks of cycling to go.

From the Sohlbergplassen, a 30 km end-of-day cycle brought me to the four-star Grimsbu Turistsenter – or, between you and me, Grimsbu Camping. It was another oasis of lush green grass. Should SW19 ever be blighted by an aggressive form of fungal turf disease, the campsites of central Norway might be a good place to come and play tennis. Had the equipment been handy, I could have easily indulged in a bit of ball tossing over a net with my German neighbours.

Instead, I busied myself by writing my notes from the two previous days of cycling, while the Germans were, well… organising themselves. And what a good job they were doing! My Teutonic neighbours, cycling tourists themselves, had elevated organisation to an art form. On the surface of my two-wheeled life on the road, everything appeared to be serene. Open a pannier, however, and chaos was often exposed. My eyes started to pay less attention to my writing and more attention to them and their ordered lives.

I needed to investigate this spectacle of organisation in more detail so went over for a chat. They were a couple in their forties and each had a smart black bike. I learnt that they had been on the road for three weeks which, bearing in mind that all their clothes and equipment looked as though they had just been delivered from the shop, was decidedly alarming. How was it possible to be so clean and organised after over 20 days on the road? Our conversation turned towards routes and I sensed that Mr Organised found my self-deprecating 'it-will-turn-out-OK' attitude to such things somewhat tiresome. They were, however, heading in the same direction as me, towards Trondheim, so it seemed likely that we would encounter each other again. He might have to contend with more tongue-biting eye-raising moments the following day.

I decided to abandon temporarily cycling route 7, as it headed off to the west alongside my nemesis, the E6 road. I was left to fathom an 'it-will-turn-out-OK' route to the east. To avoid a longish detour to the south via a town called Alvdal, the directions suggested by Google took me off-road and along an unsurfaced track, where I encountered the following idiosyncratically formatted sign:

> STRÅLSJØÅSVEIEN
> Bomavgift:
> motosykkel/moped   10,-
> pers. bil, traktor   70,-
> _____ ' _____ m/henger   70,-
> Bobil, campingv.   70,-
> lastebil, buss   100,-
> Sesongkort   1/5 -31/10
> Lastebil / buss   -kr. 700
> Alle andre   -kr. 450
> STRAFFEGEBYR: kr. 450

Beside the sign was a tall red box with a metal lid to which a pen had been attached on a piece of string. Inside were small forms that presumably needed to be completed. Was this a challenge from *The Crystal Maze*? It was clearly a private road and the numbers referred to the toll that had to be paid by motorbikes, mopeds, tractors, campervans, buses and... I couldn't work out the rest. How about bicycles? Should I pay? What should I pay? Who should I pay? Where should I pay? Should I fill in the form? How could I do that when I didn't understand what was being asked? It was all very baffling.

After pondering the matter for a few moments, I decided to adopt the 'stupid foreigner' approach and ignore it. That would be my defence should the matter ever get to court which, bearing in mind the lack of witnesses, seemed unlikely. Aside from a very small flock of sheep, the only people at risk of being called by the prosecution were the Germans, who had paused along the track to take photographs of the pretty rural scenes surrounding us.

'No need to pay; it's free for cyclists,' explained Mr O., somewhat exasperated.

A few kilometres further along the track, we were to meet again as I doubled back, thinking I had taken a wrong turning; I hadn't.

'It's that way,' he informed me, eyes heading skyward. Perhaps I was being a stupid foreigner after all.

I turned around (again), let them pass and followed from a discreet distance. I admired how they seemingly had everything planned. How much of my time did I 'waste' poring over maps and scratching my head as to which way to turn next? How many wonderful campsites did I cycle near and then away from in ignorance of their existence? My approach did have its faults, but then again, I enjoyed the day-to-day uncertainty of not knowing what was around the corner. My German friends had their way of doing things and I had mine.

Shortly after the town of Tynset, I crossed the River Glomma and started travelling in a predominantly northerly direction again. My map suggested a couple of campsites near a place called Kvikne and it was towards them that I spent the second half of the day cycling. The effort required to climb 200 m in the early afternoon was rewarded later with a long, easy cycle along a pretty, alpinesque valley with a fast-flowing river. It was this that had, presumably, attracted the fishermen who made up the majority of the other campers at Kvikne Camping where I pitched my tent and heated up a now familiar meal of affordable fresh pasta and green pesto.

The ascents and descents of the previous day had only had the net effect of bringing me down from around 700 m in Grimsbu to 500 m in Kvikne. This was good news for cycling day 74, as I was aiming for the coast and could look forward to more gentle downhill cycling for much of the day. As I set off, the snow-capped mountains were still visible over my shoulder to the south, clearly defined against the predominantly blue sky, but it wasn't too long before they had disappeared and I was again travelling through attractive lowland farms and villages. It reminded me of the Norway to which I had become accustomed in the first few days after crossing the border from Sweden. That said, when the sun crept behind a cloud, there was a distinct chill in the air, which reminded me of my increasingly northern latitude and the proximity of the sea. How many people could say they had cycled from the Mediterranean to the Norwegian Sea? I would soon be able to.

It would be a long Saturday in the saddle – 120 km – but one not without its twists and turns. After just 20 km I was confronted with my old foe, the E6, and for a further 15 km could do little to avoid it. As it was the weekend, however, the traffic was somewhat lighter. At Berkåk it was nevertheless a relief to splinter away from the E6 and move along to the more tranquil route 700 that would hopefully guide me all the way to the coast.

I could quite easily have pulled on Reggie's brakes every few minutes to take another photograph of yet another gorgeous valley, picturesque river, quaint wooden farm building, cute cow… but I restricted my stops to once every 15 minutes or so, snapping this way and that. It seemed that more energy was being expended moving the forefinger of my right hand to release the shutter of the camera than in keeping the wheels of the bike moving downhill. Life on two wheels had rarely been better, or indeed easier.

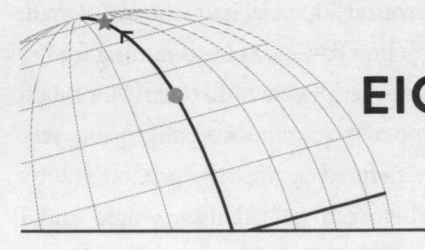

THE TWENTY-EIGHTH DEGREE
63°–64° NORTH

4–8 July

It seemed that my day had come to a fortuitous end. After completing my requisite 75 km, I could see the first of several campsites on my map just to the east of Midtskogen, beside a lake. Perfect. What's more, since the town of Grindal – some 20 km earlier in the afternoon – I had again been following cycle route 7. It was all pointing towards a trouble-free Sunday of cycling before my planned day off in Norway's third city on Monday.

Cycle route 7 branched away from route 700 in the direction of the lakeside campsite and, after a short, sharp climb, I found what I was looking for. Or had I? The location was beautiful but the campsite was in dire need of a makeover. The reception hut was shut but I was informed by a decidedly disgruntled man, whom I assumed to be a long-term resident of the site, that I could pitch the tent next to the sanitary shed or beside the entrance. The former stunk; the latter was overrun by large black flying monsters that I suspected were eyeing me up for their next meal. I was reminded of cycling in Croatia two years previously, when I thought I had come across a great campsite on the island of Pag, similarly located by a lake, only to find a cesspit of an establishment. The following day I fell ill and was forced to find a hotel and travel no further than the toilet across the corridor from my room. Not wishing to repeat my adventures of 2013, I fled the scene.

The coastal town of Orkanger was at the northern end of route 700, about 30 km from Midtskogen, although by the time it reached the sea, it had upgraded itself to route 65. The first campsite didn't exist; the next was in a scruffy town. By then the pull of the ocean was increasingly strong so I kept on cycling to the site in Orkanger. Alas, it had closed. There was, however, one last option before I would have to resort to seeking out a hotel: a campsite 10 km along the coast near the town of Viggja. I arrived there just before 8 p.m. and it was, mercifully, perfect.

Although it was busy with families, there was one other lone cyclist on site. Her name was Jeanet and she was from the Netherlands. Somewhat more relaxed about life on the road than my German neighbours back in Grimsbu, she offered me a brownie in return for using my iPad to check her flight home. This brought a level of diversity to my diet that I hadn't experienced since crossing the border from Sweden.

My plan for Trondheim was to meet up with Steve, a cycling enthusiast from Liverpool who had lived in the city for many years with his Norwegian girlfriend Anita and their young daughter Annie. He had been offering advice and guidance for several weeks via email as I cycled through Scandinavia, and Nick – the young cyclist I had met in Sweden and who had stayed with Steve – had said he was 'very good company', smiling cryptically.

Steve had offered to host me for a couple of nights and so, as I set off on the short 35 km ride to the centre of the city, I could jettison all worries about finding somewhere to stay. The cycle was a pretty one, split roughly into two parts: initially along a corniche road with sublime views across the Norwegian Sea and then inland, heading north, over an unexpectedly steep 100 m high hill before finally descending back to sea level through the suburbs to the city centre itself.

Trondheim had been very much on my mind throughout the months of 'planning' leading up to departure from Tarifa. It was the finishing line of the EuroVelo 3, the pilgrims' route, and although no pilgrim myself, I had read about the Nidaros Domkirke – the cathedral – dedicated to St Olaf and the traditional end point for those travelling from Oslo in the south. I had followed, more or less, the route of the pilgrims and encountered many on my way north. Like their counterparts in northern Spain, the vast majority had been on foot but, unlike those travelling along the Camino de Santiago, they were not walking in their hundreds. As pilgrimages went, it must surely have been an altogether quieter and more contemplative one.

That said, as I approached the impressive Gothic façade of the cathedral, a good number of walkers could be seen celebrating the completion of their 640 km hikes with relieved smiles on their faces. There was one other cyclist. He introduced himself as Jean-Philippe from Switzerland and, as it was for me, Trondheim was for him merely a pause along the way. He recounted a sad tale about his sick daughter and how, by cycling from his home in Basel to Nordkapp, he hoped to raise money for research into her condition. Then Jeanet, the brownie-trading Dutch cyclist pulled up and we continued our chat, sharing anecdotes and plans. None of us were true pilgrims but St Olaf, patron saint of Norway and, curiously, 'difficult marriage' had brought us together to have a good old natter. Perhaps that was the way he helped with marital issues too.

I had arranged to meet Steve at 5 p.m. at his house in the suburbs so, as it was still only early afternoon, I decided to find Trondheim's claim to bicycling fame, the Trampe CycloCable®. Never heard of it? Well, let me explain...

Back in the early 1990s, Jarle Wanvik was an enthusiastic cycling commuter in Trondheim but was becoming increasingly fed up with arriving at work a little hot and sweaty. Now, you and I might consider asking our bosses to install a shower, but not Jarle. His mind was working at an altogether different level of creativity and he conceived the idea of a bicycle lift to aid him in his desire to arrive perspiration-free at his desk every morning. He proposed his idea to the local public roads administration and, on 18 August 1993, the system was inaugurated in an opening ceremony attended by some 2,000 people. Clearly, Jarle wasn't the only person who'd had enough of sweating up the hill to the University of Trondheim.

I found the lift at the bottom of the Brubakken hill, close to the River Nidelva, and next to some signs assuring all potential users that the system was 'safe to use'. Along a single track sunk into the kerb, small metal plates could glide from the bottom to the top of the hill. I watched carefully as several people queued to position their right foot against one of the plates and then push a button. After a few moments the plate, cyclist and bicycle were all moved up the hill effortlessly. Simple, brilliant and not a drop of sweat was expended.

In the first 15 years of operation, 220,000 journeys had been made on the *sykkelheis* with no accidents having been recorded.

However, with Reggie still fully laden with four panniers and the tent, I suspected that the combined weight of cyclist, bike and luggage might be a test too far for the Trampe CycloCable®. I had no wish to go down in history as the first person in nearly a quarter of a million to have fallen off and rolled back down the hill in pain. I was happy to watch others having fun using the cycle lift that was now just as much a tourist attraction as it was a utilitarian piece of the local public transport network.

—

Steve's house was located a few kilometres to the south of Trondheim. He had told me to look out for a silver VW campervan and I found the small red house quite easily, tucked away along a quiet road on a hill overlooking the narrow valley through which I had just cycled.

There was something of Alexei Sayle to Steve: well-built, bald, white beard and an unmistakable Liverpool accent. In fact there was much of Alexei Sayle about Steve and over the course of the next 36 hours I wondered on more than one occasion whether the Scouse comedian hadn't upped sticks and moved to Norway under an assumed identity. Even Steve's expletive-embellished anti-establishment politics ('The road tolls are ******* extortionate... as are the ******* taxes... why don't they invest more of the ******* sovereign wealth fund?') seemed to be along the lines of those that Alexei might have expressed.

The numerous bottles of Lagerbier Hell that were consumed during the evening induced a quality of sleep that I hadn't experienced for quite some time. When I woke, it was (mercifully) rest day 14. How many more of those would I have the chance to take before I arrived at Nordkapp? Could this be the final one? Steve proposed that we absorb ourselves in Norwegian culture for the day and this involved visiting the family *hytte*, or hut. I had noticed many of these *hytter* as I cycled across the mountains of southern Norway and, according to Steve, most families had one tucked away somewhere in remote countryside. Many were 'off grid' and this was certainly the case when we arrived at Anita's family's *hytte* about an hour's drive from Trondheim. No electricity, no landline, no mobile signal, a few minutes' walk away from the rough track... How well did I know these people?

Any anxieties as to whether I was being escorted to a shallow grave in the woods were assuaged somewhat when Anita started lighting candles and laying out lunch. In the meantime, Steve decided to go for a short row on the adjacent lake in what turned out to be a forlorn attempt to catch some fish. It seemed a strange precursor to being murdered so I cast aside my negative thoughts and set about enjoying myself. As huts go, it was a spacious and comfortable one with chairs, tables, a small kitchen, green checked curtains and enough candles to keep a large Dickensian house illuminated 24/7.

The primary activity of life at the *hytte* appeared to be doing nothing and I was certainly up for a bit of that. Alas, the heavy rain meant that doing nothing had to be an activity undertaken either inside the wooden hut or on the small veranda but over the course of the next couple of hours, we seemed to manage fine, chatting about life in Norway from the perspective of a local and an expatriate.

I never really got to the bottom of what Steve did in Norway. He wasn't employed by anyone and he mentioned various business activities that he had been involved in over the years. If physically he had many of the attributes of Alexei Sayle, his CV resembled that of Eddie Grundy in *The Archers*, moving from one odd job to the next, earning a little here and a little there, with the occasional suggestion of the rules of society being bent to make ends meet. In a world where we often define people by their chosen profession, he certainly couldn't be and that was nice.

Later in the day, back at Steve's house, as my dirty clothes tumbled around the washing machine and my electrical items recharged in sockets dotted around the building, I pondered the remaining 2,000 km of the trip.

Cycling along the busy E6 road was no longer an option. This, as you might imagine, filled me with joy. Even if I *had* fancied spending several weeks pedalling alongside fast-moving cars, buses and lorries, the tunnels forbidden to cyclists made the E6 impassable to me. Instead, cycle route 1 made use of the fjord-hopping coastal roads. I envisaged this involved a good number of ferries in addition to some spectacular bridges. The Arctic Circle would be crossed at some point south of Bodø, from where a longer ferry crossing would take me onto the Lofoten islands to continue my journey north via Tromsø and Alta to Nordkapp. At least that was the plan.

Having said my goodbyes to Steve and his family early the following morning, I returned to sit opposite the façade of the cathedral in the centre of Trondheim. It was a much quieter place than it had been at the weekend and there were no identifiable pilgrims, walking or cycling, with whom I could pass the time of day. I looked up at the uninspiring grey sky that hovered over the three rows of religious luminaries immortalised in stone above the main door of the cathedral. It was a colour that seemed to guarantee heavy rain at some point in the next few hours. I hadn't experienced a Mercedes day (remember them?) in quite some time but everything about Tuesday 7 July was pointing in that direction. I was cold, my throat was sore, the weather was crap and, despite having a pannier full of clean clothes and fully charged gear, my own physical batteries were low. Too much of that beer from hell? Perhaps.

At least for the first half-hour of the cycling day I could sit and feel sorry for myself on a ferry across the 15 km wide Trondheimsfjord to a small town called Vanvikan. Upon arrival, it had indeed started to rain so I pulled on my waterproofs, stocked up on snacks at the Coop and set off north.

Perhaps what I needed to soothe my Tuesday-morning blues was a nice bit of easy, flat riding to get the adrenaline flowing and the endorphins running around my brain in a morale-boosting frenzy. What I didn't need – but I got – was an immediate steep climb from sea level to 250 m.

The remainder of the day was a struggle, up and down over hills that I wished hadn't existed and through roadworks that I wished hadn't been started. The second half of the 80 km cycled drew a line on my GPS tracker as straight as a spoke and in a direction that was almost precisely due north. In these respects, I reasoned, my pain had not been prolonged. As I zipped up the door of the tent to keep the midges at bay on a campsite near Åfjord, I could only hope that the following morning would bring respite from the rain, the sniffles, the roadworks and my own personal melancholy.

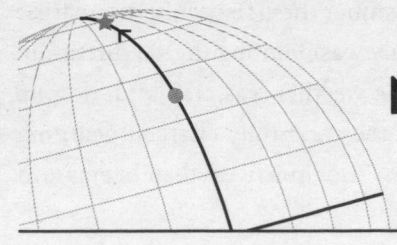

THE TWENTY-NINTH DEGREE
64°–65° NORTH

8–11 July

Solace can often be found in food, so, after packing away the tent in the rain, I cycled the short distance to the local supermarket cafeteria. The conversation with the woman behind the counter went along the following lines:

Me: '*Hei, hei!* [Which, even after nearly two weeks in Norway, still sounded far too familiar for an opening line.] Do you speak English?'

Assistant: 'Yes, a little.' [I took this to mean: 'Yes, probably more fluently than many of your fellow Brits.']

Me: 'Can I have a coffee and two of these?' [I pointed at a pastry that was described on the label as a '*kanel bolle*' but which I couldn't bring myself to mispronounce as 'cannonball'.]

Assistant: 'Here you go. That's fifty kroner.'

Me: 'If they [the cannonballs] are good, I may come back for another. My plan is to wait here until the rain stops.'

Assistant: 'That could be September.'

Never let it be said that the Norwegians lack a sense of humour. I smiled and went to eat the first of the *kanel bolle* whilst sitting on a high stool at a long bench by the window. From my elevated position I had a wonderful view of not only Reggie, whom I had left outside, untethered, but also the puddles and the rain creating them. I sat, watched and waited.

Should I have been surprised by the grim weather outside? Along with the bear situation, it was one of the few aspects of cycling in Norway that I *had* looked into prior to setting off. I had compared the key average July meteorological statistics for Bodø – roughly halfway between Trondheim and Nordkapp – with those for London. Average temperatures in London varied between a low of 14°C and a high of 24°C. In Bodø the figures were 12°C and 16°C. As far as the chances of getting wet were concerned, in London it could be expected to rain, on average, for eight days in the month and deliver 45 mm of water. In Bodø I should be prepared for it to rain on ten days but deliver 92 mm of water. So, not much colder – just colder for more of the time – and when it rained, it did so more heavily or for a longer period. My money was on the latter.

I much preferred the days when I had a destination in mind. I reached for my penultimate map – Norway North – and followed route 715 along the coast, adding up the distances marked on it in my head as my finger did the moving: 7 km, 14, 21, 25, 34, 41, 51, 54. There was a campsite at a place called Osen. After Osen, cycle route 1 continued to follow the 715 but the next site was 50 km further on. That was, if the sites existed. I triple-checked in my booklet of Norwegian campsites and did a quick online search: the site at Osen definitely existed and it looked like the kind of place I'd been dreaming about ever since I came up with the crazy idea of cycling from Tarifa to Nordkapp.

I glanced again out of the window. The puddles were still there, as was Reggie. But what was that I could see above me? Could it really be a patch of blue sky? What about the rain? A puddle was now reflecting perfectly the red-and-blue sign of the rival supermarket across the street. Had I really been sitting there all through August?

'It's stopped raining,' I called out to the woman at the counter.

'Well, it must be September then,' she replied, smiling.

In the real world, I had been sitting in the cafeteria for nearly two hours so, with a delayed departure, a cycle of just 54 km to Osen was the best option; admittedly, it was also the *only* option.

There was nothing spectacular about cycling day 77 and the weather was such that had I been on a beach holiday in Ibiza, I would have been writing to the tour operator demanding a return of my money. But I wasn't on a Mediterranean island; I was about 250 km from the Arctic Circle and at least it was no longer raining. That small but significant novelty made the cycling a joy. Yes, it was cold. Yes, the sky was grey. Yes, there were steep hills. But not a drop more rain fell.

To cap off a day that had seen a remarkable turnaround in my fortunes as well as my mood, the campsite was just as good as the photographs had suggested. The cheery bearded guy on reception invited me to pitch the tent wherever I liked and I did so in a secluded spot only a few metres from the narrow pebbly beach of the fjord. I heated some baked beans and positioned myself in the camping chair to eat them whilst watching the water retreat from the bay and the sun make its first and final appearance of the day as it edged towards a distant bridge on the horizon.

The following morning I found myself chatting to the chap in the reception hut again.

'Do you see many cyclists who are heading to Nordkapp?' I asked.

'A few, but I can't remember anyone who started their journey in Spain,' he replied, chuckling at the perceived insanity of what I was attempting. 'Here, take this.'

I thought it might be a self-help guide for those wishing to wean themselves off long-distance cycling, but no, it was of far more practical use: a small booklet entitled *Kystriksveien: The World's Most Beautiful Journey*.

The Kystriksveien was the coastal road and, over the course of the journey north to Bodø, that booklet would become my travel bible. It listed the places, the accommodation, the ferries and their timetables, and pointed out all the attractions along the way. 'Allow yourself to travel slow and explore!' it exalted in its introductory passage. Having chosen to cycle, there was no alternative than to travel slow but the reminder to explore was pertinent. Yes, after three months on the road I was eager to finish, but not at the expense of ignoring my surroundings and all they had to offer. It was wise, and timely, advice.

Namsos, some 80 km along the coastal road that was also cycle route 1, was described by my new travel guide as 'a rock and roll city with long-standing traditions in the timber industry'. I couldn't ever remember visiting a place that headlined itself in those terms so, with Namsos Camping also getting a prominent mention, I set my sights and front tyre in its direction and started pedalling.

Despite the joyous lack of rain, water could still have been the theme for the day, gathered as it was in the numerous lakes I passed and flowing along the River Luna beside which I was climbing. Every few kilometres I would stop or, at the very least, slow down to gaze at the powerful current thundering over rocky outcrops. With the traffic on the road being so slight, the waterfalls were not only the sight of the day but also the invigorating sound. I chuckled upon realising that the very same aspect of nature – water – that had my mood sinking so low only two days previously was now the icing on the cake.

The long descent over the final two-thirds of the day allowed me to pick up speed and I was able to cover a 78 km cycle in just four hours. Alas, the final hour or so was under increasingly heavy rain and the irony of seeing the wood in the large timber yards on the outskirts of Namsos being sprayed to keep it from drying out didn't escape me. The rain was also dousing my enthusiasm for a night in the tent.

But what about the rock 'n' roll? All would shortly be revealed, but not before I had discovered a rather smart, dry and surprisingly modestly priced Scandic hotel. Scandic is to Scandinavia what the Parador chain of hotels is to Spain, albeit located within your traditional, more modern hotel buildings rather than old castles and monasteries. They seemed to be a cut above the competition and for this reason I had never considered them a possibility. Arriving somewhat drenched in Namsos and noting that the name of the local Scandic hotel was the Scandic Rock City, all in the name of research, I reconsidered, paid up and booked in.

My corner room on the fourth floor had the kind of carpet-to-ceiling panoramic view over the Namsosfjord that I had thought only existed as the backdrop to purpose-built television studios at Olympic Games or royal weddings. Not bad for under 50 quid. The only blot on the landscape was the large copper-clad building next to the Scandic Rock City: Rock City itself. Once I had dried out, I went to investigate.

My coastal road bible had already informed me that some of Norway's 'best known rock artists' grew up in Namsos and that 'on 11-11-11 at 11:00, Rock City was opened, an adventure centre for rock 'n roll from Trøndelag'. This information posed more questions than answers.

Rock City was having a quiet day. Perhaps that was due to the rain but something about the place suggested that quiet days might have been the norm. I wandered through the entrance and got chatting with the two young people manning the reception area. Reluctant to fork out the 100NOK entrance fee, I was keen to imply that I had no intrinsic love for Trønder Rock (how could I when I didn't know what it was?) but was open to being persuaded.

'Let me show you around,' invited the man.

'Do I need a ticket?' I asked.

'Don't worry, you don't have to pay,' he went on, clearly eager to have at least one customer, even a non-paying one, to give him something to do.

Over the next half-hour I discovered that Trønder Rock was actually just 'rock' performed by musicians from the Trøndelag region of Norway. Of all the local rock stars, the name Åge Aleksandersen was the one to crop up most often. He, it seemed, was the Paul McCartney of Norway. Born in Namsos in 1949, he was a founding member of the group Prudence – named after the Beatles song – and was responsible for such classics as 'Drunk and Happy', the 1980 Eurovision entry 'Bjørnen sover' (or 'The Bear Sleeps', a political song aimed at the Russians who had just invaded Afghanistan; it came a respectable second place) and that favourite Norwegian ditty 'Fire pils og en pizza' or 'Four Beers and a Pizza'.

I may mock his choice of song titles (as the author of three books with *...on a Bike Called Reggie* in their name, who am I to criticise?) but he has sold over 1.5 million records during his career to date and has won a string of awards in doing so.

'He's playing the Royal Albert Hall in London next summer,' explained my guide.

'Does he have a big international following?'

'Not really but back in the 1970s he wrote a song called "It's a Long Way to Royal Albert Hall" about his struggles to make it on the music scene. To celebrate his forty years in the business, he's playing the venue.'

'But will he sell any tickets?' I queried.

'It's already sold out.'

And so it was. Not by the British but by Norwegians who, according to newspaper reports, 'filled around a dozen chartered jets from Trondheim to sing along with 27 of Aleksandersen's hits'. Åge's dream (and that of 4,300 of his fans) had come true.

I thanked my host and wandered back to my hotel room with newfound respect for ageing rockers. Especially one Norwegian rocker called, most appropriately, Åge.

The highlight of cycling day 79 was the huge buffet breakfast at the Scandic Rock City. I filled my boots (and a couple of pockets) but from then on, in most respects, it was downhill all the way. Except, alas, being downhill all the way. It was the first day of the entire trip when it rained from the beginning of my cycle to the end. Not once did the droplets of water stop falling. How nice it might have been to stay for a second night at the Scandic and spend the day investigating more stories of other Norwegian rock stars.

Instead, I plodded up the road, ticking off the kilometres. Just as a falling object quickly reaches its terminal velocity and stays there for the rest of its descent, I quickly found my terminal level of wetness and stayed there for the rest of the cycle. The only respite from the elements came at a remote café, when I took an hour-long pause to stare out over the sea and then, towards the end of the day, when I caught the Lund–Hofles ferry.

Arriving in non-descript Kolvereid, I sought out the campsite in the hope of renting a small, cheap cabin of some description but the price was not only excessive, it would have been more than I had paid for the night in the posh Scandic. The local hotel would have to suffice. Constructed from the Norwegian equivalent of Portakabins, it was at least warm and I spent the evening in my room, drying clothes whilst listening to Liberal Democrat Tim Farron MP and former Chancellor Norman Lamont debate the political comings and goings back home in the UK on Radio 4's *Any Questions?*. The panellists were politely asked: 'How has the budget affected you personally?' and 'Should the Greeks leave the Euro?' but not, alas, 'When will it stop raining in Norway?' so I looked online and... goodness. Tomorrow!

I had avoided looking at the forecast for fear that it might tell me what I didn't want to know. In reality, it was exactly what I *did* want to read.

Saturday – sunny – 11°C – 0 mm precipitation – 2 m/s wind
Sunday – sunny – 19°C – 0 mm precipitation – 2 m/s wind
Monday – sunny – 18°C – 0 mm precipitation – 2 m/s wind

I double-checked that I didn't have the location set for southern Spain. No, it was correct. Summer, it seemed, was about to arrive on the coast of northern Norway.

When I woke and thrust open the curtains the following morning, the sky was blue and the sun – remember that? – was shining. Marvellous.

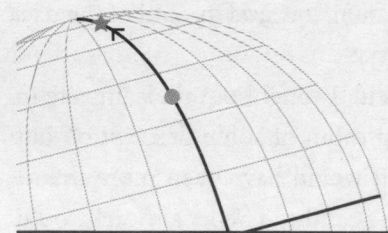

THE THIRTIETH DEGREE
65°–66° NORTH

11–13 July

The north-western coastline of Norway had so far failed to deliver. Clearly, the weather had been a factor, but the scenery had yet to live up to my high expectations. With the exception of the view of the setting sun from the campsite near Osen, much of what I had seen was nice but my jaw had yet to drop by any significant measure. Things, however, were about to change.

It was now Saturday morning and, as had been forecast, it wasn't raining and there were large blue patches in the sky, although it remained cold. But I could cope with the cold by wrapping up and keeping moving on the bike. The energy was provided in quantity via a slap-up breakfast. It may have had all the physical attributes of post-war emergency housing, but the Kolvereid Fjordhotel didn't skimp on making sure that I – their only client that morning – was fully fuelled.

Between Trondheim and the sixty-fifth line of latitude, Norway had been comparatively flat. Although my cycling route had taken me along valleys, and beside lakes and fjords, the mountains I was passing were modest in size. There was little to excite your average Munro bagger along the coast of Trøndelag and drag him from his bothy, other than the realisation that he had gone to bed in Scotland and woken up on the other side of the North Sea.

Along the coast of Nordland, however, peaks above 1,000 m were increasingly common. The greatest mountains of Norway were, of course, behind me – I had glimpsed the distant snow caps to the west as I cycled from Oslo to Trondheim but, from my own elevated position, it had been difficult to take in their true size. Here on the coast, however, from my location at sea level, every one of the 1,000 plus metres could be appreciated in their full glory.

And what a coastline it was. You may remember me commenting upon the smashed-plate nature of Denmark with its 400 islands. In comparison, Britain has over 800. Impressive, right? It's not that impressive when you consider that the estimated figure for Norway is *over 50,000* islands. That's a lot of ferries and bridges. Meanwhile, *National Geographic Magazine* reports that in 2011 the Norwegian government recalculated the length of the coastline using new technology. It grew by 18,000 km and now stands at a phenomenal 101,000 km. Perhaps news of the lengthening coastline was scaring away the masses, as the road north of Kolvereid was not just quiet, it was, at times, silent. Just the sound of me breathing, Reggie purring, water flowing, small flies buzzing and an occasional bird tweetling.

A sign that the terrain was gradually becoming more challenging, I began to encounter unavoidable long tunnels. Up until this point they had been modest affairs, just a few tens of metres in length, or longer tunnels that were easily avoided thanks to the option of using an adjacent old road. That had been the case along the shore of Lake Mjøsa. Now, however, they were black holes into which I had no alternative but to plunge, rather reluctantly. I had always assumed that the reason the cycling route to Nordkapp jumped over to the Lofoten islands after Bodø was because of tunnels on the mainland from which cyclists were prohibited. In the back of my mind, I worried that my route would one day end abruptly because of a sign banning me from continuing on two wheels. Logic dictated that by following cycle route 1, this wouldn't be an issue, but from past experience I knew that my ability to be loyal to a cycle route for 100 per cent of its length was low. Perhaps now was the time to start sticking rigidly to where I, as a cyclist, was being told to go. In most places along the coast, this wasn't difficult, as there was usually only one road to follow. Side roads would, more often than not, have taken me to a dead end at the sea or on tortuous climbs into the hills.

My first long tunnel of the entire cycle from Tarifa was the Hestnes Tunnel, about 50 km along the coast from Kolvereid. At 600 m in length and with the road taking a distinct turn to the left, there was no sign of an exit at the other end. All that was visible from the entrance was the long row of lights on the ceiling, sufficiently bright to light the road but insufficient to give a clear view of approaching traffic. Or indeed to give a clear view of me to other users of the tunnel, so I dismounted, switched on my lights and hoped for the best. I took comfort from the knowledge that up until this point of the day, the traffic had been extremely low. The flip side, however, was that a driver might not be expecting to meet a cyclist in the tunnel. Somewhat hesitantly, I set off.

The Norwegians are the undeniable masters of tunnelling and there are, according to the Norwegian Public Roads Administration, over 900 road tunnels in the country, with a cumulative length of 750 km. That's about the same distance as driving from London to

Dundee. You'd think there would come a time when the tunnellers of Norway could stand back and say, 'OK, that's it, we've finished.' But no. Of the ten longest road tunnels in Norway, eight have been opened since the year 2000. That was the year when the longest road tunnel in Norway (and, incidentally, the world) was opened. The Lærdal Tunnel cuts through 24,509 m of prime Norwegian granite and such is its length that every 6 km there is a large cave-cum-rest area. And they're not done yet. It was reported in 2016 that a system of floating tunnels is under consideration to enable ferry-free transport across seven fjords between Kristiansand and Trondheim. The concrete tunnels would float under the water at a depth of 20 m. You can't fault their ambition.

Back in the 600 m of the Hestnes Tunnel, I was beginning my slow plod to the other end. Despite the day being a dry one, the tunnel was as damp as it was dark. There were large puddles on the floor and my body collided frequently with globular drips of water from the ceiling. The temperature had also plummeted sharply. On a scorching day, this might have come as a blessed short-term respite from the heat, but with the temperature outside barely reaching double figures, it sent a chill through my body. I was, at least, spared from any other road users thundering beside me over my left shoulder. That was an experience I would gladly leave for another tunnel on another day.

Within half an hour of emerging from the gloom, I was standing alongside a quay, waiting for a ferry to take me across the fjord to Vennesund. My hope was to spend the night at the Vennesund Brygge og Camping. As the ferry neared its destination and grey skies turned to blue, I could see the campsite on the shore only a few seconds' walk from the dock. After disembarking and presenting my credentials at the reception inside a grand, white, wood-panelled building beside the water, I proceeded to pitch the wet tent in glorious sunshine.

Then Concord arrived to spoil the view. It was big, white and noisy. Perhaps that's why the manufacturers of this particular campervan had named it so. Was it really necessary to park it so close to my little inoffensive green tent overlooking the water?

I gave the elderly couple who had positioned it there the kind of hard stare from which even Paddington Bear would have recoiled. But not, it seemed, the superannuated Norwegians. They ignored me in the same way they had ignored the tent so, to make my point (as well as reinstate my personal tent space), I proceeded to unpeg and drag my little home to a nearby plot where the view wasn't obscured by a vast wall of white steel.

With the evening sun beating down to heat me from the outside and piping hot ravioli doing the same job from the inside, I was a happy man. Despite the increasing number of campervans – each arrival of the ferry deposited another handful that came to park on the grass – the views across the fjord on one side and the sea on the other were exactly what I'd come to Norway to appreciate. Looking north, the panorama was particularly enticing, with distant but seemingly ever larger mountains dominating the scene. Eight hours later I was delighted to reappear from the tent to find that things had barely changed. Only the sun had altered its position; everything else was just as I had left it, notably the deep blue sky.

Since having said goodbye to the shores of the Mediterranean some three months previously, this day was promising to be one of the best. I would be spending most of it cycling beside the coast and it turned out to be a predominantly flat route, involving two ferry crossings, increasingly magnificent mountains to the east and the seemingly endless expanse of the Norwegian Sea to the west. There was not one thing from which to take displeasure. The traffic on the roads continued to be light and the weather was simply perfect, with the only wind to speak of being that generated by my own swift movement through the air.

Such was the length of the days – on a cloudless day it was now sufficiently light to cycle without lights for 24 hours had I been so inclined – that it made sense to keep going and make the most of the almost perfect cycling conditions. Pretty, isolated towns came and went; rusty red sheds beside the water contrasted beautifully with the lush green vegetation on land, and the blue of the sea and sky. The bright white houses and churches looked resplendent. This really was the Norway I had seen in the tourist brochures and it was as welcome as it was enjoyable.

With no traffic to distract me for most of the cycle between the two ferries, my eyes could concentrate on other things. To the north I could see a distinctive long massif with several peaks rising, teeth-like, from its summit. Consulting my map I discovered that they formed an island called Alsta and that the massif itself was called the Sju søstre. I had identified a campsite on the other side of the island as a likely place to spend the night but to access it meant either an impromptu off-road hike to around 1,000 m (perhaps not...) or a more feasible but lengthy cycle around the mass of rock – 20,000 horizontal metres were much more appealing than 1,000 vertical ones and, an hour or so later, I had arrived at my destination.

'Have you seen the Seven Sisters?' asked the campsite owner, looking out from the window of his office. I couldn't see anyone, let alone seven sisters.

'No, sorry. Are they on bikes?'

'And those two,' he said, ignoring me and pointing upwards, 'are the Twins.'

'On a tandem?'

'Have you come to climb them?'

What was he suggesting? We appeared to be having two completely separate conversations.

'The Sju søstre: the Seven Sisters,' he clarified. 'Many people stay here to climb them. They are very famous in Norway.'

He was, of course, referring to the peaks on the other side of a small airport that separated the campsite from the road.

'Here, have one of these,' he said, pushing a wrapped boiled sweet into my hand in the same way he might donate one to a rather dim child to keep them amused for a while.

'Thanks.'

It had been a long day – nine hours of cycling, waiting for ferries and gazing out to sea from ferries – but I had covered some 125 km. I had so far cycled 6,400 km and today's efforts had pushed the average over 81 days to nearly 79 km per day. The plan was still to arrive at Nordkapp by the one-hundredth day. If my calculation of 7,500 km from Tarifa was anywhere near accurate, I might even arrive quite a few days before that.

But then again, why would I want to rush things? '*Travel slow and explore*' had declared my little guide and if what lay ahead was anything like I'd experienced on cycling day 81, I had no incentive to do anything apart from taking my time and enjoying the ride.

That night I was surrounded by hikers.

'We've climbed one of them,' explained my immediate neighbour.

'I've done two today,' added another, 'and I met someone who is doing all seven. He's probably still up there.'

I had no plans to summit any of the Sisters but the fact that I had cycled from southern Spain brought nods of appreciation. It was good to share adventures.

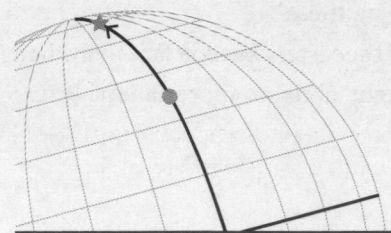

THE THIRTY-FIRST DEGREE
66°–67° NORTH

13–16 July

I'd never thought about why the Arctic Circle was where it was. 'Because to the north of the Arctic Circle it gets bloody cold!' would probably have been my rather flippant answer. Unsurprisingly, that's not it.

Most of us were taught at school that the equator is the point on Earth where the sun is directly overhead at noon. Well, not quite. In 2015 the sun was directly overhead at the vernal and autumnal equinoxes on 20 March and 22 September respectively. But let's not quibble; it wasn't far off on the other 363 days as well. The sun is directly overhead at the Tropic of Cancer on 21 June and the Tropic of Capricorn on 21 December.

The imaginary line on the Earth that we refer to as the Arctic Circle is marked out on maps at 66°34′ north of the equator. The Tropic of Capricorn is about 23°26′ south of the equator. If you add 66°34′ and 23°26′ together, you get exactly 90°, or a right angle. This means that when the sun is directly overhead at the Tropic of Capricorn on 21 December, it is not visible from the Arctic Circle.

There is a period of 24 hours during which the sun never appears above the horizon.

South of the Arctic Circle, providing it's not cloudy, you are always guaranteed to see at least a bit of sun on every day of the year. North of the Circle, the period of darkness is increasingly long until you arrive at the North Pole, where there is a period of six months of 'darkness' kicking off on 25 September. It's not total darkness, as for most of those six months, the sun isn't far below the horizon and lights the sky. Total darkness at the Pole lasts 'just' 11 weeks, from mid-November to late January.

The reverse is true during the summer, of course, when there is continuous daylight for increasingly long periods north of the Arctic Circle. If I were to see the midnight sun at my final destination, I would need to arrive there on or before 28 July. Shortly after leaving the campsite opposite the Seven Sisters on the island of Alsta, I would cross the sixty-sixth degree of latitude. There were slightly over five degrees between me and my destination at 71°10', and just 15 days before my last chance of seeing the midnight sun at Nordkapp. It was entirely possible that I might witness the midnight sun *before* I arrived in Nordkapp but it would be a fitting end to the journey if I could also do so at the Continent's most northerly point.

When I examined my route north of Alsta, it continued to twist and turn around the fragmented coastline just as it had been doing to an increasing extent since leaving Trondheim. There were plenty of fjords to cycle along, bridges to cross and ferries to catch. One of these ferries would be from Kilboghamn to Jetvik. I was enjoying the opportunity afforded by the ferries of taking a break from moving under my own steam, and what was special about the Kilboghamn–Jetvik ferry was that it crossed the point 66°34' north of the equator.

It looked as though I wouldn't be cycling across the Arctic Circle; I would be sailing across it. But not until the following day. Instead, I set my sights on cycling to within a short ride away of Kilboghamn, with a view to catching the ferry at some point on the morning of cycling day 83.

Having pitched the tent on a slight incline, I woke repeatedly during the night, each time with a different dream still fresh in my mind. Perhaps it was the long-distance nature of the trip but quite why Michael Palin was chasing the diminutive Miriam Margolyes around that large house remains a mystery to this day. In the real world, I had my own chasing to do, along and across a series of fjords.

The Helgeland Bridge spanning the Leirfjord was as impressive as it was long. I paused along the causeway that linked its southern end to the island to take in its slender lines. The two towers were a masterclass in how to construct something so elegant out of concrete. From a distance they resembled the eyes of two needles, the road being the cotton threaded delicately through the openings. 'In a mountainous country cut apart by deep fjords, bridge building is a virtue of necessity,' explained our friends at the Norwegian Public Roads Administration who are responsible for over 18,000 bridges spanning gaps amounting to nearly 450 km. The tunnels might get you to Dundee but add in the bridges and your drive from London will see you all the way to John O'Groats.

In many other countries, where such infrastructure would be expected to carry a constant stream of traffic to justify the expense, the kilometre-long Helgeland Bridge would never have been built in the first place. After pedalling through the two heavy-duty needles, I turned to appreciate the bridge's beauty, silhouetted against the cloudless sky, for one last time. It was empty. Just Reggie and me.

On such quiet roads, it was difficult to miss the sudden passage of perhaps 20 cars, vans, lorries and buses. It was a sign that a ferry ahead had just arrived and all the vehicles had disembarked. Would I make it to the dock before the ferry once again set off? Alas, no. I pulled up to see the boat slowly edge away from the shore.

There could be far worse places to spend an hour than sitting beside a Norwegian fjord in the sunshine. When I arrived at Nesna on the other side of the fjord, nearly two hours had passed and my body was entering a state of repose. Should I abandon the day there and then? But I'd only cycled and ferried 50 odd kilometres. No, I would continue. I may have been feeling lethargic but it had been easy cycling for days and why waste the opportunity of riding in the sun?

Within the hour, I was being reminded just how long and steep some Norwegian roads could be. Geography was giving me a sharp kick up the backside by forcing me to climb some 300 metres. Mother Nature was also in on the act, sending down squadrons of large black flies in their hundreds. Such were their numbers that any attempt at swatting them away was comically futile, as it merely sufficed to stir the swarm. Dragging my Buff over my head and pulling down the sleeves of my shirt were the only solutions to keep them from landing on my skin and biting, scratching, sniffing and crapping. Surely the nearby cows would have been far better prey?

I exchanged notes and food with a German cyclist from Hamburg at the top of the hill. Travelling south, he was as delighted as me to be informed that a rapid descent was imminent. As we attempted to catch our breath at the high viewpoint, the magnificent vista snatched it away. The climb had been worth every rapid beat of the heart, as we both feasted our eyes upon a deep, iconic Norwegian coastal valley.

The mouth of the Sørfjord that we were looking down upon was just 2 km wide. However, with no obliging ferry or bridge to make life easy, travelling from one lip to the other required a 40 km detour along the length of the fjord and then back again. Six of these kilometres would be through tunnels – initially a modest 400 m but then 2,780 m and 2,870 m through the Sjona and Sila tunnels respectively. Their lengths alone made them a foreboding prospect but they were also darker and colder, as well as appearing narrower than the ones through which I had cycled so far. It was also almost inevitable that I would meet traffic.

Taking the same precautions as I had done previously, I set off through the first and it wasn't long before a vehicle could be heard in the distance. The sound reverberated around the stone tube to such an extent that it was all but impossible to determine what it was, how far away it was or even the direction in which it was moving. Seeing no lights ahead of me, I assumed it was behind but the level of sound continued to increase until... *BEEEEP* – a loud blast on the horn by the driver of a... I still wasn't sure. Then it thundered past, exposing my eardrums to levels of noise that they hadn't experienced since the day I had run over the Japanese tourist in Paris. It was a lorry and it had been a frightening experience.

As to why the driver had thought it wise to use his horn, I had no definitive answer. Did he think I hadn't noticed him? Was he being friendly? Or was he ticking me off for being in the tunnel in the first place? I suspected the latter but he had no reason to be doing so. Cycle route 1 continued to be regularly signposted along the road and there had been no signs banning bicycles from the tunnel. Whatever his motivation, he had only succeeded in making an already unpleasant experience even worse.

The long day ended after nearly 130 km, at a campsite opposite the small island of Aldra that didn't offer much to write home about, so I'll spare you most of the details. It was, at least, quiet. I escaped the rough patch of ground behind the '*Mote & amping*' (the sign was as neglected as the rest of the establishment) early the following morning in the knowledge that this would be the day I crossed the Arctic Circle. How many people could say that?

On the 9 a.m. boat from Kilboghamn, not many at all. It was another ferry that had pretensions of being an aircraft carrier in style, if not necessarily in size. There was ample space remaining on the runway/deck after I had boarded and joined just three motorised vehicles: two cars and a tractor. The hour-long sailing trip to Jetvik was the longest yet of the journey but, at only £4.50, certainly not the most expensive. Tourist information was thrown in for free.

'Look!' announced rather suddenly the man selling tickets. Two men from one of the cars were, like me, poised with their cameras, waiting to capture the moment we passed through the invisible line. 'Can you see the white globe?'

I could, just. It was several hundred metres away on shore and marked, presumably, 66°34' north. With only one identifiable point on the line, however, it would be impossible to say when the ferry entered the circle. Clarification came a few moments later in the form of a loud blast from the ship's whistle. Ouch. My eardrums hadn't yet recovered from the lorry incident in the tunnel.

There had been nothing much to see at Trafalgar, nor Waterloo, nor that famous cycling street in Münster. It was the same here on the Arctic Circle. Had there been no kind ferryman pointing out the relevant distant object, or his equally diligent colleague pulling his hooter upstairs on the bridge, I would have been scrambling for a GPS signal on the phone. I could have been left guessing as to when I had passed through the Arctic Circle but would it have mattered if I'd been out by a few metres? Of course not. It was once again the human mind imposing significance upon a particular place for what it represented. I liked that.

The roads were getting busier, but not so much with anything four-wheeled. I had been surprised as to how few cyclists I'd seen as I travelled across Germany, Denmark, Sweden, and southern and central Norway. Here in Nordland, however, they were increasingly common and welcome sights. Some even appeared to be collaborating.

POLSKI's!
I took the ferry at 16.45!
I'm gonna camp about 5 km after the ferry!
If we don't meet tonight, we can meet at the next ferry at Ågskardet
tomorrow between 10 and 11 a.m.! Otherwise maybe 12!
DAVID!

So read the large handwritten note below the sign for cycle route 1 near the dock in Jetvik. I could only assume that David did a lot of shouting. Or perhaps he was American.

I never knowingly met David, but a Dutch cyclist heading south recommended the campsite at Furøy. 'It's a good place to relax,' she explained, and so it was. After another long tunnel – at 3.2 km the longest yet – and a second ferry, Furøy Camping was only five minutes from the dock. As a place to rest, recuperate, wash and dry my clothes, and recharge all the batteries, it was perfect.

It was at Furøy that I first encountered Hans and Veronika. The weather had now taken a turn for the worse and I noticed two cyclists arrive quite late in the evening. He had a greying beard and was in his late fifties. She was in her twenties. I assumed that they were father and daughter, and wondered in which direction they were travelling. Once their tent had been erected, they sensibly hid from the rain and we never spoke. In the morning, their tent had disappeared but my curiosity remained.

When the rain abated, I packed my stuff away and fell into conversation with a Scottish family who were travelling in a burgundy Range Rover. All three of their children were being given instructions as to what to pack where; given that the oldest was probably no more than 12 years old, they had been well trained.

'We caught the Newcastle to Amsterdam ferry,' said the man. I was curious because, with only a couple of weeks of my own trip remaining, I had yet to make any plans to travel back home from Nordkapp.

'It's such a pity that the Newcastle–Bergen route no longer operates,' I noted.

'Yes, but it is, apparently, possible to travel on a cargo freighter from Bergen to Immingham,' he explained.

That would be an adventure in itself. I put it down in the column of 'possibles'. I really wanted to avoid the hassle of taking the bike on a plane.

For the first time in many days, the cycle route deviated from the number 17 coastal road north of Furøy. The 'coastal' FV17 was replaced with the 'even-more-coastal' FV452. The downside of not being on a main road was that ferries from Vassdalsvik to Ørnes were far less frequent. Having missed the boat at 10.50 a.m., when I arrived at the dock at lunchtime, I still had over two hours to wait for the next one at 2.25 p.m. Time wouldn't be wasted, however. The two cyclists I'd seen at the campsite were also waiting and we got chatting.

'I'm Hans, and this is my daughter Veronika,' explained the man, 'and we're cycling to Nordkapp.'

'Perhaps,' interjected Veronika.

Did I detect tension? There couldn't be many women her age who would relish a cycle-camping holiday with their father in northern Norway.

After about half an hour we were joined by a familiar face: Jean-Philippe, the Swiss cyclist I had met outside the cathedral in Trondheim who was also en route to Nordkapp. A little later two German women in their early thirties arrived. They too were cycling to Nordkapp. This was turning into quite a convention of like-minded travellers. I quickly got out my notebook, formally opened the session and started taking minutes. There was much to discuss.

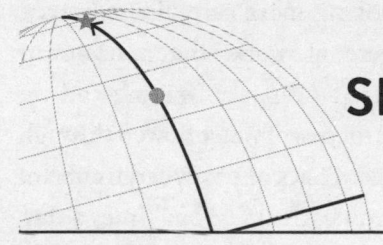

THE THIRTY-SECOND DEGREE
67°–68° NORTH

16–17 July

After a night spent in a half-built campsite, I was within a day's cycle of Bodø, the town from where I could catch a ferry to the Lofoten islands. The sun had disappeared from the sky, and the low cloud and drizzle that replaced it gave a slightly eerie edge to the morning. Isolated houses were dotted along the shores of the fjords, fishing boats sat motionless in the water, mist hung low on the cliffs and the bridges began to take on an almost contorted nature, bending and angling themselves in ways that common sense would dictate they shouldn't. I had become accustomed to roads that swept around mountainsides with curving artistic beauty but to see bridges doing similar things was verging on the disconcerting.

Although the route never climbed higher than 200 m above the sea, the up-and-down nature of the day was sapping. It came as no surprise to discover later that, over the course of the day, my cumulative ascent was nearly 1,000 m. Even the steep bridges were a challenge, none more so than the achingly beautiful structure at Saltstraumen. It arched itself over and across a narrow stretch of water, which, at a casual glance, was just another pretty gap between two outcrops of land. Looking more carefully, however, I noticed that strange forces were at work: the maelstroms of Saltstraumen.

Every six hours, 400 million cubic metres of water flowed through the narrow channel below the bridge. That's one very large cube of water measuring about 750 metres on each side. Four times a day, the direction of the tide changed, but with very large volumes of water moving in and out of such a narrow channel, incoming and outgoing currents interacted in a way that created large whirlpools. I poked my head over the side of the bridge but guessed it wasn't tide changeover time. The only whirlpools to be seen were modest in size. I was left to imagine just how foreboding they could be when the water started flowing in the opposite direction or when the combined efforts of the sun and the moon came together to have their greatest impact upon the tides.

I went to ponder over nature's maelstroms whilst eating a vegetable tart at a nearby swish café called Magic. The panoramic windows offered a cracking view, and I watched as people walked over the hump of the bridge and stared into the waters below, just as I had done a few minutes earlier. There were even two cyclists, an older man and a younger woman… Hang on. Those were Hans and Veronika. They continued across the bridge, spotted the café and came in to take shelter from the cool, damp conditions outside. I greeted them with a smile and we got chatting.

'Veronika is my middle daughter,' explained Hans. 'The other two are not interested but we've always cycled together. Last year we cycled from Bergen to Trondheim and this year we're completing the trip by cycling from Trondheim to Nordkapp.'

Hans worked as the research boss at a manufacturer of silicon in southern Germany and Veronika was a student of psychology in Austria. They had flown out to Trondheim via Oslo but I was curious as to how they were planning on returning home.

'There's an airport at Alta. Once we've arrived at Nordkapp, we'll cycle back there to catch a plane south again,' explained Veronika.

'I haven't made any plans to travel home yet,' I admitted, going on to detail my complete lack of preparation in that area. I mentioned the cargo ship to Immingham and Hans smiled.

'Good luck with that.'

It was obvious that he thought such a plan might require more than just turning up at the dock in Bergen and thumbing a lift. Even if it were a possibility, I would still be required to travel south to Bergen in the first place. There were no trains north of Bodø that connected with southern Norway and although coaches did link Nordkapp with the rest of the country, did I really want to end this epic trip by spending days travelling back south on a cramped bus?

—

The winding route along the coast had managed to turn a direct 35 km into a cycle of 86 km. I couldn't remember if, when working out my estimated distance of 7,500 km for the entire trip, I had taken the twisting nature of the journey in northern Norway into account. Arriving in Bodø, my cumulative kilometre count stood at 6,734. Were there only another 750 km left to cycle to Europe's most northerly point?

Cycling as far as Bodø felt much more significant than crossing the Arctic Circle. Until a few days before arriving at 66°34', I would have been hard-pressed to pinpoint the Circle accurately on a map. Bodø was different. Both Bodø and the southern point of the string of Lofoten islands were easily identifiable on a map. They had been on my mind for months, arguably more than Nordkapp itself which, in my consciousness, remained a distant outpost at the point where Norway stopped and the sea started.

So, it was with a modest sense of satisfaction that I rolled down the long finger of land at the end of which Bodø and a ferry to the islands were located. As with many other towns through which I had passed along the coast, Bodø was a functional kind of place. It was clean and tidy but ultimately a little drab, with no easily located spot where a casual traveller like me could sit, glance around and imagine what life might have been like prior to about 1950. The architecture of the second half of the twentieth century dominated.

Despite earlier inclinations towards finding a hotel, the lure of the tent was too great and Bodøsjøen Camping, on the other side of the 3 km wide peninsula of land, turned out to be a good place to spend the night. By the time the light had stopped making an effort to get any dimmer – I hadn't experienced real darkness for some time – the free camping area was packed with perhaps two dozen campers, most of them travelling by bike. I chatted to a Danish architect about the buildings I had seen in Oslo and then, unsurprisingly, Hans and Veronika arrived, and I spent a little time with them. They were becoming welcome familiar faces whenever I chose to stop.

'I can charge you more if you want,' explained the man selling tickets for the ferry the following morning.

I had just expressed surprise that, for the 100 km crossing to the Lofoten islands, I would only have to pay 186NOK, or around £17.

The ferry itself – the *Landegode* – had something of a French high-speed TGV train about it, with a pointed bow and a somewhat less effective long blue go-faster stripe along its edge. I lashed Reggie to the unnamed bikes of Hans and Veronika, who were also on board, and settled back in a comfortable armchair for a leisurely, if a little bumpy, cruise across the Norwegian Sea.

Upon arrival on the Lofoten islands, I was keen not to cycle with Hans and Veronika. I liked them a lot; they were good, interesting and fun company but my preference, as is almost always the case, was to cycle alone and interact with others when we happened to meet up at the end of the day or at pit stops along the way. As I cycled down the ramp and off the ferry, Hans and Veronika had already set off and when I saw them turning left in the direction of the curiously named Å, I was happy to turn right and start the long journey back towards the mainland via the fragmented string of islands. We would meet up again, no doubt, at some point in the future. That said, I did wonder why they were cycling to Å. With such a brief and alphabetically challenged name, it could surely only be home to scores of taxi firms and skip hire companies.

The Lofoten islands were immediately distinctive. The mountains remained a dominant feature of the landscape but whereas on the mainland settlements had grown to cover broad lowland coastal strips, here on the islands there were no broad lowland strips to expand into. The small settlements were limited to narrow pieces of land by the coast or had been built upon small offshore islands, linked to the larger islands by bridges and causeways. The mountains rose steeply to heights approaching 1,000 m within a piece of lake-dotted land that was, at times, barely 5 km wide.

Just as they had been for much of the previous day or so, the peaks were shrouded in mist. Smart buildings, predominantly reddish-brown but sometimes yellow, orange or green, were strewn along the shore in a chaotic yet pleasing fashion. Numerous wooden jetties linked small windowless sheds to the sea where fishing boats, small and large, bobbed silently on the water. Many of the sheds had been built upon stilts – half on rock, half in the ocean – and next to most of them were unpainted wooden platforms. These were the frames for the drying of cod and they would become a familiar feature of the landscape over the next few days.

Once the immediate rush of traffic from the ferry had disappeared into the distance, the tranquil charm of the Lofoten islands returned and for the next couple of hours I was able to indulge in a thoroughly enjoyable ride along the coastal road north. The distinct look and feel of the islands had injected a shot of excitement into my veins. This was Norway but not quite Norway as I knew it.

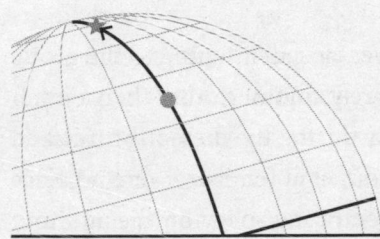

THE THIRTY-THIRD DEGREE
68°–69° NORTH

17–20 July

The cluster of islands along which I was cycling was split into two groups: the Lofoten to the south and west, and the Vesterålen to the north and east. I would cross from one to the other by taking a short ferry from Fiskebøl to Melbu, with all of the other constituent islands being accessible via bridges and tunnels. The plan was an easy one: continue to follow cycle route 1 as far as Andenes before catching another ferry back to the mainland.

The Lofoten islands were not lacking in campsites so as I continued my journey north from the ferry, I wasn't concerned about finding one when the time came for me to pull on the brakes and pause for the night. That moment arrived at around 4 p.m., after having cycled just 30 km. It was now rare to come across a campsite that didn't cater for people who wanted more watertight accommodation, and the Ramberg Gjestegård was no exception, having rooms in the main building as well as small cabins facing out to sea. There were, however, a good number of campers and I squeezed my own tent into one of the few remaining patches of green grass within spitting distance of the beach. And what a beach it was.

Sitting on sand dunes with my eyes closed, listening to the gentle lapping of waves on the sand was rarely anything other than a joy. It had been a favoured leisure activity during the previous three and a half months of travelling. Yet the dunes at Ramberg were no place to sit with your eyes closed. Concentrating solely on the auditory pleasures would have been time misspent, as the visual ones were equally soothing.

Had I been immune to the temperature, I could have been easily fooled into thinking that I was beside the Caribbean rather than the Norwegian Sea on a cloudy day. The long white beach curved away to the north with parabolic precision. A band of fine, off-white sand was sandwiched between the greenery of the shore and a transparent turquoise sea. The waves were rolling gently over the beach and, in the distance, on the far side of the semicircle of sand, was a small line of white, pale green and light orange houses. The mountains beyond completed the almost perfect tropical vista. The day's cycle had already answered any questions I might have had as to why the Lofoten islands were so popular with tourists; the beach and its surroundings made me wonder why there weren't even more of them around.

I then heard screams and turned to see a tanned couple in their sixties running across the sand in the direction of the sea. Both were dressed for a beach holiday in Barbados rather than one nearly 200 km north of the Arctic Circle. They were being followed, rather more sedately, by a group of fully clothed friends who were cheering them on. As they arrived at the water's edge, both the man and the woman dived into the ocean and more screams ensued.

I had become accustomed to getting cold and wet on the bike, but couldn't imagine how utterly chilling such a swim might be. I wondered what was being celebrated. Retirement? Marriage? A significant birthday? Or even the end of a great journey? Whatever the reason, the leap into the Norwegian Sea must have been a memorable one. Assuming I made it to Nordkapp, I had my own celebration approaching. What would I do? Diving from the high cliffs that I had seen in photographs probably wasn't an option. Yet it would be nice to mark the event with a reward to myself in some way, shape or form.

The next morning, I was inside the campsite restaurant tucking into a pastry, drinking coffee and staring out of the window, trying to predict the weather for the day. It remained cloudy but of greater concern was the wind and my eyes were focussed upon a thin Norwegian flag hoisted high on a post at the entrance. It was far too horizontal for my liking, its end whipped around by the gusts. What's more, it was pointing south-west. By unhappy coincidence, I had a day of cycling north-east ahead of me.

I concluded that I needed to wrap up and so, with three layers beneath my windproof jacket, a beanie on my head, a Buff around my neck and long trousers covering what remained, I set off into the wind. However, this proved to be a rather rash decision, as within the hour, with the sun beginning to shine through the rapidly disappearing clouds and the temperature rising, I stopped to de-layer. After four days of on-off rain and cloud, I was hopeful that the weekend ahead would be climatically blessed. Dealing with the wind as I cycled was a price worth paying for the good job that it was doing, blowing the unseasonal weather south.

The beach beside the campsite at Ramberg had been exceptional but by no means an exception. Even when the necessity to keep moving along the chain of islands took me a little inland for most of what remained of the morning, the sights around me were still more than sufficient to keep a souvenir shop well stocked in postcards. By the time I arrived in the small town of Napp, I was visually exhausted. What followed was something of an antidote.

I had already cycled through numerous tunnels but up until this point they had all been through mountains. I had yet to cycle through an undersea tunnel. I knew that in order to access the island of Nordkapp at the very end of my journey, I would need to travel through a 7 km undersea tunnel. The prospect of doing so was somewhat of a daunting one, not so much for its length (although it would, I imagined, be the longest of the cycle through Norway) as for its depth. It was over 200 m below sea level. Whereas tunnels through mountains were, in general, built on the flat or with only a gentle gradient, I had a 9 per cent gradient to look forward to at either end of the Nordkapp tunnel. It was something that I had been trying to blank from my mind.

At least the undersea tunnel at Napp would give me an insight into cycling in such a hostile environment. At 1,780 m, it was much shorter than its counterpart near Nordkapp and also much less deep, at only 60 m. But with a maximum gradient of 8 per cent on each side, it was barely less steep. Before entering the tunnel, I double-checked that I had the right to be there (yes, no signs telling me that cyclists were banned, I was still on the cycle route and there were no alternative bridges or ferries), turned on my lights and plunged into the semi-darkness.

The good news was that the tunnel, especially the road surface, was much drier than those I had previously encountered. Slipping and the consequences of doing so didn't bear thinking about. There was, however, a fair amount of traffic in both directions and the noise was beyond unpleasant. The gradient kicked in immediately, although initially my issue was with keeping my speed down rather than up. All seemed to be going well.

As expected, at the halfway point, the gradient started to reverse and more effort was required. I slowed to a gradual plod but maintained my position to the right of the roadway. I sensed that a large vehicle behind me had also slowed and after a few moments I dared to take a glance to my left. It was a coach full of people from a cruise ship. I couldn't understand why the driver wasn't passing me, as the gaps between oncoming cars were large. Then, just as the lorry driver had done in the previous tunnel, he gave a long, deafening blast of his horn. This in itself could have knocked me off poor Reggie but I remained vertical, albeit with my heart racing for all the wrong reasons. Eventually, the driver passed me. I saw him glance in my direction and raise his eyebrows. What had I done wrong?

Worse was to come. Behind the coach, a short queue of cars had developed. They had no hesitation in passing, and zoomed off at speed and at close quarters. Idiots. Except, that is, for the final driver in the five-car queue. He slowed to my speed, pulled up beside me, lowered the passenger window and shouted at me in Norwegian. He was looking straight at me – one hand on the wheel, one hand remonstrating in my direction. I had no idea what he was saying but he was clearly not a happy man; he appeared more focussed on giving me a piece of his mind than on looking at where he was driving. A few more seconds passed and then he too sped off up the gradient of the tunnel. The encounter had been as bewildering as it was frightening.

I had done nothing wrong. I had the right to be in the tunnel, was clearly visible and kept to the right. Some of the tunnels I was to make use of in the coming days had buttons at their entrances for cyclists to press and illuminate a warning sign. This one hadn't. The mystery as to why the drivers were so irked with my presence and my actions remains a mystery to this day. Answers, as they say, on a postcard.

The goings-on in the tunnel had dented my mood somewhat but as I progressed north and east, the width of the Lofotens increased and much of the traffic chose alternative routes. Shortly after Leknes, I bumped into a cyclist called Brad. We had exchanged emails earlier in the summer about cycling through Norway. His plan was to cycle from Nordkapp to Bergen with his girlfriend Anna and earlier in the week, in our most recent exchange of messages, it became apparent that our paths would cross somewhere on the Lofotens.

'Andrew?' I heard someone shout from the other side of the road. We got chatting.

'It's been sunny but cold further north,' he explained, 'and Nordkapp is very different from the fjords, green valleys and snow-capped mountains down here.'

It was inevitable that I would ask about the Nordkapp Tunnel.

'It was hard, especially as it was our first tunnel. The steepness, the darkness, the noise; I had the feeling we'd be squashed every time a vehicle approached.'

He added that to get to Nordkapp they had taken a flight to Oslo, another to Trondheim and a final one to Honningsvåg. Three flights with bikes? The inconveniences of flying with a bicycle – the dismantling, the wrapping, the idiosyncratic rules of the airlines – are not to be underestimated. I was having palpitations at the thought of just one flight, never mind three.

After our chat we continued in our respective directions; his and Anna's wind-assisted, mine most definitely not. Much of what remained of the day was spent imagining what the final ten days of the cycle would be like: Nordkapp, the tunnel, the weather, the landscape and that looming journey back to the UK.

I camped near Kabelvåg on the southern side of the Lofotens. The site wasn't anywhere near as stunningly located as the previous one by the beach but served its purpose. In the morning I felt tired and my back was aching. The few kilometres into the centre of the town were a real struggle but coffee and a couple of pastries had a vaguely therapeutic effect. I really couldn't see cycling day 88 turning into one of epic proportions but I eventually set off again on what was rapidly developing into a drizzle-infused, gloomy day. So much for the previous day's wind blowing everything south.

My final 40 km on the Lofoten islands were quiet and subdued, although the now much less touristy hamlets and villages were still worthy of slowing down for and admiring. The buildings were becoming less pristine but that did at least suggest the isolation and remoteness you'd expect of northern Norway.

Upon arriving by ferry in the port of Melbu, it was immediately obvious why the Lofoten islands pulled in the punters to a much greater extent than the Vesterålen. The most striking difference was the height of the mountains, which no longer dominated every view. Large, flat areas by the coast had been given over to farming, although it seemed a harsh place in which to earn your living from the land.

Taking a short detour into the centre of Stokmarknes to find food, I was surprised to find a large boat sitting not beside but on top of the quay. It was small by cruise ship standards but a curious sight nevertheless. On its bow was its name, the *Finnmarken*. It was initially a little difficult to work out what it was doing there but I then noticed a sign: *Hurtigrutemuseet*.

Way back in April near Burgos, in northern Spain, you may remember I met a chap called Peter who used to work at the BBC World Service. He was one of the first people to tell me that he had been to Nordkapp. 'How did you get there?' was the obvious question. 'On one of the Hurtigruten ships,' he replied. Such was his enthusiasm for travelling on the Hurtigruten that he had done so three times. Locking Reggie outside to a lamppost, I went inside to investigate the museum.

The Hurtigruten shipping line had been founded in Stokmarknes in 1893 and it operated a dozen or so ships between Bergen in the south and Kirkenes close to the border with Russia. Each ship had exactly the same route and timetable, and they operated all-year round, ferrying people, goods and even the mail from port to port along the coast. The service stopped at 34 ports and a voyage from Bergen to Kirkenes took about six days.

As I wandered around the scale models, decommissioned bells, posters, costumes and all other kinds of nautical curiosities, I could feel myself being sucked into the romance of life on board one of the 'coastal steamers'. '*The World's most wonderful voyage*' extolled one of the old adverts. I imagined it still was. Could I have found my perfect post-Nordkapp way south? It was very tempting.

—

If, as I cycled over the long bridge to the island of Langøya, I had known that I was still only halfway through the cycling day despite having already passed the 70 km mark, I might have been somewhat disheartened. The cycle along the coast to Sortland was, compared to the previous couple of days, pretty standard stuff. My expectations of Sortland weren't high but at least it had a campsite.

'They tried to charge me two hundred and fifty kroner so I didn't stop,' one female cyclist told me in the mid-afternoon rain. 'It wasn't that great either.'

Oh dear... I arrived in the centre of Sortland, which, under the rain, wasn't looking its best. The fact that it was Sunday didn't help, as most places were closed; a pizza place and a kebab shop were the only establishments showing any signs of life. I sat on a bench, pulled out my phone, took a picture of Reggie and some of the drab buildings, and tweeted the following:

I have discovered #Norway's least inspiring town: #Sortland... #cycling

I then dared to look at the reviews for Sortland Camping on TripAdvisor. *'Expensive'*, *'unfriendly'*, *'flee'*, *'we are never going back'* and *'to avoid'* were some of the comments. One reviewer even suggested the site might prove to be a good incentive for people to start wild camping, something that I had still not managed to do.

I found a nearby petrol station and bought some highly calorific food. Perhaps, with the rain, it wasn't the day to launch my belated wild-camping career. However, the adventurer in me was alive and kicking, and I had yet to make use of the very long days. There was no reason why I shouldn't carry on cycling until... another campsite? The next one on my map was at least 40 km away.

Throwing caution to the wind (yes, it was still blowing), I set off. The ride along the coast was a remote one in the slowly dimming light but three hours later, after a day in the saddle that had stretched to nearly 140 km, I arrived at the Andøy Outdoor Centre, pitched the tent, prised open my emergency can of ravioli and went to bed a tired but happy traveller. Little did I know that back in Sortland, the locals were about to become a little less contented with life. Or, more specifically, me.

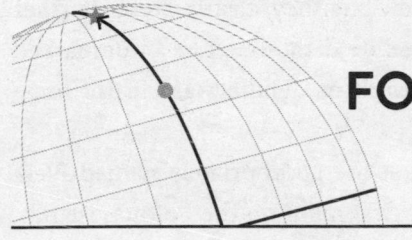

THE THIRTY-FOURTH DEGREE
69°–70° NORTH

20–25 July

Andøya, the northernmost of the Vesterålen island chain, didn't just *feel* remote; it *was* remote. It would be my home for most of cycling day 89, and I discovered it to be a place of mystery and intrigue. Only the hardiest of tourists had made it this far. With low hanging mist and constant heavy drizzle, I had wrapped up for the ride. This time no de-layering took place. Barely any skin was visible and from the neck down I was waterproofed.

My bleak, sparsely populated route was as silent as it was still. No noise to speak of. No howling wind. Few animals revealing their presence. Even fewer cars on the road. The subdued level of light that managed to penetrate the clouds was insufficient to make the colours shine, and the landscape was one of dull, dark greens and browns. In the final scenes of *Skyfall*, 007 drives through the similarly bleak Scottish Highlands. It could have been Andøya. I loved it. I was James Bond, on a touring bike.

The presence of two large military listening stations added an extra layer of mystery and intrigue to the island. 'No photography' signs were the only written indication that the curious arrays of masts and wires were top secret, but they clearly were. Further north, a remote collection of satellite dishes next to an unmarked truck had my mind working overtime. There was clearly some serious eavesdropping going on.

The views from the campsite at the appropriately named Bleik were reminiscent of those of my first night on the Lofoten islands. Again, I was able to pitch the tent near a white sandy beach and look out across the vastness of the Norwegian Sea, with my back to the mountains.

I fell into conversation with my neighbour. He was from the Netherlands and travelling with his family in a Land Rover that supported two tents on its roof, accessible via ladders at either end of the vehicle.

'I bought it when I lived in South Africa,' he explained. 'It's designed to keep you safe from wild animals.'

'What did you do there?' I asked.

'I worked in personnel for the Dutch foreign ministry,' he replied.

I didn't believe a word of it. 'Personnel'? He wasn't fooling me. He was clearly a spy. Andøya was the kind of place where secret agents took their holidays.

Aside from the drab island of Langøya, the Lofoten and Vesterålen had been great places along which to cycle and I had enjoyed almost all of my time there. I was also beginning to appreciate northern Norway through the filter of weather that wasn't always so great. It had been such a pity about 'uninspiring' Sortland. Talking of which, I had received an email from a journalist called Sanne. She worked for the *Sortlands Avisa*, the local newspaper. *Could I talk?* Yes, but perhaps away from the electronic ears of Andøya. I didn't want to cause a diplomatic incident. I replied, asking her to call me the following morning.

There were more listening stations, a military base and a curious tunnel with an uncountable number of wires feeding into it (as well as more 'No photography' signs…) squeezed into the 10 km between Bleik and Andenes. The ferry to what I assumed was the mainland departed from the end of a tentacle of land that formed the northernmost point of the Vesterålen islands. Four hours after having left the campsite, I was back on dry land at Gryllefjord, on the island of Senja. I hadn't reached the mainland after all.

I had suggested a time of 11 a.m. for Sanne to get in touch with me. I took her call whilst sitting on the crash barrier of a deserted bridge across the Gryllefjord, immediately in front of what appeared to be a brand new tunnel through the mountain.

'I really don't want to make any enemies in Sortland,' I explained, a little anxious that my tweet may have gone viral amongst the chattering classes of the town.

'Don't worry. I want the article to be positive, to stimulate debate,' she assured me, and started asking questions. 'Why was Sortland uninspiring? What suggestions do you have for improvements? How does it compare with other places in Norway?'

I must have only been in Sortland for under an hour. Perhaps I had been a little rash: the poor weather, everything closed as it was Sunday, the campsite… I tried to emphasise the extent to which I had enjoyed cycling through most of the rest of the country. Just not Sortland.

As I made my way through the tunnel, I wondered if any of my words could be misconstrued. I hoped not but only time would tell; I'd soon find out, when the article was published the following week. It would quickly be forgotten, right?

Senja's west coast consisted of a series of long fingers of land and narrow fjords. Some I would have to cycle along but with others I could cut through the knuckles via a tunnel. Towards the end of my 80 km ride across the island, the cycle route sliced off three of the fingers by climbing away from the coast a little and then falling back down to the ferry terminal at Botnhamn.

These were, however, no mere fingers of land. They were none other than the teeth of the Devil himself. Or so said an information board reminding me that I was again following one of the National Tourist Routes. Further south I had been taken aback not only by the spectacular view from one of the designated viewing platforms along the Turistveger, but also by the viewing platform itself. I had similar feelings at the Bergsbotn *utsiktsplattform*, where a slender structure of wood and metal enabled a casual fjord gazer such as me to move away from the land. Raised from the platform was an arc formed from curved wooden planks, elevating me to a position where the platform itself was almost out of sight. I never thought that art could be expressed in a simple viewing platform. Norway had proved me wrong.

Upon arrival in Botnhamn I was delighted to find that Hans and Veronika were already waiting for the ferry. I hadn't seen them since the previous Friday and we spent time catching up on our journeys along the Lofoten and Vesterålen islands. I avoided any mention of Sortland. They had embraced wild camping in a way that I hadn't and they planned to wild camp again somewhere near Brensholmen, on the next island of Kvaløya. Would I ever reach the mainland?

Not far from the ferry terminal on Kvaløya, I paused next to a bright yellow distance sign. Just one destination was listed:

Tromsø 55

There had been something of a turnaround in the weather and my body cast a long shadow on the road in the direction of Tromsø. It was 7 p.m. and I had already cycled 90 km. My shadow would, however, only increase in length very slowly over the subsequent few hours. Indeed, it might never disappear; this was, after all, the land of the midnight sun. I saw no reason to stop.

As evening rides go, it was a memorable one. There was no wind to speak of and, with the sun on my back, I powered over the island like a salmon returning to spawn. The route was by no means flat, but rarely anything other than spectacular – big mountains, big valleys, big sea – and, at times, alarmingly remote. Could Norway's eighth city really be within cycling distance? Descending from the hills, I first spotted signs of its existence at around 9.30 p.m., when one of the long bridges to the small island upon which Tromsø had been built finally came into view.

Although the campsite near Tromsø was inundated with campervans, all parked up in lines on a vast expanse of tarmac, the free camping area was beside a stream, and full of nooks and crannies, overgrown paths, small open patches of ground and more secluded woods. The cycle had put me in a good mood and the campsite had gilded it, so it was no surprise that late the following morning I could be seen cycling over the long bridge back into the centre of Tromsø with a broad smile on my face. Was I being prematurely happy? The straight-line distance to Nordkapp was still over 300 km, significantly more via cycle route 1. Perhaps 500 plus? It was difficult, however, to fight the urge to celebrate my achievement just a little.

That said, my celebrations were modest and initially came in the shape of food and coffee at the Helmersen Delikatesser, where I ate and drank away a couple of hours watching the world go by and the seagulls try to steal my lunch. Tromsø had a charm that had been absent from so many of the other coastal towns. The buildings were smart and colourful, with many having their origins in the nineteenth century. Yet there was nothing claustrophobic about the place, with its wide avenues and open spaces that made full use of the abundant sunlight. Smart, modern constructions along the fjord complemented but didn't detract from the older ones and, from beside the water, perhaps Tromsø's greatest asset was on display: its location.

In an almost continuous 360-degree ring, snow-capped mountains surrounded the city. There may have been hints of southern Scandinavia whilst strolling down the *Storgata*, or main street, but cast your gaze beyond the pretty buildings and there was immediate confirmation that this was unmistakably northern Norway.

The employee of the *delikatesser* was not a great fan of Tromsø – 'Too quiet, nothing ever happens here...' – but I most certainly was. After so many disappointing small towns, it was good to find one that ticked most of my boxes. One of these was to locate a nice place for a beer so I reached for my guidebook to see what was recommended. The Amundsen Restauranthus, former home of the explorer Roald, of South Pole fame? The Blå Rock Café? Or the Ølhallen Pub adjoining the Mack Brewery, the world's most northerly? How could I turn down the opportunity of tasting the world's most northern beer?

The brewery had been opened by the entrepreneurial Ludwig Markus Mack who, in 1877, realised the potential of brewing beer in a city that was rapidly growing rich from the 'seemingly inexhaustible' natural resources of the Arctic Sea. Soon, the beer that he was producing in his brewery was considered *the* beer of northern Norway and so it remained. Well, according to Mack. The company was still in the family and now the fifth generation of Macks were in charge, although the boss himself went by the name of Bredrup. Somehow a pint of Mack sounded better than a pint of Bredrup.

The Ølhallen – 'beer hall' – Pub, located in the cellar of the brewery, was opened in 1928 by a previous boss, one Lauritz Bredrup, who persuaded the town council that it would be so much better if people could drink inside and under control rather than out on the street. Ever the rebel, after ordering my pint of Mack I chose to sit and drink it outside on the terrace, presumably much to the disapproval of any passing town councillors.

The view was somewhat obliterated by a second brewery building opposite where I was sitting and supping, but my eye wandered in the hope of being amused. After a few minutes, I noticed a sign across the road upon which the crest of the United Kingdom was emblazoned. Around its edge it read: 'British Consulate'. A quick Google search revealed a curious fact. Not only was the local consulate for the United Kingdom located in the brewery, but the 'head of mission' – the honorary consul – was listed as a certain Haakon Bredrup of the fourth generation of Macks, father of the current boss and chairman of the board. Should a diplomatic incident take place with the Sortland tweet issue, I would at least know who to call. If nothing else, he might allow me to drown my sorrows with his beer. Perhaps that was the recommended course of action with troubled visitors from Britain and the key thing on his CV that had got His Excellency Mr Bredrup the job in the first place.

It wasn't a long session of boozing, as the Ølhallen Pub closed in the late afternoon. I pushed Reggie back through the centre of Tromsø, cycled over the long bridge for the final time and returned to the campsite to plan the final stage of the journey to Nordkapp. I found Hans and Veronika in the communal cooking room doing the same thing and we combined our thoughts as we bent over my last map, Norway North Cape. Tromsø was on the left-hand edge and Nordkapp was at the top. Although only one and half degrees of latitude separated us from our ultimate destination, the greater challenge would be in cycling across the nearly seven degrees of longitude that remained. What's more, such was the twisting nature of the coastal route that we would pass through the line of 70 degrees of latitude not once but three times, the final crossing being just north of Alta. This would be the next, and last, major town en route to Nordkapp. What remained after Tromsø would have made a decent cycling expedition by itself.

Although we had agreed on probable locations where to stop overnight, I was still keen to cycle independently, at my own pace. And so, it seemed, were the Germans, as when I set off at around 9.30 a.m., they were already long gone. The busy E8 out of Tromsø reminded me of the horrible E6 further south but, after a while, the cycle route split away to follow the almost deserted ferry-hopping coastal road. My senses could drift away from monitoring the cycling to admiring the mountainous scenery that had been visible from the centre of Tromsø. Most peaks were now well in excess of 1,000 m and covered with fresh snow. If cycling day 91 were to be replicated over the final week of the trip, I was in for a memorable and fitting finale to the cycle from Tarifa.

After the second ferry crossing – much longer and choppier than the first – I was alarmed to see that the cycle route would now follow the dreaded E6. Such was the thinning nature of what remained of Norway that it was perhaps inevitable that our paths would again coalesce. I'd done a pretty decent job of avoiding major roads for most of the cycle from Lillehammer but here I would have to admit defeat.

A simple, isolated, mosquito-ridden site near Rotsundelv would be home for the night. Hans, Veronika and I were the only campers and in the morning we again set off at different times. The fickle weather had taken a turn for the worse and cloud hung low in the sky, obliterating the dramatic views of the previous day.

Although most of the cycling in recent days had been much flatter than I had expected, it was punctuated by short, sharp climbs. None more so than the energy-sapping ascent from sea level to 400 m to a viewing point beside the Badderfjord. However, even the clouds couldn't diminish the panoramic vista of mountains and fjords that stretched away in all directions. At the top, a large hotel-restaurant, the Gildetun, served a constant stream of holidaymakers from the cruise ships that were heading in the same direction as me. Adjacent to its large car park was the burnt-out stump of a tree that had been fashioned into a sign. Etched into one of its remaining three branches was the information I'd been looking out for since leaving Tromsø:

NORDKAPP 370 km

At the bottom of the hill, I found Hans and Veronika scratching their heads, trying to find the campsite that I was also aiming for. We pooled our ideas and within the hour had found what we were looking for, near Sekkemo.

Aside from the viewing point, it had been a subdued day and I suspected that my fellow long-distance cyclists were having similar thoughts. After eating, we retreated to our tents early but I couldn't sleep. I was certainly tired. Was it excitement? Anticipation? Yes, but tinged with a certain amount of sadness that my transcontinental adventure would soon be finished. A strange maelstrom of emotions was keeping my mind active and I remained wide awake.

In the early hours I reached for my iPad, wirelessly tethered it to my phone and went online. There was a Hurtigruten ship, the MS *Lofoten* – the smallest and oldest of the fleet – leaving the port of Honningsvåg on the island of Nordkapp at 5.45 a.m. on Thursday 30 July. My ETA at Nordkapp was the end of cycling day 96, on Tuesday 28. I reached for my credit card and booked a passage to Bergen. Not only did I now have a ticket to travel south, but I also had a deadline to meet. Not arriving at Nordkapp by Wednesday at the very latest would be a costly mistake. With that worry added to the maelstrom, there was little chance of me drifting off into the land of slumber, and I didn't.

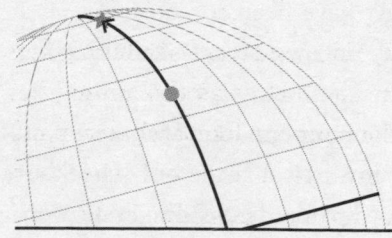

THE THIRTY-FIFTH DEGREE
70°–71°10'21" NORTH

25–28 July

I crossed over the seventieth degree of latitude for the first time about 25 km into the morning's ride from Sekkemo after a climb to over 250 m and a freewheel ride back down to sea level. It was to be the only serious hill of the day. My main physical battle was against the wind, which, after I turned east to cycle along the Langfjord, was doing its best to push me back to where I had started. I persevered and won. It wasn't easy, dressed as I was in my full waterproof body armour. The drivers of passing vehicles must have questioned the wisdom of cycling anywhere in such wet and windy conditions. It was certainly what I was thinking myself.

Before setting off I had spent a while admiring the time and effort that Hans and Veronika had put into preparing what I considered a lavish breakfast. My own strategy of buying a banana and pastries, and washing them down with coffee from a local shop or café had worked well on almost every day since leaving Tarifa. Until now. No longer was it easy to find those shops and cafés, and although on this occasion Hans had offered to share what they had, it didn't seem fair for me to guzzle down their food so I politely turned down his offer. Perhaps I shouldn't have been so courteous, as I was still searching for a place to buy my own breakfast after having cycled over 80 km.

Salvation came in the form of a Coop supermarket at about 1 p.m. Unfortunately, I managed to time my arrival at the only checkout just moments after a coachload of Spaniards. So desperate were my taste buds to consume something other than water that, while waiting to be served, I opened and drank the entire contents of the bottle of Coke that I was holding.

'Sorry, do you speak English?' I asked the girl when it was finally my turn. She smiled and shook her head but I continued anyway. 'You haven't charged me for the Coke,' I explained.

'Å pante...' she replied, pointing to a hole in the wall near the entrance. It was a 'reverse vending' machine where empty bottles could be inserted and the deposit returned in the form of a voucher.

'No...'

Lacking the mental energy to try to explain through words, I mimed taking the bottle from the shelf and drinking it, much to the bemusement of a few Spanish stragglers who were now behind me in the queue.

After all those days on the road, I remained, at heart, a somewhat inept traveller. At least it felt that way.

With the confusion sorted out, I went outside to eat what I had bought, only to be joined on my bench by two of the Spaniards, who lit up cigarettes. I gave them a hard stare but it had no effect. I couldn't believe that at this late stage of the journey I was having another Mercedes day. I should have been jubilant, joyful, eager, enthused to be within touching distance of Nordkapp. Yet I wasn't. I put my grumpiness down to lack of sleep, lack of food, the weather and the uninspiring landscape through which I was passing. It was in complete contrast to what I had experienced elsewhere since leaving Tromsø.

A tunnel from which cyclists were banned was the icing on the cake. The alternative route added an extra 10 km to the cycle but the incident had me reflecting upon distances travelled more generally and, when I sat down at the campsite later in the day near Alta, I noticed that I had now cycled 7,500 km. Having seen a nearby sign informing me that the distance from Alta to Nordkapp was only 240 km, I realised that my initial back-of-an-envelope guestimate had actually been quite accurate. That brought a smile to my face. As did clean clothes and warm food.

Hans and Veronika's efforts with breakfast had inspired me to make more of an effort with my evening meal and I went inside the campsite kitchen to conjure up a feast fit for someone who was about to finish cycling the length of a continent. My attempt was familiar – 'fresh' pasta (from a packet) and pesto, bread and cheese – but not bad. However, it paled into insignificance compared with what my fellow campers in the kitchen had knocked up. They were all from a large Italian family that spanned across at least three generations and their evening meal could have been served up in a restaurant. It was, it seemed, a day when I was never going to win.

It was now Sunday morning and I was keen not to be left bereft of breakfast for a second consecutive day. However, a cycle around the deserted centre of Alta revealed nowhere to buy so much as a cup of coffee. On my map I noticed a large airport to the north of the town; it was the one from where Hans and Veronika were planning on flying south. Surely there must be something open there.

I was saved by an Esso garage near the entrance of the airport. Outside I bumped into a young Norwegian cyclist who had just arrived from Nordkapp.

'How was the tunnel?' I enquired. It was now my stock question for anyone I met who was travelling south.

'Hard: three km down at nine per cent, then a little bit flat, then four km up at ten per cent,' he explained, adding a little detail to what I knew already. 'But for you it should be easier going from south to north.' He made a good, if minor, point.

I stopped for a second time only a few hundred metres down the road at a Shell station, this time to stock up on chocolate. The 100 km road from Alta to Olderfjord, along which I was about to start cycling, appeared on my map to be as remote a road as I had yet to encounter. Two large bars of chocolate should see me through any dietary emergencies. Once supplemented with more food from a small supermarket slightly further north that had, by some miracle, chosen to open on a Sunday morning, my survival seemed guaranteed.

As I moved away from the western side of the peninsula, I also began to climb. The gradient was never severe but it had been quite some time since I had been required to maintain such a constant and prolonged effort on the bike. Momentary relief came when I arrived at a large lake where the road flattened out and I could begin to catch my breath. For a few minutes I relaxed.

I had been noticing birds of prey high in the sky all morning; their presence indicated just how remote the area was becoming. Beside the lake it was no different and, as I cycled, I watched one bird as it descended to its nest high on the cliff ahead of me on the left. Or rather that's what I thought it was doing. As I approached the section of the road nearest to the cliff, the bird continued to descend. It then pulled away sharply and climbed, but not for many metres, before once again swooping down. It repeated this action three or four times, on each descent getting closer to… my head.

I suddenly realised that the large brown bird in the sky was aiming its displeasure at me. Either that or it saw in me a hefty lunchtime snack. Somewhat alarmed at a distant, graceful and majestic animal becoming a rather frightening sharp-taloned beast only a few metres from my scalp, I started to cycle as I have rarely cycled before. Such was the proximity of the bird that I could hear its wings flapping above my head. Would this be it? After over 7,500 km, thwarted in my efforts to reach Nordkapp by a… bird?

I dared not look behind me but in front I could see a small wood beside the lake. Two people were sitting on its shore. The cover of the trees should, I reasoned, dissuade the bird from pursuing me and if it didn't, the two people could help me to fight it off before it started plunging its beak into my flesh.

'Did you see that?' I panted, my voice shaking. I had dispensed with any pleasantries and assumed they could speak English.

'Yes, it was very interesting,' replied the man, calmly. 'I don't understand why the bird has chosen to nest by the road,' he mused.

'It was attacking me,' I gasped.

'You were never in any danger. It just wanted to scare you off.'

'Do you know what breed of bird it was?' I asked, my heart still racing.

'I think in English it's called a rough-legged buzzard.'

I didn't know whether to be more impressed at the man's relaxed manner – he had, after all, just witnessed a near-death experience, or so I thought at the time – or the fact that he, as a Norwegian, knew the English for 'rough-legged buzzard'. It had been a disturbing incident.

I remained wary of birds, but animals rooted to the ground would be far more prevalent as I edged north. Within a few minutes of leaving the wood, I noticed an elk beside the road. My pulse quickened slightly. Remembering the conversation I had had with the woman after my previous elk encounter north of Oslo, I was relieved that the adult was by itself. Then, on the other side of the road, I spotted a small elk, presumably the adult's calf. I hesitantly moved into the centre of the road and slowed to a crawl. Thankfully, they both ignored me.

After having reached the high point of the day, the road descended slowly back in the direction of the eastern side of the peninsula. The landscape had now changed radically. Gone were the trees; low-level vegetation covered the ground and in the distance, dark mountains gently rose to meet the sky. This, I assumed, was perfect for the reindeer that wandered, seemingly aimlessly, in herds across the land, their bells jingling as they strolled. They ignored me too. I much preferred it that way.

At Skadi the road split into two, with the E6 continuing east. This was the first settlement I had encountered since moving away from the west coast and I paused at a large café for a mid-afternoon break. The bikes outside were familiar; I found Hans and Veronika chatting to a Polish cyclist inside.

'I've cycled from Irun in Spain,' he explained, 'and I haven't washed for two weeks.'

I noticed Hans raise an eyebrow, while Veronika struggled to keep a straight face.

We all agreed to cycle together to the campsite at Olderfjord, which was by then only 20 km away, but when we arrived, the Polish chap had disappeared. I guessed that staying somewhere with hot running water just wasn't his style.

All that remained was to cycle the 100 km to Honningsvåg on the Monday, stay overnight in the town and complete the short 30 km ride to Nordkapp itself on the Tuesday morning.

The weather had got into a rhythm of one day OK, one day bloody awful – and so it was to continue. Had I ever cycled in such appalling conditions? I doubted it. I fortified myself before heading out into the wall of water by indulging in a three-course breakfast in the restaurant at the campsite-hotel. The map gave every indication that there would be no opportunities to buy food before arriving in Honningsvåg; the road would be as coastal as it could be without falling into the sea until it shimmied around the headland and plunged into the horrors of the Nordkapp Tunnel. Close inspection of the map also revealed a second long tunnel immediately before Honningsvåg but it was, at least, not an undersea one.

Was I procrastinating? It seemed highly likely. Eventually, with a heavy stomach, but a growing sense of excitement, I set off, leaving Hans and Veronika still cooking their breakfast in the campsite kitchen.

The headwind made cycling in the heavy rain painful. I can only imagine I would have stayed drier and warmer if I had volunteered to have buckets of cold water continuously thrown in my face for five hours. The road had been cut into the cliff, revealing fascinating layers of geological history. In order to drag my mind away from obsessing about the tough cycling conditions, I tried to imagine how and why each layer had been deposited. It's usually the case that such slices of world history are evidence of the area being part of a tropical forest or sea. Really? Here? Could things have changed so drastically over the course of hundreds of millions of years? Yes, they probably could, but it did seem to be a line of thought so utterly removed from reality.

In the back of my mind was the tunnel – *THE* tunnel – the Nordkapp Tunnel. As envisaged, it was tucked away from the coastal road but visible after a short cycle over the headland. As with all the tunnels through which I had cycled, from a distance its simple exterior appearance was understated.

Then came the warning signs.

Tåke i tunnel
Fog in tunnel

Low Gear
9%

Before a final confirmation of its vital statistics:

6870 m
212 m.u.h.

After pausing to switch on and check my lights, I entered the black hole.

Initially, it was a relief to be inside, out of the rain and wind. But not the cold. The chill was immediate, as was the incentive to keep moving to try to maintain at least some warmth. Yet with a nine per cent hill in front of me, gloom all around and a wet, potentially slippery surface beneath the bike, I couldn't help but grip the brakes tightly.

Traffic was mercifully light – this just wasn't the day for a casual drive to the northernmost point of the Continent – but when a car or coach did appear, such were the crazy echoes that it was impossible to tell from which direction they would emerge. Eventually, I could feel the road surface flatten out and there was a modest sense of elation at having completed one of the three stages of this tunnel of terror.

Then came the stark realisation of where I was and what was above me, 200 m below the level of the sea. The lowest point of the trip from Tarifa. *How can this be a good thing? What is keeping the rock above me in place? What would happen if...?* No. Those were not good thoughts.

Part 3 was the long climb, all 3 km of it. I had already been in the tunnel for over 15 minutes and was keen to gasp fresh air. How could anyone cycle through here and not experience a few moments of claustrophobia? Experiencing more than my fair share, I felt the bike zigzagging slightly from side to side as I attempted to make the incline more hospitable. *One slipped zigzag... Stop thinking the unthinkable!*

Then, in the distance, was the light and after a few minutes I emerged into the open. The wind and the rain returned but the chill abated; I had been underground for over 30 minutes. It had been an experience I wouldn't, indeed couldn't, have avoided but also one that I had found simply bone-chillingly scary.

The light at the end of the tunnel was, of course, of double significance. It had signalled the end of a thoroughly unpleasant section of the ride but also my arrival on the island of Nordkapp. Now I just needed to find Nordkapp itself.

Via the second, much less threatening, tunnel, I cycled into the centre of Honningsvåg and found a café where I was able to eat, warm up and, to a certain extent, dry out. The plan had been to stay on the campsite but, bearing in mind the poor weather conditions, I decided to reserve a room at the local hostel. I had been in the tent for 16 consecutive nights and had earned the right to reacquaint myself with a mattress for one final time before the end of the trip.

My guidebook spoke glowingly of Honningsvåg but I was struggling to see its charms. Dominating the seascape were two large cruise ships, one of which was a Hurtigruten; it would be from here that I would start my journey south early on Thursday morning. After all this time on two wheels, it was strange to be contemplating a long journey by any other means.

When I arrived at the five-storey hostel on the edge of town, Hans and Veronika had caught up with me and, for similar reasons to mine, they too had opted out of camping. We compared notes on a journey that had been just as gruelling for them as it had been for me and looked forward to the final push the following morning. Although the forecast looked promising, I still worried that the clouds would prevent us from witnessing the fabled midnight sun. Experiencing that was, perhaps, hoping for too much.

As with the other Norwegian islands along which I had cycled, Magerøya, the island of Nordkapp, had its own unique identity. I set off at 9 a.m. and within a few kilometres was climbing through a treeless landscape. The mountains were all now behind me and here hills rolled modestly over the contours of the rock from which they had been formed. Herds of reindeer and elk roamed in the distance, wisely keeping themselves away from the road and its traffic of cars, motorhomes and, of course, bicycles like Reggie.

The drama of Magerøya came in its location, isolated from the rest of the continent – a point where the land stopped, and the sea started and continued for many thousands of kilometres on a journey to the North Pole and onwards to the northern shores of Alaska. My own journey had started within sight of Africa but when I glanced to the west, to the east and, as I neared the cluster of buildings at Nordkapp itself, to the north, I could see nothing but a vast expanse of water.

It was approaching midday on Tuesday 28 July and the journey was entering its final few minutes. These were the precious moments that I had found almost impossible to imagine as I cycled along the causeway in Tarifa. The blank canvas of events was now nearing completion. As Reggie's tyres rolled over the loose gravel surrounding the Nordkapphallen tourist centre, my mind was split between looking back over the 7,776 km cycled and forward at the remaining 100 m. It was a confusing mix of memories and emotions but as I slowed to a halt next to the iconic metal globe on its plinth, the overriding feeling was that of calm satisfaction. I had been travelling for nearly four months. I had achieved my objective. I had arrived.

I dismounted from Reggie and went to sit on Europe's most northerly bench. For a few moments, I was the continent's most northerly man. I smiled. Job done.

—

The journey may have ended, but the day had not. The night of 28 July would be the final opportunity of the year to see the midnight sun at Nordkapp. The weather had been kind, much kinder than in recent days, but as the afternoon progressed, the clouds remained. Nevertheless, the crowds – from their cars, motorhomes, cruise ships and bicycles – gathered.

I was joined by my new friends Hans and Veronika. The tents were erected outside the gates of the carpark – at last, a night of wild camping – and together we celebrated our arrival with peach schnapps.

As midnight approached, the clouds still covered the sky. The crowd started to thin but then, as the sun edged towards the horizon, as the clocks struck 12 and as we all held our breath, the bright orange globe in the sky broke through to reveal what we'd all come here to witness: the magical midnight sun. I couldn't have wished for a more fitting finale for a cycle from Tarifa in Spain to Nordkapp in Norway, across 35 degrees of Europe.

EPILOGUE

28 July–8 August

On previous European trips, I had bundled up poor Reggie, stuffed him into a box or wrapped him in cling film at the airport and flown back to Britain. Not so this time.

Even before I could board the MS *Lofoten* at Honningsvåg on Thursday morning, I needed to cycle back to the town. I did so with my brakes wearing thin and my enthusiasm for cycling dented somewhat by having just arrived and celebrated the end of a long, long journey. Much more for mental reasons than physical ones, the return trip to Honningsvåg was an arduous one.

Hans invited me for dinner in town that evening and, along with Veronika, we enjoyed a wonderful celebratory feast of seafood by the harbour. It was a nice way to start my reintegration back into polite society. Although my preference had always been to travel alone on the trip to Nordkapp, the two Germans – father and daughter – had made those final two weeks of the trip so much more enjoyable. We shook hands and embraced; the following morning they had to cycle back to Alta, and I had a rendezvous with a ship.

The MS *Lofoten* was an adventure in itself. Built in 1964, she could only accommodate a maximum of 140 people in her berths, although as we cruised from port to port, locals joined and left the ship without staying overnight. There was something of Agatha

Christie's *Death on the Nile* about the experience: intriguing characters of differing nationalities and diverse social standings mingling together on the two decks. Just no dead bodies.

When the ship docked for a two-hour pause in Hammerfest, I disembarked and went to explore. At the Museum of Reconstruction for Finnmark and North-Troms I was to discover why the towns through which I had cycled were often lacking when it came to historical charm. The area was considered to be of strategic importance by the Nazis and of all the regions in Norway, Finnmark and North-Troms hosted the most German soldiers. As a consequence, many towns were heavily bombed by the Allies. In the later stages of the conflict, much of what remained was razed to the ground by retreating German troops on the direct orders of Hitler. An aerial photograph of Hammerfest taken in 1946 showed a town only recognisable by the streets separating the bare patches of land. In Honningsvåg the only remaining building had been the church. At the end of the war, the population, which included 75,000 refugees in their own country, was left to pick up the pieces. Bearing all this in mind, they had done a remarkable job since.

—

Back on the ship, an email had arrived from Sanne, the journalist from Sortland; the article had appeared in the newspaper and gone live online. She had sent me the link to the story. The headline, beside the photograph of Reggie and the drab buildings that I had posted on Twitter, read:

Engelsk forfatter slakter Blåbyen

I ran it through an online translator: *'English writer butchers the blue city'*. Oh dear…

The article, however, was a fair reflection of what I had said to Sanne in our interview. In the coming days several hundred comments were posted on Facebook, debating whether I was right or wrong in my opinions. 'Sortland has become a ghost town,' wrote one local. 'He has just put into words what many of us think about Sortland,' remarked another.

Others weren't so happy. A follow-up article focussed on the thoughts of a prestigious architect who had once lived in Sortland. She disagreed with my general sentiment, although admitted that the port area needed sprucing up. Another article by a high-profile journalist argued that 'Sortland is not ugly. It is rough around the edges… If I had met Sykes, I'd have told him to give it more time'. And finally, two college students, Petter and Kim, had been out onto the streets of Sortland to debate the issue and had produced a short documentary with their findings. In reference to my tweet, their film had been given the title *"Uninspiring"*.

Things may, however, be moving forward. Sortland is known as 'the blue city' by locals because of a project instigated by an artist called Bjørn Elvenes. Following criticism of the town by Lonely Planet and Rough Guides in the 1990s, he took on the mission of sprucing things up by painting 17 blocks of the town centre in different shades of blue. He chose the colour as a symbol of Sortland's maritime links. By posting my comments on Twitter, I was clearly hitting a raw nerve. However, shortly after my interview appeared in the *Sortlands Avisa*, it was reported by the newspaper that, as a result of 'vigorous debate in recent weeks about whether Sortland centre is inviting or not', Bjørn was keen to complete his unfinished project. 'It is now time that something happened again,' he was quoted as saying, adding, 'Only a quarter of the buildings in my plan were ever painted blue.'

To anyone in Sortland I might have offended, I apologise. I'd like to think that, by prompting a little discussion, some good might have come out of that one, simple tweet. One day I will return to Sortland for a better, longer look. I'm sure I will be surprised, especially if Bjørn has been busy again with his brush.

—

The MS *Lofoten* docked in Bergen the following Monday afternoon. I stayed overnight in the city before catching a ferry to Hirtshals, in Denmark. Following a somewhat convoluted train-hopping journey down the length of Jutland, I returned to Hamburg to pay a second visit to my friends Dominic, Annet and their children. More beer was consumed before I caught a succession of trains through Germany and the Netherlands in the direction of the coast. There I discovered that 'Rotterdam' as defined by P&O Ferries differed by some 20 km from my definition of Rotterdam so it was back on Reggie for a short, flat trip along the river to where the overnight ferry to Hull was waiting beside the dock.

A total of 164 days after having touched down in Malaga, Spain, I arrived back in Britain to build a new life in my home county of Yorkshire. As one adventure finished, another was about to begin.

ACKNOWLEDGEMENTS

As with all long journeys, this cycle from Tarifa to Nordkapp was made not just pleasurable but memorable because of the many people I had the opportunity of meeting as I travelled. Alas there are far too many to list here but I would particularly like to thank those mentioned below.

My Uncle Ronald and his wife Beatrice who not only provided me with a base in southern Spain immediately prior to setting off on the trip but also somewhere to store Reggie whilst I was studying in Cádiz.

The friends I had the opportunity of meeting up with along the way; Liz near Tours, my former colleagues Kerrie, David and Sarah (and the students of Gillotts School in Henley-on-Thames) who I met in Paris; Janina in Cologne and especially Dominic, Annet, Leni and Nick in Hamburg who had me knocking on their door not once but twice.

The online friends – many via WarmShowers – who, although we had never met before, were kind enough to offer a bed for the night; Juan in Palencia, Chris and Audrey in La Rochelle, Kevin and Cheryl near Brussels, Andrea and Matthias in Düsseldorf, Dirk and Anita in Münster, Franziska and Klaus in Flensburg and Steve, Anita and Annie in Trondheim.

Thanks also to Dirk from Hannover for introducing me to life as a pilgrim in Spain, fellow cyclist Javier from Argentina and to Peter and Linda for their advice and good conversation in Burgos.

The biggest thanks must, however, go to Hans and Veronika from Munich with whom I had the pleasure of sharing many evenings during the final two weeks of the journey. Their unwavering cheeriness was infectious and kept a smile on my face as we neared the northern end of the continent.

Reggie would like to thank Roman of Yep Bikes in San Pedro (Spain), Christophe and François of Fun Bike in Maubuisson (France), Patrice of VéloSpot in Saumur (France), the quiet, un-named mechanic at Détours de Loire in Tours (France), Wilhelm of Hü4 in Hamburg (Germany), the mechanics at Fri Bikeshop in Stege (Denmark) and Petter of Sykkelsporten in Sarpsborg (Norway) for keeping him on the road. (And so would I.)

Finally, to all the wonderfully supportive and helpful people at Summersdale who have allowed me to bring this story to the page. Thanks to Debbie for having the courage to sign me up, the unflappably positive Claire who has flawlessly co-ordinated the publishing process, to Jen for her honest and thorough edit and to Daniela for her forensic checking of the manuscript. Please blame the author for any errors that remain.

Have you enjoyed this book?
If so, why not write a review on your favourite website?

If you're interested in finding out more about our
books, find us on Facebook at **Summersdale Publishers**
and follow us on Twitter **@Summersdale.**

Thanks very much for buying this Summersdale book.

www.summersdale.com

Inside cover photos: 1. Reggie the bike / 2. Conil de la Frontera, Spain /
3. Saint-Jean-Pied-de-Port, France / 4. Couture-sur-Loir, France /
5. Binche, Belgium / 6. Redalen, Norway / 7. Folldal, Norway /
8. Schleswig-Holstein, Germany / 9. Benavente, Spain /
10. Kruså, Denmark / 11. Castrojeriz, Spain /
12. Halland, Sweden / 13. Ramberg, Norway /
14. Redalen, Norway